U·X·L Encyclopedia
of World Mythology

VOLUME 4: M–P

U·X·L Encyclopedia of World Mythology

VOLUME 4: M–P

U·X·L
A part of Gale, Cengage Learning

GALE
CENGAGE Learning™

Detroit • New York • San Francisco • New Haven, Conn • Waterville, Maine • London

U·X·L Encyclopedia of World Mythology

Product manager: Meggin Condino

Project editor: Rebecca Parks

Editorial: Jennifer Stock, Kim Hunt

Rights Acquisition and Management: Kelly A. Quin, Scott Bragg, Aja Perales

Composition: Evi Abou-El-Seoud

Manufacturing: Rita Wimberley

Imaging: Lezlie Light

Product Design: Jennifer Wahi

For product information and technology assistance, contact us at Gale Customer Support, 1-800-877-4253.
For permission to use material from this text or product, submit all requests online at cengage.com/permissions.
Further permissions questions can be emailed to permissionrequest@cengage.com.

Cover photographs reproduced by permission of Purestock/Getty Images (picture of Statue of Poseidon); Voon Poh Le/Dreamstime.com (drawing of paper cut dragon); Werner Forman/Art Resource, NY (picture of an incense burner of a sun god); Charles Walker/Topfoto/The Image Works (photo of a papyrus drawing of Anubis weighing the heart); and The Art Archive/Richard Wagner/Museum Bayreuth/Gianni Dagli Orti (photo of a drawing of a valkyrie).

While every effort has been made to ensure the reliability of the information presented in this publication, Gale, a part of Cengage Learning, does not guarantee the accuracy of the data contained herein. Gale accepts no payment for listing; and inclusion in the publication of any organization, agency, institution, publication, service, or individual does not imply endorsement of the editors or publisher. Errors brought to the attention of the publisher and verified to the satisfaction of the publisher will be corrected in future editions.

LIBRARY OF CONGRESS CATALOGING-IN-PUBLICATION DATA

U*X*L encyclopedia of world mythology
  p. cm.
  Includes bibliographical references and index.
  ISBN 978-1-4144-3030-0 (set) -- ISBN 978-1-4144-3036-2 (vol. 1) -- ISBN 978-1-4144-3037-9 (vol. 2) -- ISBN 978-1-4144-3038-6 (vol. 3) -- ISBN 978-1-4144-3039-3 (vol. 4) -- ISBN 978-1-4144-3040-9 (vol. 5)
  1. Mythology—Encyclopedias, Juvenile. I. Title: UXL encyclopedia of world mythology. II. Title: Encyclopedia of world mythology.

BL303.U95 2009
201'.303—dc22   2008012696

Gale
27500 Drake
Farmington Hills, MI 48331-3535

ISBN-13: 978-1-4144-3030-0 (set)   ISBN-10: 1-4144-3030-2 (set)
ISBN-13: 978-1-4144-3036-2 (Vol. 1)   ISBN-10: 1-4144-3036-1 (Vol. 1)
ISBN-13: 978-1-4144-3037-9 (Vol. 2)   ISBN-10: 1-4144-3037-X (Vol. 2)
ISBN-13: 978-1-4144-3038-6 (Vol. 3)   ISBN-10: 1-4144-3038-8 (Vol. 3)
ISBN-13: 978-1-4144-3039-3 (Vol. 4)   ISBN-10: 1-4144-3039-6 (Vol. 4)
ISBN-13: 978-1-4144-3040-9 (Vol. 5)   ISBN-10: 1-4144-3040-X (Vol. 5)

This title is also available as an e-book.
ISBN-13: 978-1-4144-3846-7 ISBN-10: 1-4144-3846-X
Contact your Gale, a part of Cengage Learning sales representative for ordering information.

Printed in the United States of America
1 2 3 4 5 6 7 12 11 10 09 08

Table of Contents

Table of Contents by Culture

Reader's Guide

The *U·X·L Encyclopedia of World Mythology* examines the major characters, stories, and themes of mythologies from cultures around the globe, from African to Zoroastrian. Arranged alphabetically in an A–Z format, each entry provides the reader with an overview of the topic as well as contextual analysis to explain the topic's importance to the culture from which it came. In addition, each entry explains the topic's influence on modern life, and prompts the reader with a discussion question or reading/writing suggestion to inspire further analysis. There are five different types of entries: Character, Deity, Myth, Theme, and Culture. The entry types are designated by icons that are shown in a legend that appears on each page starting a new letter grouping so that you can easily tell which type of entry you are reading.

Types of Entries Found in This Book

Character entries generally focus on a single mythical character, such as a hero. In some cases, character entries deal with groups of similar or related beings—for example, Trolls or Valkyries. Deities (gods) are found in their own unique type of entry.

Deity entries contain information about a god or goddess. An example would be Zeus (pronounced ZOOS), the leader of the ancient Greek gods. Deities are very similar to other mythical characters, except that they often appear in many different myths; each Deity entry provides a summary of the most important myths related to that deity.

Myth entries focus on a specific story as opposed to a certain character. One example is the entry on the Holy Grail, which tells the legend of the vessel's origins as well as the many people who sought to locate it. In some cases, the myth is primarily concerned with a single character; the entry on the Golden Fleece, for example, features Jason as the main character. Like the Holy Grail entry, however, this entry focuses on the legends surrounding the object in question rather than the character involved.

Theme entries examine how one single theme, idea, or motif is addressed in the mythologies of different cultures. An example would be the Reincarnation entry that examines different cultural depictions of this eternal cycle of death and rebirth.

Culture entries contain a survey of the myths and beliefs of a particular culture. Each entry also provides historical and cultural context for understanding how the culture helped to shape, or was shaped by, the beliefs of other cultures.

Types of Rubrics Found in This Book

Each entry type is organized in specific rubrics to allow for ease of comparison across entries. The rubrics that appear in these entries are: *Character/Myth/Theme Overview*; *Core Deities and Characters*; *Major Myths*; *[Subject] in Context*; *Key Themes and Symbols*; *[Subject] in Art, Literature, and Everyday Life*; and *Read, Write, Think, Discuss*. In addition, the character, deity, and myth entries all have key facts sections in the margins that provide basic information about the entry, including the country or culture of origin, a pronunciation guide where necessary, alternate names for the character (when applicable), written or other sources in which the subject appears, and information on the character's family (when applicable).

Character Overview offers detailed information about the character's place within the mythology of its given culture. This may include information about the character's personality, summaries of notable feats, and relationships with other mythological characters. *Myth Overview* includes a summary of the myth being discussed. *Theme Overview* provides a brief description of the theme being discussed, as well as a rundown of the major points common when examining that theme in different mythologies.

Core Deities and Characters includes brief descriptions of the main deities and other characters that figure prominently in the given culture's mythology. This is not a comprehensive list of all the gods or characters mentioned in a particular culture.

Major Myths features a brief summary of all the most important or best-known myths related to the subject of the entry. For example, the entry on Odin (pronounced OH-din), chief god of Norse mythology, includes the tale describing how he gave up one of his eyes in order to be able to see the future.

[Subject] in Context provides additional cultural and historical information that helps you understand the subject by seeing through the eyes of the people who made it part of their culture. The entry on the weaver Arachne (pronounced uh-RAK-nee), for instance, includes information on the importance of weaving as a domestic duty in ancient Greece.

Key Themes and Symbols outlines the most important themes in the tales related to the subject. This section also includes explanations of symbols associated with the subject of the entry, or which appear in myths related to the subject. For example, this section may explain the meaning of certain objects a god is usually shown carrying.

[Subject] in Art, Literature, and Everyday Life includes references to the subject in well-known works of art, literature, film, and other media. This section may also mention other ways in which the subject appears in popular culture. For example, the fact that a leprechaun (pronounced LEP-ruh-kawn) appears as the mascot for Lucky Charms cereal is mentioned in this section of the Leprechauns entry.

Read, Write, Think, Discuss uses the material in the entry as a springboard for further discussion and learning. This section may include suggestions for further reading that are related to the subject of the entry, discussion questions regarding topics touched upon in the entry, writing prompts that explore related issues and themes, or research prompts that encourage you to delve deeper into the topics presented.

Most of the entries end with cross-references that point you to related entries in the encyclopedia. In addition, words that appear in bold within the entry are also related entries, making it easy to find additional information that will enhance your understanding of the topic.

Other Sections in This Book

This encyclopedia also contains other sections that you may find useful when studying world mythology. One of these is a "Timeline of World Mythology," which provides important dates from many cultures that are important to the development of their respective mythologies. A glossary in the front matter supplements the definitions that are included within the entries. Teachers will find the section on "Research and Activity Ideas" helpful in coming up with classroom activities related to the topic of mythology to engage students further in the subject. A section titled "Where to Learn More" provides you with other sources to learn more about the topic of mythology, organized by culture. You will also encounter sidebars in many of the entries; these sections offer interesting information that is related to, but not essential to, your understanding of the subject of the entry.

Comments and Suggestions

We welcome your comments on the *U·X·L Encyclopedia of World Mythology* and suggestions for other topics to consider. Please write to Editors, *U·X·L Encyclopedia of World Mythology,* Gale, 27500 Drake Rd., Farmington Hills, Michigan, 48331-3535.

Introduction

On the surface, myths are stories of gods, heroes, and monsters that can include fanciful tales about the creation and destruction of worlds, or awe-inspiring adventures of brave explorers in exotic or supernatural places. However, myths are not just random imaginings; they are cultivated and shaped by the cultures in which they arise. For this reason, a myth can function as a mirror for the culture that created it, reflecting the values, geographic location, natural resources, technological state, and social organization of the people who believe in it.

Values

The values of a culture are often revealed through that culture's myths and legends. For example, a myth common in Micronesian culture tells of a porpoise girl who married a human and had children; after living many years as a human, she decided to return to the sea. Before she left, she warned her children against eating porpoise, since they might unknowingly eat some of their own family members by doing so. Myths such as these are often used to provide colorful reasons for taboos, or rules against certain behaviors. In this case, the myth explains a taboo among the Micronesian peoples against hunting and eating porpoises.

Geography

Myths often reflect a culture's geographic circumstances. For example, the people of the Norse culture live in a region that has harsh, icy winters. It is no coincidence that, according to their myths, the being whose death led to the creation of the world was a giant made of frost. By contrast, the people of ancient Egypt lived in an dry, sunny land; their most important gods, such as Ra, were closely associated with the sun. Geographic features are also often part of a culture's myths, or used as inspiration for mythological tales. Spider Rock, a tall peak located at Canyon de Chelly National Monument in Arizona, is said by the Hopi people to be the home of the creation goddess Spider Woman. The Atlas mountains in northern Africa took their name from the myth that the Titan Atlas (pronounced AT-luhs) had once stood there holding up the heavens, but had been transformed to stone in order to make his task easier.

Natural Resources

Myths can also reflect the natural resources available to a culture, or the resources most prized by a certain group. In Mesoamerican and American Indian myths, maize (commonly referred to as corn) often appears as a food offered directly from gods or goddesses, or grown from the body of a deity. This reflects not only the importance of maize in the diets of early North and Central American cultures, but also the ready availability of maize, which does not appear as a native plant anywhere else in the world. Similarly, the olive tree, which is native to the coastal areas along the Mediterranean Sea, is one of the most important trees in ancient Greek myth. The city of Athens, it is said, was named for the goddess Athena (pronounced uh-THEE-nuh) after she gave its citizens the very first domesticated olive tree.

Sometimes, myths can reflect the importance of natural resources to an outside culture. For example, the Muisca people of what is now Colombia engaged in a ceremony in which their king covered himself in gold dust and took a raft out to the middle of a local lake; there he threw gold trinkets into the water as offerings to the gods. Gold was not commonly available, and was prized for its ceremonial significance; however, when Spanish explorers arrived in the New World and heard of this practice, they interpreted this to mean that gold must be commonplace in the area. This led to the myth of El Dorado, an entire city made of gold that many Spanish explorers believed to exist and spent decades trying to locate.

Technology

A culture's state of technological development can also be reflected in its myths. The earliest ancient Greek myths of Uranus (pronounced

YOOR-uh-nuhs) state that his son Cronus (pronounced KROH-nuhs) attacked him with a sickle made of obsidian. Obsidian is a stone that can be chipped to create a sharp edge, and was used by cultures older than the ancient Greeks, who relied on metals such as bronze and steel for their weapons. This might suggest that the myth arose from an earlier age; at the very least, it reflects the idea that, from the perspective of the Greeks, the myth took place in the distant past.

Social Order

Myths can also offer a snapshot of a culture's social organization. The Old Testament tale of the Tower of Babel offers an explanation for the many tribes found in the ancient Near East: they had once been united, and sought to build a tower that would reach all the way to heaven. In order to stop this act of self-importance, God caused the people to speak in different languages. Unable to understand each other, they abandoned the ambitious project and scattered into groups across the region.

Besides offering social order, myths can reinforce cultural views on the roles different types of individuals should assume in a society. The myth of Arachne (pronounced uh-RAK-nee) illustrates a fact known from other historical sources: weaving and fabric-making was the domestic duty of wives and daughters, and it was a skill highly prized in the homes of ancient Greece. Tales of characters such as Danaë (pronounced DAN-uh-ee), who was imprisoned in a tower by her father in order to prevent her from having a child, indicate the relative powerlessness of many women in ancient Greek society.

Different Cultures, Different Perspectives

To see how cultures reflect their own unique characteristics through myth, one can examine how a single theme—such as fertility—is treated in a variety of different cultures. Fertility is the ability to produce life, growth, or offspring, and is therefore common in most, if not all, mythologies. For many cultures, fertility is a key element in the creation of the world. The egg, one of the most common symbols of fertility, appears in Chinese mythology as the first object to form from the disorder that previously existed in place of the world. In many cultures, including ancient Greece, the main gods are born from a single mother;

in the case of the Greeks, the mother is Gaia (pronounced GAY-uh), also known as Earth.

For cultures that relied upon agriculture, fertility was an important element of the changing seasons and the growth of crops. In these cases, fertility was seen as a gift from nature that could be revoked by cruel weather or the actions of the gods. Such is the case in the ancient Greek myth of Persephone (pronounced per-SEF-uh-nee); when the goddess is taken to the underworld by Hades (pronounced HAY-deez), her mother—the fertility goddess Demeter (pronounced di-MEE-ter)—became sad, which caused all vegetation to wither and die.

For the ancient Egyptians, fertility represented not just crop growth and human birth, but also rebirth into the afterlife through death. This explains why Hathor (pronounced HATH-or), the mother goddess of fertility who supported all life, was also the maintainer of the dead. It was believed that Hathor provided food for the dead to help them make the long journey to the realm of the afterlife.

For early Semitic cultures, the notion of fertility was not always positive. In the story of Lilith, the little-known first wife of Adam (the first man), the independent-minded woman left her husband and went to live by the Red Sea, where she gave birth to many demons each day. The myth seems to suggest that fertility is a power that can be used for good or evil, and that the key to using this power positively is for wives to dutifully respect the wishes of their husbands. This same theme is found in the earlier Babylonian myth of Tiamat (pronounced TYAH-maht), who gave birth to not only the gods but also to an army of monsters that fought to defend her from her son, the hero Marduk (pronounced MAHR-dook).

These are just a few of the many ways in which different cultures can take a single idea and interpret it through their own tales. Rest assured that the myths discussed in this book are wondrous legends that capture the imagination of the reader. They are also mirrors in which we can see not only ourselves, but the reflections of cultures old and new, far and near—allowing us to celebrate their unique differences, and at the same time recognize those common elements that make these enchanting stories universally beloved and appreciated by readers and students around the world.

Timeline of World Mythology

c. 3400 BCE Early Sumerian writing is first developed.

c. 3100 BCE Egyptian writing, commonly known as hieroglyphics, is first developed.

c. 2852–2205 BCE During this time period, China is supposedly ruled by the Three Sovereigns and Five Emperors, mythical figures that may have been based on actual historical leaders.

c. 2100 BCE Earliest known version of the *Epic of Gilgamesh* is recorded in Sumerian.

c. 1553–1536 BCE Egyptian pharaoh Akhenaten establishes official worship of Aten, a single supreme god, instead of the usual group of gods recognized by ancient Egyptians.

c. 1250 BCE The Trojan War supposedly occurs around this time period. Despite the war's importance to Greek and Roman mythology, modern scholars are not sure whether the war was an actual historical event or just a myth.

c. 1100 BCE The Babylonian creation epic *Enuma Elish* is documented on clay tablets discovered nearly three thousand years later in the ruined library of Ashurbanipal, located in modern-day Iraq.

c. 800 BCE The Greek alphabet is invented, leading to a flowering of Greek literature based on myth.

c. 750 BCE The Greek epics known as the *Iliad* and the *Odyssey* are written by the poet Homer. Based on the events surrounding the

Trojan War, these two stories are the source of many myths and characters in Greek and Roman mythology.

c. 750 BCE The Greek poet Hesiod writes his *Theogony*, which details the origins of the Greek gods.

c. 563–480 BCE According to tradition, Gautama Buddha, the founder of Buddhism, is believed to have lived in ancient India and Nepal during this time.

525–456 BCE The Greek dramatist Aeschylus writes tragedies detailing the lives of mythical characters, including *Seven Against Thebes*, *Agamemnon*, and *The Eumenides*.

c. 500–100 BCE The oldest version of the *Ramayana*, the Hindu epic about the incarnation of the god Vishnu named Rama, is written.

c. 496–406 BCE Ancient Greek playwright Sophocles creates classic plays such as *Antigone* and *Oedipus the King*.

c. 450 BCE The Book of Genesis, containing stories fundamental to early Christianity, Judaism, and Islam, is collected and organized into its modern form.

c. 431 BCE Greek builders complete work on the temple of Athena known as the Parthenon, one of the few ancient Greek structures to survive to modern times.

c. 150–50 BCE The Gundestrup cauldron, a silver bowl depicting various Celtic deities and rituals, is created. The bowl is later recovered from a peat bog in Denmark in 1891.

c. 29–19 BCE Roman poet Virgil creates his mythical epic, the *Aeneid*, detailing the founding of Rome.

c. 4 BCE–33 CE Jesus, believed by Christians to be the son of God, supposedly lives during this time period.

c. 8 CE Roman poet Ovid completes his epic work *Metamorphoses*. It is one of the best existing sources for tales of ancient Greek and Roman mythology.

c. 100 CE The *Mahabharata*, a massive epic recognized as one of the most important pieces of literature in Hinduism, is organized into its modern form from source material dating back as far as the ninth century BCE.

c. 570–632 CE The prophet Muhammad, founder of Islam, supposedly lives during this time.

c. 800–840 CE The oldest surviving remnants of *The Book of One Thousand and One Nights*, a collection of Near Eastern folktales and legends, are written in Syrian.

c. 1000 CE The Ramsund carving, a stone artifact bearing an illustration of the tale of Sigurd, is created in Sweden. The tale is documented in the *Volsunga* saga.

c. 1010 CE The oldest surviving manuscript of the Old English epic *Beowulf* is written. It is recognized as the first significant work of English literature.

c. 1100 Monks at the Clonmacnoise monastery compile the *Book of the Dun Cow*, the earliest written collection of Irish myths and legends still in existence.

c. 1138 Geoffrey of Monmouth's *History of the Kings of Britain* is published, featuring the first well-known tales of the legendary King Arthur.

c. 1180–1210 The *Nibelungenlied*, a German epic based largely on earlier German and Norse legends such as the *Volsunga* saga, is written by an unknown poet.

c. 1220 Icelandic scholar Snorri Sturluson writes the Prose Edda, a comprehensive collection of Norse myths and legends gathered from older sources.

c. 1350 The *White Book of Rhydderch*, containing most of the Welsh myths and legends later gathered in the *Mabinogion*, first appears.

1485 Thomas Malory publishes *Le Morte D'Arthur*, widely considered to be the most authoritative version of the legend of King Arthur.

c. 1489 *A Lytell Geste of Robin Hode*, one of the most comprehensive versions of the life of the legendary British character of Robin Hood, is published.

c. 1550 The *Popol Vuh*, a codex containing Mayan creation myths and legends, is written. The book, written in the Quiché language but using Latin characters, was likely based on an older book written in Mayan hieroglyphics that has since been lost.

1835 Elias Lonnrot publishes the *Kalevala*, an epic made up of Finnish songs and oral myths gathered during years of field research.

1849 Archeologist Henry Layard discovers clay tablets containing the Babylonian creation epic *Enuma Elish* in Iraq. The epic, lost for centuries, is unknown to modern scholars before this discovery.

1880 Journalist Joel Chandler Harris publishes *Uncle Remus, His Songs and Sayings: the Folk-Lore of the Old Plantation*, a collection of myths and folktales gathered from African American slaves working in the South. Many of the tales are derived from older stories from African myth. Although the book is successful and spawns three sequels, Harris is accused by some of taking cultural myths and passing them off as his own works.

Words to Know

benevolent: Helpful or well-meaning.

caste: A social level in India's complex social class system.

cauldron: Kettle.

chaos: Disorder.

chivalry: A moral code popularized in Europe in the Middle Ages that stressed such traits as generosity, bravery, courtesy, and respect toward women.

constellation: Group of stars.

cosmogony: The study of, or a theory about, the origin of the universe.

deity: God or goddess.

demigod: Person with one parent who was human and one parent who was a god.

destiny: Predetermined future.

divination: Predicting the future.

dualistic: Having two sides or a double nature.

epic: A long, grand-scale poem.

fertility: The ability to reproduce; can refer to human ability to produce children or the ability of the earth to sustain plant life.

hierarchy: Ranked order of importance.

hubris: Too much self-confidence.

immortal: Living forever.

imperial: Royal, or related to an empire.

indigenous: Native to a given area.

Judeo-Christian: Related to the religious tradition shared by Judaism and Christianity. The faiths share a holy book, many fundamental principles, and a belief in a single, all-powerful god.

matriarchal: Female-dominated. Often refers to societies in which a family's name and property are passed down through the mother's side of the family.

mediator: A go-between.

monotheism: The belief in a single god as opposed to many gods.

mummification: The drying and preserving of a body to keep it from rotting after death.

nymph: A female nature deity.

omen: A mystical sign of an event to come.

oracle: Person through whom the gods communicated with humans.

pagan: Someone who worships pre-Christian gods.

pantheon: The entire collection of gods recognized by a group of people.

patriarchal: Male-dominated. Often refers to societies in which the family name and wealth are passed through the father.

patron: A protector or supporter.

pharaoh: A king of ancient Egypt.

polytheism: Belief in many gods.

primal: Fundamental; existing since the beginning.

prophet: A person able to see the plans of the gods or foretell future events.

pyre: A large pile of burning wood used in some cultures to cremate a dead body.

resurrected: Brought back to life.

revelation: The communication of divine truth or divine will to human beings.

rune: A character from an ancient and magical alphabet.

seer: A person who can see the future.

shaman: A person who uses magic to heal or look after the members of his tribe.

sorcerer: Wizard.

syncretism: The blending or fusion of different religions or belief systems.

tradition: A time-honored practice, or set of such practices.

underworld: Land of the dead.

utopia: A place of social, economic and political perfection.

Research and Activity Ideas

Teachers wishing to enrich their students' understanding of world mythologies might try some of the following group activities. Each uses art, music, drama, speech, research, or scientific experimentation to put the students in closer contact with the cultures, myths, and figures they are studying.

Greek Mythology: A Pageant of Gods

In this activity, students get to be gods and goddesses for a day during the classroom "Pageant of the Gods," an event modeled after a beauty pageant. Each student selects (with teacher approval) a deity from Greek mythology. Students then research their deity, write a 250-word description of the deity, and create costumes so they can dress as their deity. On the day of the pageant, the teacher collects the students' descriptions and reads them aloud as each student models his or her costume for the class.

Materials required for the students:

Common household materials for costume

Materials required for the teacher:

None

Optional extension: The class throws a post-pageant potluck of Greek food.

Anglo-Saxon Mythology: Old English Translation

Students are often surprised to learn that *Beowulf* is written in English. The original Old English text looks almost unrecognizable to them. In this activity (which students may work on in the classroom, in the library, or at home), the teacher begins by discussing the history of the English language and its evolution over the past one thousand years (since the writing of *Beowulf*). The teacher then models how a linguist would go about translating something written in Old English or Middle English (using an accessible text such as *The Canterbury Tales* as an example), and makes various resources for translation available to the students (see below). The class as a whole works on translating the first two lines of *Beowulf*. The teacher then assigns small groups of students a couple lines each of the opening section of *Beowulf* to translate and gloss. When each group is ready with their translations, the students assemble the modern English version of the opening of *Beowulf* and discuss what they learned about the various Old English words they studied.

Materials required for the students:

None

Materials required for the teacher:

Copies of an Old English version of the first part of *Beowulf* for distribution to students.

There are multiple Old English dictionaries available online, so student groups could work on this activity in the classroom if a sufficient number of computer workstations with Internet access are available. There are also many Old English dictionaries in print form. If none is available in the school library, some can be checked out from the public library.

Egyptian Mythology: Mummify a Chicken

The ancient Egyptians believed preserving a person's body ensured their safe passage into the afterlife. The process of Egyptian mummification was a secret for many centuries until ancient Greek historian Herodotus recorded some information about the process in the fifth century BCE. Archaeologists have recently refined their understanding of Egyptian mummification practices. In this activity, students conduct their own mummification experiment on chickens.

The teacher contextualizes the activity by showing students a video on mummies and asking them to read both Herodotus's account of mummification and more recent articles about mummification that center on the research of Egyptologist Bob Brier.

Once students understand the basics of mummification, groups of five or six students can begin their science experiment, outlined below. The teacher should preface the experiment with safety guidelines for handling raw chicken.

Materials required for students:

Scale

One fresh chicken per group (bone-in chicken breast or leg may substitute)

Disposable plastic gloves (available at drugstores)

Carton of salt per group per week

Spice mixture (any strong powdered spices will do; powdered cloves, cinnamon, and ginger are good choices)

Extra-large (gallon size) air-tight freezer bags

Roll of gauze per group (available at drugstore)

Disposable aluminum trays for holding chickens

Cooking oil

Notebook for each group

Materials required for the teacher:

Video on mummies. A good option is: *Mummies: Secrets of the Pharaohs* (2007), available on DVD.

Reading material on mummies, including Herodotus's account. See: http://discovermagazine.com/2007/oct/mummification-is-back-from-the-dead; http://www.nationalgeographic.com/tv/mummy/; http://www.mummytombs.com/egypt/herodotus.htm

Plenty of paper towels and hand soap.

Procedure

1. All students put on plastic gloves.

2. Weigh each chicken (unnecessary if weight printed on packaging) and record the weight in a notebook. Record details of the chicken's appearance in the notebook.

3. Remove chicken organs and dispose of them. Rinse the chicken thoroughly in a sink.

4. Pat the chicken dry with paper towels. Make sure the chicken is completely dry, or the mummification process might not work.

5. Rub the spices all over the chicken, both inside and outside, then salt the entire chicken and fill the chicken cavity with salt.

6. Seal the chicken in the air-tight bag and place it in the aluminum tray.

7. Remove gloves and wash hands thoroughly with soap and water.

8. Once a week, put on plastic gloves, remove the chicken from the bag, dispose of the bag and accumulated liquid, and weigh the chicken. Record the weight in a notebook and make notes on changes in the chicken's appearance. Respice and resalt the chicken, fill the chicken cavity with salt, and seal it in a new bag. Remove gloves and wash hands. Repeat this step until no more liquid drains from the chicken.

9. When liquid no longer drains from the chicken, the mummy is done! Wipe off all the salt and rub a light coat of cooking oil on the mummy. Wrap it tightly in gauze.

Optional extension: Students can decorate their mummies using hieroglyphics and build shoebox sarcophagi for them.

Near Eastern Mythology: Gilgamesh and the Cedar Forest

The story of Gilgamesh's heroics against the demon Humbaba of the Cedar Forest is one of the most exciting parts of the *Epic of Gilgamesh*. In this activity, students write, stage, and perform a three-act play based on this part of the epic. Necessary tasks will include writing, costume design, set design, and acting. The teacher can divide tasks among students as necessary.

Materials required for the students:

Household items for costumes

Cardboard, paint, tape, and other materials for sets

Copy of the *Epic of Gilgamesh*

Materials required for the teacher:

None

Hindu Mythology: Salute the Sun

The practice of yoga, an ancient mental and physical discipline designed to promote spiritual perfection, is mentioned in most of the Hindu holy texts. Today, the physical aspects of yoga have become a widely popular form of exercise around the world. In this activity, the students and teacher will make yoga poses part of their own daily routine.

The teacher introduces the activity by discussing the history of yoga from ancient to modern times, by showing a video on the history of yoga, and by distributing readings from ancient Hindu texts dealing with the practice of yoga. After a class discussion on the video and texts, the teacher leads students through a basic "sun salutation" series of poses with the aid of an instructional yoga video (students may wish to bring a towel or mat from home, as some parts of the sun salutation involve getting on the floor). Students and the teacher will perform the sun salutation every day, preferably at the beginning of class, either for the duration of the semester or for another set period of time. Students will conclude the activity by writing a summary of their feelings about their yoga "experiment."

Materials required for the students:

Towel or mat to put on floor during sun salutations.

Materials required for teacher:

A DVD on the history of yoga. Recommended: *Yoga Unveiled* (2004), an excellent documentary series on the history of yoga.

An instructional yoga video that includes the "sun salutation" sequence (many available).

Handouts of ancient Indian writings on yoga. See *The Shambhala Encyclopedia of Yoga* (2000) and *The Yoga and the Bhagavad Gita* (2007).

African Mythology: Storytelling

Anansi the Spider was a trickster god of West African origin who was known as a master storyteller. In this activity, students work on their own storytelling skills while learning about the spread of Anansi stories from Africa to the Americas.

The teacher begins this activity by discussing the ways that oral traditions have helped the African American community preserve some part of their West African cultural heritage. The spread of stories about Anansi around Caribbean and American slave communities is an example, with the Uncle Remus stories of Joel Chandler Harris being a good demonstration of how the Anansi tales have evolved. The class then conducts a preliminary discussion about what the elements of a good spoken story might be, then watches or listens to models of storytelling. After listening to the stories, the class discusses common elements in the stories and techniques the storytellers used to keep the audience's attention and build interest.

Students then read a variety of Anansi and Uncle Remus stories on their own. With teacher approval, they select one story and prepare it for oral presentation in class (several students may select the same story). After the presentations, students can discuss their reactions to the various oral presentations, pointing out what was effective and ineffective.

Materials required for the students:

Optional: props for story presentation

Materials required for the teacher:

Background reading on West African oral traditions.

Recordings or videos of skilled storytellers. See *The American Storyteller Series* or the CD recording *Tell Me a Story: Timeless Folktales from Around the World* (which includes an Anansi story).

Optional extension: The teacher may arrange for students with especially strong oral presentations to share their stories at a school assembly or as visiting speakers in another classroom.

Micronesian and Melanesian Mythology: Island Hopping

The many islands that make up Micronesia and Melanesia are largely unfamiliar to most students. In this activity, students learn more about these faraway places.

The teacher introduces this activity by hanging up a large map of the South Pacific, with detail of Micronesian and Melanesian islands. The teacher explains that, during every class session, the class will learn the location of and key facts about a particular island. Each day, one student is given the name of an island. It is that student's homework assignment that night to learn the location of the island, its population, and its key industries. The student must also learn two interesting facts about the island. The next day, the student places a push pin (or other marker) on the map showing the location of his or her island. The student presents the information to the class, writes it down on an index card, and files the index card in the class "island" box. In this way, the students learn about a new Micronesian or Melanesian island every day and build a ready resource of information about the islands.

Materials required for the students:

None

Materials required for the teacher:

Large wall map with sufficient detail of Micronesia and Melanesia
Index cards
Box for island index cards
Push pins, stickers, or other markers for islands

Northern European Mythology: The Scroll of the Nibelungen

The *Nibelungenlied* is an epic poem set in pre-Christian Germany. The tale contains many adventures, fights, and triumphs. In this activity, students prepare a graphic-novel version of the *Nibelungenlied*.

To introduce this activity, the teacher gives students a synopsis of the *Nibelungenlied* and describes the various interpretations of the saga (including Richard Wagner's opera and J. R. R. Tolkien's *Lord of the Rings* triology). The teacher then explains that the class will create a graphic novel of the *Nibelungenlied* on a continuous scroll of paper. The teacher shows models of various graphic novels and discusses the conventions of graphic novel representations.

Students are divided into groups of three or four, and each group receives one chapter or section of the *Nibelungenlied* as its assignment.

After reading their sections, the groups meet to discuss possible graphical representations of the action in their chapters and present their ideas to the teacher for approval. After gaining approval, student groups work, one group at a time, to draw and color their chapters on the scroll. When the scroll is finished, each group makes a short presentation explaining what happens in their chapter and how they chose to represent the action. The final scroll can be displayed around the classroom walls or along a school hallway.

Materials required by the students:

None

Materials required by the teacher:

Easel paper roll (200 feet)

Markers, colored pencils, and crayons

Copies of *Nibelungenlied* chapters for students (or refer students to http://omacl.org/Nibelungenlied/)

Inca Mythology: Make a Siku

A siku is an Andean pan pipe. Pipes such as these were important in Inca culture, and remain a prominent feature in Andean music. In this activity, students will make their own sikus.

The teacher begins this activity by playing some Andean pan pipe music, showing students the Andes on a map, and discussing the ways in which Inca culture remains part of the lives of Native Americans in countries like Peru. The teacher shows a picture of a pan pipe (or, ideally, an actual pan pipe) to the students and explains they will build their own.

Students need ten drinking straws each (they can bring them from home, or the teacher can provide them) and a pair of scissors. To make the pipe:

1. Set aside two of the straws. Cut the remaining straws so that each is one-half inch shorter than the next. The first straw is uncut. The second straw is one-half inch shorter than the first. The third is one inch shorter than the first, and so on.

2. Cut the remaining straws into equal pieces. These pieces will be used as spacers between pipe pieces.

3. Arrange the straws from longest to shortest (left to right) with the tops of the straws lined up.
4. Put spacer pieces between each part of the pipe so they are an equal distance apart.
5. Tape the pipe in position, making sure the tops of the straws stay in alignment.
6. The pipe is finished. Cover in paper and decorate if desired. Blow across the tops of straws to play.

Materials required by the students:

Ten drinking straws

Scissors

Tape

Materials required by the teacher:

Andean pipe music

Pictures of a pan pipe or an actual pan pipe

Picture of the Andes on a map

U·X·L Encyclopedia of World Mythology

VOLUME 4: M–P

M

 Character

 Deity

 Myth

 Theme

 Culture

Nationality/Culture
Hindu

Pronunciation
muh-hah-BAHR-ruh-tuh

Alternate Names
None

Appears In
The *Mahabharata*

Mahabharata, The

Myth Overview

The *Mahabharata* (pronounced muh-hah-BAHR-ruh-tuh) consists of a collection of legends and tales revolving around the great Bharata War between the Kauravas and the Pandavas, two branches of an ancient Indian dynasty. The stories—which involve gods and **heroes**—contain elements of myth, philosophy, and religious teachings. A section of the epic called the ***Bhagavad Gita*** (Song of God) is one of the most important religious texts of Hinduism.

The *Mahabharata* is set in the kingdom of Kurukshetra (pronounced khuh-rook-SHAY-truh) on the northern plains of India along the Ganges River. The opening parvans (books) explain the ancestry of the major characters and provide background for the central conflict of the work. That conflict begins when the rightful heir to the throne of Kurukshetra, a blind prince named Dhritarashtra (pronounced dree-tuh-RAHSH-truh), is passed over in favor of his younger brother Pandu (pronounced PAN-doo). Instead of taking the throne, however, Pandu goes to the Himalaya mountains to live as a hermit, leaving Dhritarashtra on the throne after all.

Before Pandu left Kurukshetra, his two wives gave birth to five sons, who became known as the Pandavas (pronounced PAHN-duh-vuhz). They lived at the royal court with their cousins, the one hundred sons of Dhritarashtra known as the Kauravas (pronounced KOW-ruh-vuhz).

659

When the Pandavas came of age, the eldest, Yudhisthira (pronounced yoo-DIS-thuh-ruh), demanded the throne from his uncle, claiming that he was the rightful heir. A feud broke out between the two branches of the family, and the Kauravas eventually forced the Pandavas into exile in the forest.

While in exile, the Pandavas entered a tournament to win the hand of a beautiful princess named Draupadi (pronounced DROW-puh-dee). The Kauravas also entered the contest, but the Pandava brother Arjuna (pronounced AHR-juh-nuh) won the princess, who became the common wife of all five Pandavas.

After the tournament, King Dhritarashtra called the Pandavas back to his court and divided the kingdom among them and his own sons. Unhappy with this settlement, the Kauravas challenged the Pandavas to a game of dice and won back the entire kingdom by cheating. Once again, the Pandavas were forced into exile.

After many years of wandering, the Pandavas returned to reclaim the kingdom, but the Kauravas refused to give up control and both sides prepared for war. The god **Krishna** (pronounced KRISH-nuh) supported the Pandavas. Although he took no part in the fighting, he served as charioteer for the Pandava brother Arjuna and gave him advice. Their conversations prior to battle make up the section of the *Mahabharata* known as the *Bhagavad Gita*.

The Pandavas and Kauravas met in a series of battles on the plains of Kurukshetra. In the end, the Pandavas emerged victorious after killing all their cousins. The Pandavas gained the kingdom, and the oldest brother, Yudhisthira, took the throne.

The Pandavas ruled peacefully, although their uncle Dhritarashtra mourned the loss of his sons and frequently quarreled with his nephews. Dhritarashtra eventually went to live in the forest and died there. Some time later, Yudhisthira gave up the throne and went with his brothers and their wife, Draupadi, to live on Mount Meru, the abode of the god **Indra** (pronounced IN-druh).

The conflict between the Pandavas and Kauravas makes up only a portion of the *Mahabharata*. The work includes many other tales about deities and heroes and covers an enormous range of topics. The stories present complex philosophical ideas that form the basis of the Hindu faith—codes of conduct, social duties, and religious principles.

The *Mahabharata* in Context

One of the major epics of India and the longest poem in the world, the *Mahabharata* is a sacred Hindu text. Although tradition holds that an ancient sage, or wise man, called Vyasa (pronounced vee-YAH-sah) authored the *Mahabharata*, it was almost certainly composed by a number of different poets and then collected into a single work sometime between 400 BCE and 200 CE. The epic reached its present form about two hundred years later. It contains nearly one hundred thousand verses and is divided into eighteen books called *parvans*. The work reflects Hindu beliefs about the historical rulers of a region of northern India, and also provides details about worship and codes of conduct in ancient Hindu culture.

Key Themes and Symbols

The main theme of the *Mahabharata* is the idea of sacred duty. Every character in the epic is born into a particular social group, or caste, that must follow the duty prescribed to it by sacred law. The characters who perform their sacred duty are rewarded, while those who do not are punished. This is the great lesson that Lord Krishna gives Arjuna when he begins to doubt his role in the battle. Obeying one's sacred duty is a key pillar of the Hindu religion.

The *Mahabharata* in Art, Literature, and Everyday Life

The *Mahabharata* is immensely popular in India and throughout Southeast Asia. The work inspired many ancient works of art, such as Indian miniature paintings and the elaborate sculptures of the ancient temples of Angkor Wat and Angkor Thom in Cambodia. Today the *Mahabharata* remains an important Hindu epic and continues to serve as the foundation for Hindu religious faith and mythology.

Read, Write, Think, Discuss

In the *Mahabharata*, Draupadi is married to five brothers at the same time. Many modern cultures have laws prohibiting marriage to more than one person at a time. What purpose do you think laws such as this serve? How does a society benefit from limiting marriage to a single person? Should a woman be allowed to marry two or more men if all the participants agree? Why or why not?

SEE ALSO *Bhagavad Gita*; Hinduism and Mythology; Indra; Krishna

Mahadevi

See **Devi.**

Manco Capac

Nationality/Culture
Incan

Pronunciation
MAHN-koh kah-PAHK

Alternate Names
None

Appears In
Inca creation myths

Lineage
Son of Inti, the sun god

Character Overview

In the mythology of the Incas, Manco Capac was the founder of the Inca nation and a culture hero who set the Incas on the road to glory. He was the son of the **sun** god Inti (pronounced IN-tee) and the supreme teacher of the ways of civilization. There are several versions of Manco Capac's story. The best-known source, *The Royal Commentaries of the Inca* by El Inca Garcilaso de la Vega, relates that the sun god was distressed because the people of earth did not live in a civilized way. As he crossed the sky each day, he saw that they wore only leaves and animal skins for clothing, lived in caves, and gathered wild plants and berries for food. So the sun god decided to send his son, Manco Capac, and daughter, Mama Ocllo (pronounced MAH-muh oh-KEE-oh), to teach the people how to improve their way of life. He gave his children a golden rod and told them to push it into the ground wherever they stopped to rest. When they reached a spot where the rod sank completely into the ground with a single push, they should build a sacred city of the sun, to be named Cuzco (pronounced KOOZ-koh).

Setting out from Lake Titicaca (pronounced tee-tee-KAH-kah), Manco Capac and Mama Ocllo wandered across the land and finally came to a valley where the golden rod sank easily into the soil. There they gathered all the people from near and far and taught them how to build homes, weave cloth, make tools, and grow crops. They also taught

Manco Capac was the son of the Incan sun god, who came to earth to teach the people how to live better. THE ART ARCHIVE/MUSEO PEDRO DE OSMA LIMA/MIREILLE VAUTIER. REPRODUCED BY PERMISSION.

the people how to use weapons so that they could defend themselves and defeat others.

Another version of the myth says that Manco Capac was one of six siblings who emerged from a cave near Cuzco. The siblings gained control over the people of the earth, and Manco Capac became the first ruler of the Incas. Still another tale says that Manco Capac deceived people into believing that he was the son of the sun god. He did this by standing on a mountain wearing gold plaques that shone in the sun and made him look like a god.

Manco Capac in Context

The myth of Manco Capac reflects the Inca belief in the naturally primitive state of humans. Before Manco Capac arrives, humans live without clothing, houses, or agriculture. According to the Inca people, Manco Capac was an actual ruler who lived in the twelfth or thirteenth century. It is possible that Manco Capac was a human ruler, or series of rulers, who oversaw the basic changes that led to a well-defined Inca society, and was later granted a godlike status for his accomplishments.

When the Spaniards came to the land of the Incas, they removed the preserved bodies of many dead Incan rulers to keep people from worshipping them. They were not able to find the body of Manco Capac, however, because his body was buried outside the city of Cuzco. The Incas believed that his body turned into a stone, and this stone became one of their holiest objects.

Key Themes and Symbols

One of the main themes of the myth of Manco Capac is guidance, or teaching. Manco Capac descends to earth, shows the people the best place to live, and teaches them how to do all those things necessary for civilization: build houses, grow food, make clothes, and defend their land. In this way, Manco Capac is a symbol of everything the Incas achieved as a society.

Manco Capac in Art, Literature, and Everyday Life

Manco Capac is perhaps the most important figure in **Inca mythology** but has appeared only rarely in art and literature outside the Inca culture. He is mentioned in a short story by Herman Melville, the author of *Moby Dick*, and was a character in the 1987 *Uncle Scrooge* comic book story "The Son of the Sun," featuring Disney's Scrooge McDuck and his nephews Huey, Dewey, and Louie.

Read, Write, Think, Discuss

The Inca people believed that the natural state of humankind was uncivilized and crude. This suggests that without a strong leader a society will fall back into disorder and lawlessness. Do you think humans require guidance from a central figure in order to maintain civilized behavior? Why or why not? Similarly, do you think specific individuals, such as inventors, are mostly responsible for human progress, or do large groups of people acting together help bring about advances in human societies?

SEE ALSO Inca Mythology

Manticore

Character Overview

The manticore was a mythical animal with a human head and face, a lion's body, and a scorpion's tail. According to legend, this fast, powerful, and fierce beast attacked and devoured people. Although believed to have originated with the Persians—who said the creature lived in India—the manticore is best known from the writings of Greek historians.

First described by the Greek physician Ctesias in the late fifth or early fourth century BCE, the manticore was said to be mostly red with pale blue or gray eyes and three rows of sharp teeth stretching from ear to ear. The manticore's voice sounded like a combination of a trumpet and a reed pipe. Its tail was equipped with stinging quills that the creature could shoot like arrows. An unfortunate traveler who happened upon a manticore in the woods—its preferred habitat—would be subdued by the manticore's quills and eaten whole, bones, clothing, and all.

The Manticore in Context

In the first century CE, the Roman writer Pliny the Elder included the manticore in his book *Natural History*, which was meant to be a document of known living creatures in the ancient world. This reflects the common opinion that manticores were real beasts; indeed, Pliny was considered such a reliable source of information that people well into the Middle Ages believed the manticore to be real.

Key Themes and Symbols

In ancient Greek culture, the manticore represented the unknown lands of Asia, the area it was said to inhabit. In later times, the manticore was recognized by many Europeans as a symbol of the devil or of the ruthless rule of tyrants. This may have originated in the practice of using manticores as royal decorations.

The Manticore in Art, Literature, and Everyday Life

During the Middle Ages, the manticore appeared in a number of bestiaries, books containing pictures or descriptions of mythical beasts.

Nationality/Culture
Persian/Greek

Pronunciation
MAN-ti-kor

Alternate Names
Martichora

Appears In
Pliny the Elder's *Natural History*, Pausanias's *Description of Greece*

Lineage
Unknown

The manticore was a man-eating monster that had the head of a man, the body of a lion, and the tail of a scorpion. © SCIENCE MUSEUM/SSPL/THE IMAGE WORKS.

The manticore was also featured in medieval heraldry—designs on armor, shields, and banners that indicated the group or family to which a knight belonged. Zoologists used the name *manticora* for a genus of African tiger beetles with large, fierce-looking jaws. In modern times, the creature has appeared in numerous works of fantasy, including Salman Rushdie's *The Satanic Verses* and J. K. Rowling's Harry Potter novels. The creature also appears symbolically in the 1972 Robertson Davies novel *The Manticore*. The manticore was even the subject for a 2005 monster movie, titled *Manticore*, created for the Sci-Fi Channel.

Read, Write, Think, Discuss

Why do you think ancient Greek sources state that the manticore can be found in India? What does this suggest about Greek exploration of India and Asia? Why do you think that Europeans in the Middle Ages were so willing to believe that the manticore was a real creature?

SEE ALSO Animals in Mythology

Manu

Character Overview

In Hindu mythology, **Brahma** (pronounced BRAH-muh) split himself in two to create Manu, the first man, and Shatarupa (pronounced shuh-TAH-roo-puh), the first woman. Manu and Shatarupa gave life to all humans. According to legend, Manu was the earth's first king and the ancestor of all the kings of India.

The most famous tale involving Manu tells of a great flood that destroyed everything on earth. One day Manu was washing his hands in a bowl of water when he saw a tiny fish there. The fish pleaded with Manu to be placed in a larger vessel of water to survive. In return, the fish promised to save Manu from a great flood that was to come and carry away all living beings. Manu put the fish in a bigger bowl, but the fish grew so rapidly that he had to transfer it to an even larger tank. The fish continued to grow until Manu eventually threw it into the sea. At that point, the fish—who was actually a form of the god **Vishnu** (pronounced VISH-noo)—told Manu that he should build a great ship to save himself from the coming flood. He also instructed Manu to take into the ship two of each animal on the earth as well as seeds from every kind of plant.

When the flood came, Manu used a rope to tie his boat to a large horn growing out of the fish. Pulling the ship through the rough waters, the fish came to the Himalaya mountains. There it told Manu to tie the ship to one of the mountains and wait until the waters receded. After the flood, Manu became lonely because only he and the animals aboard the ship had survived. He offered a **sacrifice** and was rewarded with a wife, with whom he began to repopulate the earth.

Manu in Context

As the first man, Manu is also credited as the inventor of many of the basic rules of social and religious conduct. In this way, Manu served as ultimate authority on proper behavior among ancient Hindus. The traditions credited to Manu reflect the culture in which they were written, and many are noted by modern scholars as attempts to restrict the freedom of women.

Nationality/Culture
Hindu

Pronunciation
MAN-oo

Alternate Names
Satyavrata

Appears In
The *Mahabharata*

Lineage
Created from Brahma

Key Themes and Symbols

One of the main themes of the myth of Manu is destruction and renewal. All living things on earth, with the exception of those taken aboard by Manu, are killed in the flood. Manu must then repopulate the earth with the living things he saved. In Hindu mythology, Manu represents truth, wisdom, and virtue. Manu also serves as a father figure for all humankind.

Manu in Art, Literature, and Everyday Life

Although Manu was the father of mankind, he is not featured heavily in Hindu art, literature, or worship. He is believed to be the author of the ancient book called the *Manusmriti* (pronounced mah-noo-SMRIT-ee). This book contains basic codes of behavior for all Hindus to follow.

Read, Write, Think, Discuss

One of the main themes of the myth of Manu is destruction and renewal, or death and birth. As a major concern among humans everywhere, this theme is central to most world religions. Hinduism and Christianity have very different views of life and death, and of life after death. Using your library, the Internet, or other available resources, research how issues of life and death are depicted in Hinduism and Christianity. What are the similarities and contrasts? Do you think that what people believe about the **afterlife** influences the way they live their lives?

SEE ALSO Adam and Eve; Floods; Hinduism and Mythology; Noah

Marduk

Nationality/Culture
Babylonian/Mesopotamian

Pronunciation
MAHR-dook

Alternate Names
Bel

Appears In
The *Enuma Elish*

Lineage
Son of Ea and Damkina

Character Overview

The chief god of the Babylonians (pronounced bab-uh-LOH-nee-uhnz) and Mesopotamians (pronounced mess-uh-puh-TAY-mee-uhnz), Marduk created an ordered world out of the original state of chaos and disorder. He was a powerful and fierce god who punished sinners, but was also merciful toward his followers. His exploits are described in the Babylonian creation epic known as the ***Enuma Elish***.

Major Myths

Before the birth of Marduk there were two ancient gods: Apsu, god of the sweet waters; and his wife **Tiamat** (pronounced TYAH-maht), goddess of the salt waters. This pair produced children, who in turn gave birth to Marduk and other gods. In time, a great conflict arose between the young gods and the ancient gods. Tiamat created an army of demons to attack and destroy the young gods. After giving her son Kingu (pronounced KIN-goo) the tablets of destiny, which allowed him to command the gods in her service, Tiamat placed him in charge of the army. The young gods chose Marduk as their champion to do battle with Tiamat. He accepted on the condition that he be named the leader of all the gods.

Armed with a net, a bow, a mace (a type of club), and the four winds, Marduk went out to face Tiamat. She appeared in the form of a dragon. Marduk caught Tiamat in his net, but she opened her mouth to swallow him. At that point, Marduk drove fierce winds into her mouth, causing her body to blow up like a balloon. He then shot an arrow at Tiamat's heart and killed her. After splitting her body into two pieces, he set one piece in the sky to create the heavens and the other at his feet to form the earth.

Marduk took the tablets of destiny from Kingu and placed them on his own chest to proclaim his power over the gods. Then he created time by establishing the first calendar. Finally, he killed Kingu and used his blood to create humans as servants of the gods. In recognition of his power, the other gods built a great temple to Marduk in the city of Babylon, located in Mesopotamia.

Marduk in Context

Marduk was long considered the protector god of the city of Babylon. When the city became the center of the ancient world, Marduk likewise became the center of Mesopotamian myth. Scholars suggest that the myth described in the *Enuma Elish* was written to justify Marduk's place at the head of the pantheon (collection of recognized gods), which was only fitting for a god associated with the most important city in the land.

Key Themes and Symbols

In ancient Mesopotamian myth, Marduk represents the supreme power of the gods over humans. According to myth, he created humans for the sole purpose of doing labor for the gods, thus allowing the gods to rest and play. Marduk also represents youth and strength, which overcome the army of the older gods and Tiamat.

Marduk in Art, Literature, and Everyday Life

Marduk is best known as the hero of the creation myth documented in the *Enuma Elish*. The god may have also been the source of the name Mordechai. In modern times, the name Marduk is used in many fantasy-based video games and television shows, though most have little to do with the ancient god. Marduk did appear as a character within another character's body in an episode of the animated series *Sealab 2021* (2002).

Read, Write, Think, Discuss

Using your library, the Internet, or other available resources, find out where the ruins of ancient Babylon are located and what their current status is. During the recent war in Iraq, what happened to Babylon and the archeological treasures that once lay within its ruins? What is the United Nations, through the United Nations Educational, Scientific and Cultural Organization (UNESCO), trying to do to restore the beauty and importance of Babylon? Write a short paper on the state of "modern Babylon."

SEE ALSO Creation Stories; *Enuma Elish*; Tiamat

Mars

See **Ares.**

Masewi and Oyoyewi

Nationality/Culture
American Indian/Acoma

Pronunciation
mah-SEH-wee and oh-yo-YEH-wee

Alternate Names
None

Appears In
Acoma creation myths

Lineage
Sons of Iatiku

Character Overview

Masewi and Oyoyewi are twin brothers who play a prominent role in the creation myths of the Acoma people of the American Southwest. In these stories, their mother, Iatiku (pronounced ee-ah-TEE-koo), gave birth to people, and they emerged into the light from underground at a place called Shipap. Masewi and Oyoyewi, Iatiku's warrior sons, became the leaders of the people. As **heroes**, they performed many great deeds, such as summoning rain and instructing others how to make offerings to beneficial spirits called **kachinas** (pronounced kuh-CHEE-nuhz). Like **twins** in other American Indian traditions—such as the Zuni Ahayuuta brothers and the Navajo warrior twins—Masewi and Oyoyewi sometimes indulged in irresponsible and mischievous behavior between their acts of heroism.

One Acoma story tells how Masewi and Oyoyewi were responsible for bringing rain. Each night they danced outside their mother's house to ensure that the water in her medicine bowl did not dry up. However, Iatiku grew tired of the dancing, so the twins went away to prove that they controlled the rains. After they left, the water in the bowl dried up, and Iatiku asked everyone for help in bringing rain. Desperate, she pleaded with her children to return. They finally did, but only after many years of drought had led to starvation among their people. The return of the twins brought rain, and the people realized the power of Masewi and Oyoyewi.

Masewi and Oyoyewi in Context

For the Southwest American Indian agricultural tribes such as the Acoma, rain was a critical part of life. The desert conditions of the area mean that all life relies heavily upon rainfall to survive. As bringers of rain, Masewi and Oyoyewi held an important place in Acoma society. Similarly, the story of Iatiku becoming upset at the twins can be seen as a supernatural explanation for real droughts the Acoma faced.

Key Themes and Symbols

In Acoma mythology, Masewi and Oyoyewi are associated with the morning and evening stars, which are names given to the planet Venus as it appears at dawn and dusk. They are also closely associated with rainfall, and when they left the land, they caused a drought. As warriors, the twins symbolize courage and strength.

Masewi and Oyoyewi in Art, Literature, and Everyday Life

Masewi and Oyoyewi appear as wooden carvings in Acoma and Zuni art. They are considered sacred objects and are placed in shrines to be reclaimed slowly by the elements of nature. Some of these sacred objects have been stolen from tribal shrines and sold to collectors around the world; this practice is becoming less common thanks to stricter international laws regarding the selling of cultural artifacts.

Read, Write, Think, Discuss

The pueblos are one of the most fascinating features of the American Southwest. Using your library, the Internet, or other available resources, research one of the contemporary pueblo cultures. How far back in history do they go? What are some of their myths and ceremonies related to climate, weather, and water issues? Why do you think these issues are important and are central to their religious ceremonies?

SEE ALSO Creation Stories; Kachinas; Native American Mythology; Twins

Maui

Nationality/Culture
Polynesian

Pronunciation
MOU-ee

Alternate Names
None

Appears In
Polynesian creation myths

Lineage
Son of Tangaroa

Character Overview

In **Polynesian mythology**, Maui was a powerful trickster god best known for creating the Pacific islands. A son of the god Tangaroa (pronounced tan-guh-ROH-uh) and a woman, he performed many deeds to improve the lives of humans, such as making the sky higher and the days longer. Endowed with magical powers, this small but strong god tried to achieve immortality, or the ability to live forever.

Major Myths

Maui created the islands while out on a fishing trip with his brothers. First he fashioned a magic fishing hook from his grandmother's jawbone. Then, as his brothers looked on, Maui cast the hook into the water and began to pull up from the ocean floor the islands on which the Polynesians now live.

On another occasion, Maui was out walking and came upon a girl who complained that the sky was so low it kept falling on her, preventing her from doing her chores. Eager to impress the girl, Maui pushed hard and succeeded in raising the sky.

In order to give people more hours of daylight to tend their gardens, cook their food, and make cloth, Maui made the days longer. With the help of his brothers, he caught the **sun** in a net and beat it with his grandmother's magic jawbone. The sun was so bruised and bloodied by this battering that from that time on it could only limp slowly across the sky.

Maui tried to become immortal by tricking Hina, the goddess of the moon, death, and rebirth, as she lay sleeping. He crawled into her body and tried to pass through it, but the goddess was awakened by the call of a bird and promptly crushed Maui to death.

Maui in Context

Maui fills a role common in many tribal cultures: he helps his people become social beings. Maui's story reminds the people of their distant, mythic past—before they created their society and became fully human. Maui brought to Polynesians the cultural skills they needed to live in social groups, thus differentiating themselves from animal groups. Maui provides extra light for people to complete their work, and in some myths he even shows humans how to make **fire** from the friction of two pieces of wood. Before he came, it is noted, people simply ate food raw. Also common in many tribal cultures is the hero whose divine status is uncertain; Maui is sometimes mentioned as a god, and sometimes as a human. This may indicate that the legend is based on an actual figure who ruled over one of the cultures of the Pacific Islands.

Key Themes and Symbols

In Polynesian mythology, Maui is seen as a friend and helper of mankind. He makes the days longer and pushes the sky higher in order to make life easier for people. He can be seen as a symbol of social behavior.

Mortality is an important theme in the myths of Maui. Although he is the son of a god and possesses great strength, he knows he will die someday. This leads him in search of a way to live forever, which ultimately brings about his death. His fate indicates a belief that it is impossible for mortals to cheat death.

Maui in Art, Literature, and Everyday Life

Maui is perhaps best known for lending his name to Maui, one of the Hawaiian Islands, and he sometimes appears in the artistic carvings of Pacific Islanders. His hook, which was used to pull the islands to the surface of the ocean, is also a popular object represented in Polynesian art.

Read, Write, Think, Discuss

Maui typifies the culture hero, a type of character found in myths throughout the world. In their own societies, culture **heroes** perform a role much like today's politicians—helping the members of their society. Using your library, the Internet, or other available resources, research several culture heroes from different societies around the world. What characteristics or qualities do they have in common? What kinds of things do they do for their people? Now select a popular political figure in your own society and compare his or her qualities to those of the mythic figures. What does the contemporary figure do for his or her society? Does he or she live up to the traditional role of culture hero?

SEE ALSO Polynesian Mythology; Tricksters

Mayan Mythology

Mayan Mythology in Context

The Mayan civilization flourished in Mesoamerica—an area roughly corresponding to Central America—from around 300 BCE until the Spanish conquest of the early 1500s CE. The mythology of the Maya had many elements in common with those of other civilizations of the region, but the Maya developed their own unique pantheon, or collection of gods and goddesses. They also created their own stories about these deities, the image of the universe, and the place of humans in it.

The earliest known images of Mesoamerican gods were created by the Olmec civilization of Mexico. Emerging sometime after 1400 BCE, the Olmecs lived along the southern coast of the Gulf of Mexico for roughly a thousand years. They built pyramids that were sacred places where the human realm touched the realm of the gods. They also carved enormous stone heads as images of their leaders and created a long-distance trade network across Mesoamerica to obtain valued items, such as jade.

The Olmec pantheon probably included gods of rain, **corn**, and **fire**, as well as a feathered serpent god. These figures reappeared in the myths of later Mesoamerican peoples. Olmec art included images of jaguars and of creatures that were part jaguar, part human. People of the region believed that magicians could turn themselves into jaguars.

The Zapotecs, Toltecs, and Aztecs were among the Mesoamericans who inherited and built upon Olmec traditions. So did the Maya, who were concentrated in the lowlands of Mexico's Yucatán Peninsula and in a highland region that extends from the present-day states of Tabasco and Chiapas into Guatemala. The Maya enjoyed their greatest wealth, power, and success from around 300 to 900 CE. Historians call this the Classic period. During this time, the Maya built vast stone cities and the ceremonial centers of Tikal and Palenque. After the Classic period, Toltecs from central Mexico arrived in the Yucatán and eventually merged with the Maya. Their influence shaped late Mayan civilization at Chichén Itzá (pronounced chee-CHEN EET-suh) and Mayapán (pronounced mah-yuh-PAHN).

The Maya shared in a common Mesoamerican culture. The peoples of the region believed in the same gods and myths, built temples in the form of pyramids, and had an interest in astronomy. They also had a ball game in which teams competed to pass a ball of solid rubber through a stone ring or hoop. Only certain men and gods could play this game. Sometimes it was simple sport, sometimes a sacred ritual. Scholars do not know the full meaning of the Mesoamerican ball game, but it may have represented the movement of the heavenly bodies or a symbolic kind of warfare that ended in human **sacrifice**.

The Maya also shared the elaborate calendar system used across much of Mesoamerica. One part, called *Haab* by the Maya, was a 365-day calendar based on the **sun**'s annual cycle. The other, called *Tzolkin* (pronounced zol-KEEN), was a 260-day sacred calendar. The two calendars meshed in a cycle known as the Calendar Round, which repeated every fifty-two years. The Maya used the calendar both for measuring worldly time and for sacred purposes, such as divination. Each day in the Calendar Round came under the influence of a unique combination of deities. According to the Maya, the combination that occurred on a person's date of birth would influence that person's fate.

Mayan Deities

Ah Puch (Yum Cimil): god of death and destruction, brought disease and was associated with war.

Chac: rain god.

Cizin (Kisin): god of death, linked with earthquakes.

Hun-Hunahpú (Ah Mun): god of maize and vegetation.

Hunahpú and Xbalanqúe: twin sons of Hun-Hunahpú, tricked the lords of the underworld.

Itzamná: chief god, ruler of heaven, of night and day, and of the other deities.

Ixchel: goddess of fertility, pregnancy, and childbirth.

Kinich Ahau: sun god, sometimes considered an aspect of Itzamná.

Kukulcan (Quetzalcoatl): Feathered Serpent, god of learning and crafts.

Like other Mesoamerican cultures, the Maya used a writing system based on symbols called glyphs that represented individual syllables. They recorded their mythology and history in volumes known as codices. Although the Spanish destroyed most Mayan documents, a few codices have survived. Other written sources of Mayan mythology include the ***Popol Vuh***, the sacred book of the Quiché Maya of Guatemala, and the *Chilam Balam* (*Secrets of the Soothsayers*), writings by Yucatecan Maya from the 1600s and 1700s that contain much traditional lore. Accounts by Spanish explorers and missionaries—such as Diego de Landa's description of Mayan life and religion in the Yucatán with the first key to the written language (ca. 1566)—provide useful information. Inscriptions found at archeological sites are also helpful.

Like many peoples, the Maya pictured a universe consisting of heavens above and underworlds below, with the human world sandwiched between. The heavens consisted of thirteen layers stacked above the earth, and the earth rested on the back of a turtle or reptile floating in the ocean. Four brothers called the Bacabs (pronounced bah-KAHBZ), possibly the sons of **Itzamná**, supported the heavens. Below the earth lay a realm called Xibalba, an **underworld** in nine layers. Linking the three realms was a giant tree whose roots reached into the underworld and branches stretched to **heaven**. The gods and the souls of the dead traveled between worlds along this tree.

Core Deities and Characters

The chief god of the Maya was Itzamná (pronounced eet-SAHM-nah)—ruler of the heaven, of day and night, and of the other deities. Itzamná was a culture hero, a figure credited with giving people basic tools of civilization, such as language and fire. Said to have been the first priest and the inventor of writing, Itzamná was also linked to healing. His wife, Ixchel (pronounced eesh-CHEL), was goddess of fertility, pregnancy, and childbirth. Women made pilgrimages to her shrines.

Ah Puch (pronounced ah-PWAH-SH), often shown with decomposing flesh and a head like a skull, was the god of death and destruction. He brought disease, was associated with war, and ruled the lowest level of the Mayan underworld, or land of the dead. The modern Maya call him Yum Cimil (lord of death). Cizin (pronounced SEE-sen), meaning "stinking one," is another death god. He is linked in particular with earthquakes, which often strike Mesoamerica with devastating force. The ancient Maya depicted him as a dancing skeleton with dangling eyeballs. His opponent was the god of maize and vegetation, called Ah Mun or Hun-Hunahpú (pronounced wahn-WAHN-uh-pwah), often shown with an ear of maize growing from his head.

The sun god was Kinich Ahau (pronounced kee-nich AH-wah), sometimes said to be one aspect of Itzamná. He was associated with jaguars. The rain god, a major figure in all Mesoamerican mythologies, was called Chac (pronounced CHAK) by the Maya. He was often portrayed as a fisherman or as a figure with the features of a fish or reptile. Like Itzamná and other Mayan deities, Chac could appear in four forms, each associated with a particular color and compass direction. **Quetzalcoatl** (pronounced keht-sahl-koh-AHT-l), the Feathered Serpent, called Kukulcan (pronounced koo-kool-KAHN) by the Maya, was also a figure of great importance throughout Mesoamerica.

Major Myths

The Maya believed that creation was related to divination, or attempts to read the future through various signs, and they often referred to their **heroes** and creator gods as diviners. The men and women who practiced divination regarded it as a form of creation similar to the divine miracle

The Maya played a ball game in which teams competed to pass a rubber ball through a stone ring or hoop. Although the meaning of the games is not clear, the players may have represented the struggle between light and dark, and the ball may have symbolized the movement of the stars through the heavens. ERICH LESSING/ART RESOURCE, NY.

that produced the world and humankind. Like the Aztecs and other Mesoamericans, the Maya believed that the present world is only the most recent in a series of creations. The earlier ones perished, or were destroyed one after the other, just as this world will one day come to an end also.

According to the *Popol Vuh*, creation began with the god Huracan (pronounced wah-ruh-KAHN), who blew as a great wind over the ancient ocean, causing the earth to rise from the depths. Then Xpiyacoc (pronounced shpee-YAH-kok) and Xmucane (pronounced SHMOH-kah-nay), "old man and old woman," performed magical rituals that helped Huracan and other creator deities form plants, animals, and eventually the human race. The gods fashioned the first man out of clay, and he melted into the water. The next race of people, made of wood, were dull, spiritless, and easily destroyed by fire. For their third attempt, the gods mixed yellow and white maize flour together and made the First Fathers, the ancestors of men, from the dough.

The First Fathers were worshipful, handsome, and wise—too wise, the gods decided. Fearing that their creations would become too powerful, the gods blew fog into the First Fathers' eyes, taking away some of their knowledge. The gods then made the First Mothers. Finally they created the sun to bring light to the world.

One section of the *Popol Vuh* tells the myth of the Hero Twins, sons of the maize god Hun-Hunahpú. The lords of death, seeing the maize god and his twin brother playing the ball game constantly, grew annoyed and summoned the two to Xibalba (pronounced shi-BAHL-buh), the land of the dead. The brothers fell into a series of tricks and traps, which allowed the lords of death to sacrifice them and to hang Hun-Hunahpú's head from a tree. But the maize god's twin sons, Hunahpú (pronounced WAH-nuh-pwuh) and Xbalanqúe (pronounced shi-BAY-lan-kay), grew up to be even more skilled ballplayers.

When in turn the lords of death summoned the twin sons to the underworld, **Hunahpú and Xbalanqúe** had tricks of their own. They played the ball game every day, and each night they passed some test. Eventually, they decided to set a trap for the lords. In the final part of their trick, the **twins** cut themselves in pieces and then restored themselves to wholeness. The underworld gods wanted to try the same trick. However, after the twins cut up the gods, they simply left them in pieces. The twins then restored their father and their uncle to life before passing into the sky to become the sun and moon.

Key Themes and Symbols

As with many Mesoamerican cultures, sacrifice was a key theme in Mayan mythology. They believed that humans had been put on earth to nourish the gods. Human sacrifices served this purpose. So did the ritual called bloodletting, in which priests or nobles pierced parts of their bodies and offered the blood to the gods or to ancestors in exchange for guidance. Clouds of smoke from burning blood offerings were thought to summon the Vision Serpents, images of snakes with Mayan gods and ancestors coming from their mouths. Such visions probably symbolized the renewal and rebirth made possible by sacrifice.

The cycle of death and rebirth, in fact, is another key theme in Mayan mythology. This is shown by the Mayan calendar system, which includes many repeating cycles of various lengths, up to fifty-two years. It is also evident in Mayan creation myths, which suggest that the current world is only the latest in a series, and that the gods had made previous attempts to create humans.

The number four is also a recurring theme in Mayan mythology. Many gods have four forms in which they can appear. The four cardinal directions—north, south, east, and west—are important designations in Mayan mythology, and each one is associated with different characteristics.

Mayan Mythology in Art, Literature, and Everyday Life

Striking images of the deities and myths of Mayan civilization can be found today in archeological sites. Southern Mexico and northern Central America are dotted with the remains of great stone cities and temples that are still yielding a wealth of information about the history and culture of the ancient Maya. Some of these sites have become tourist attractions and educational centers.

Other remnants are literary. Mayan texts—those recorded by both Native American and Spanish chroniclers in the years after the Spanish conquest, as well as new translations of inscriptions and codices—are available to interested readers. Some have inspired modern writers. Stories in Charles Finger's *Tales from the Silver Lands* and Miguel Angel Asturias's *Men of Maize* are based on the *Popol Vuh*.

There is a living Mayan legacy as well. The descendants of the Maya number about five million today. Proud of their heritage, they still tell old myths at festivals and funerals, although perhaps less often than they used to. Some of them remember the old gods, asking Chac for rain, thanking Hun-Hunahpú for a good harvest, and fearing that Ah Puch is prowling about, hungry for victims. In the Yucatán, a television series called *Let Us Return to Our Maya Roots* promoted traditional language and customs. The mythology that once expressed the visions and beliefs of much of Mesoamerica remains part of a culture that is still alive.

Read, Write, Think, Discuss

The Bird Who Cleans the World: And Other Mayan Fables by Victor Montejo (1991) offers twenty traditional tales taken from Mayan mythology. The book, which focuses on tales of animals and lessons learned, also contains images of authentic Mayan art and artifacts.

SEE ALSO Aztec Mythology; Hunahpú and Xbalanqúe; Itzamná; Mexican Mythology; *Popol Vuh*; Quetzalcoatl; Twins

Medea

Character Overview

In **Greek mythology**, Medea was an enchantress and witch who used her magic powers to help **Jason** and the **Argonauts** (pronounced AHR-guh-nawts) in their quest for the **Golden Fleece**. Later, after Jason betrayed her, she used her witchcraft to take revenge. The daughter of Aeëtes (pronounced aye-EE-teez), king of Colchis (pronounced KOL-kis), Medea first saw Jason when he arrived at the king's palace to request the Golden Fleece. According to some accounts, **Hera** (pronounced HAIR-uh), queen of the gods, persuaded **Aphrodite** (pronounced af-ro-DYE-tee), the goddess of love, to make Medea fall in love with the young hero.

Aeëtes had no intention of handing over the Golden Fleece but pretended that he would do so if Jason successfully performed a series of tasks. He was to yoke fire-breathing bulls to a plow, sow a field with **dragons**' teeth, and then fight the armed warriors who grew from those teeth. In return for his promise to marry her, Medea gave Jason a magic ointment to protect him from the bulls' fiery breath and told him how to confuse the warriors so they would fight among themselves. Following Medea's instructions, Jason completed the tasks he had been set.

Aeëtes promised to hand over the Golden Fleece, but Medea knew that he would not keep his word. She led Jason and the musician **Orpheus** (pronounced OR-fee-uhs) into the sacred grove where the fleece was kept, guarded by a vicious serpent. Orpheus sang the serpent to sleep, enabling Jason to escape with the fleece. Medea then joined Jason and the Argonauts as they set sail in the *Argo*, pursued by her brother Apsyrtus (pronounced ap-SUR-tuhs). When Apsyrtus caught up with them, he promised to let Jason keep the Golden Fleece if he would give up Medea. Jason refused and killed Apsyrtus.

U•X•L Encyclopedia of World Mythology

Nationality/Culture
Greek

Pronunciation
me-DEE-uh

Alternate Names
None

Appears In
Ovid's *Metamorphoses*, Ovid's *Heroides*, Euripides' *Medea*

Lineage
Daughter of King Aeëtes

Eventually the Argonauts arrived at Iolcus (pronounced ee-AHL-kuhs), which was ruled by Jason's uncle Pelias (pronounced PEEL-ee-uhs). Pelias had gained the throne by killing Jason's father, King Aeson (pronounced EE-son). Medea brought Aeson back to life by boiling his remains in a pot with magical herbs. In this way, she tricked Pelias's daughters into thinking that they could restore their father to youth by cutting him up and boiling him in a pot. Pelias died a gruesome death, and the furious inhabitants of Iolcus drove out Medea and Jason.

The couple married and settled in Corinth, where they raised several children. Their happy days ended when Creon (pronounced KREE-ahn), the king of Corinth, offered Jason his daughter Glauce (pronounced GLAW-see) in marriage. Anxious to please the king, Jason abandoned Medea and prepared to marry Glauce. Medea took her revenge by sending Glauce a poisoned wedding gown that burned her alive. By some accounts, before fleeing to Athens, she also killed the children she had borne to Jason.

Aegeus (pronounced EE-joos), the king of Athens, agreed to protect Medea if she married him and bore him children. They produced a son, Medus (pronounced MEE-duhs), who stood to inherit the throne. However, Aegeus was unaware that he already had a son, **Theseus** (pronounced THEE-see-uhs), from a previous marriage. When Theseus came to Athens to claim the throne, Medea recognized him, persuaded Aegeus that Theseus planned to kill him, and prepared a cup of poisoned wine for the young man. Just as Theseus was about to drink the wine, Aegeus recognized the sword that Theseus carried, realized that Theseus was his son, and knocked the cup from the young man's hand. By some accounts, Medea then fled to a region in Asia that came to be known as Media in her honor, and whose inhabitants became known as Medes.

Medea in Context

The myth of Medea reveals much about relationships between men and women in ancient Greece. For one, Medea's escape with Jason after he agrees to marry her was a clear violation of the tradition of family-arranged marriages. Women seldom had input into whom they married, and never did so without the knowledge of their parents. Next, while a woman was duty-bound to remain with her husband until death, a man could renounce his wife publicly for any number of reasons. When Jason fails to do even that before taking a new wife, it may have been seen as an even greater insult to Medea.

Key Themes and Symbols

One important theme in the myth of Medea is exile. Medea leaves her home in Colchis after helping Jason, knowing that her father would view her acts as betrayal. Later, both Jason and Medea are exiled from Iolcus after she tricks Pelias's daughters into murdering him. When Jason later marries Glauce, Medea murders Glauce and flees to Athens. Finally, Medea flees from Athens after her failed attempt to kill Theseus.

Murder and magic are also themes that run throughout the tale of Medea. She provides Jason with a magic ointment of protection so he can subdue the fire-breathing bulls. Although she does not directly kill Pelias, she is responsible for his death by tricking the man's daughters into killing him as part of a magic ceremony. She is also responsible for the death of Glauce by way of a magically cursed gown, and for the attempted murder of Theseus by way of poison.

Medea was an enchantress who fell in love with the hero Jason, but he later abandoned her. KUNSTHISTORISCHES MUSEUM, VIENNA, AUSTRIA/THE BRIDGEMAN ART LIBRARY.

Medea in Art, Literature, and Everyday Life

The myth of Medea is best known through the stage play written by the ancient Greek dramatist Euripides (pronounced yoo-RIP-i-deez). Over the centuries, the story has been adapted countless times in books and on the stage. Several operas, ballets, and musicals based on the story of Medea have also been produced, most notably a ballet suite by composer Samuel Barber. A film adaptation based on the Euripides play was made for television in 1988 by Danish director Lars von Trier. The character of Medea also appears in the 1963 film *Jason and the Argonauts*.

Read, Write, Think, Discuss

In Greek myth, Medea is a witch and a murderer. However, she also helps Jason obtain the Golden Fleece and tries to help him regain his rightful throne. These seemingly contradictory aspects of Medea's character makes it difficult to categorize her as definitively "good" or "bad." Do you think Medea was intended to be a sympathetic character to the ancient Greeks, or was she intended as a villain? What do you think Greek writers were trying to say by making their characters so ambiguous? Select a popular figure from a contemporary Western novel and compare the way the author depicts his or her main character to the way the ancient Greeks portrayed their **heroes** and heroines.

SEE ALSO Argonauts; Golden Fleece; Jason; Theseus

Medusa

Nationality/Culture
Greek

Pronunciation
meh-DOO-suh

Alternate Names
None

Appears In
Hesiod's *Theogony*, Ovid's *Metamorphoses*

Lineage
Daughter of Phorcys and Ceto

Character Overview

Medusa, one of three sisters in **Greek mythology** known as the **Gorgons** (pronounced GOR-guhnz), had a destructive effect upon humans. In many myths she appeared as a horribly ugly woman with hair made of snakes, although occasionally she was described as being beautiful. In both forms Medusa's appearance was deadly: any person who gazed directly at her would turn to stone.

Although the two other Gorgons were immortal (able to live forever), Medusa was not. One of the best-known legends about her tells how the Greek hero **Perseus** (pronounced PUR-see-uhs) killed her. Perseus and his mother, **Danaë** (pronounced DAN-uh-ee), lived on the island of Seriphos (pronounced SEHR-uh-fohs), which was ruled by King Polydectes (pronounced pol-ee-DEK-teez). The king wanted to marry Danaë but Perseus opposed the marriage. Polydectes then chose another bride and demanded that all the islanders give him horses as a wedding gift. Perseus, who had no horses, offered to give Polydectes anything else. Because no man had ever survived an encounter with the Gorgons, Polydectes challenged Perseus to bring him the head of Medusa.

With the help of the goddess **Athena** (pronounced uh-THEE-nuh) and a group of **nymphs** (female nature deities), Perseus obtained special equipment for his task: a sharpened sickle, or curved blade, a cap that made the wearer invisible, and a pair of winged sandals. He also polished

Medusa, the most famous Gorgon, was beheaded by Perseus. IMAGNO/HULTON ARCHIVE/GETTY IMAGES.

his bronze shield so he could see Medusa's reflection in it without gazing directly at her. Wearing the magic cap and following Medusa's reflection in his shield, Perseus crept up on the Gorgons. He cut off Medusa's head in one swipe and put it in a bag. The drops of blood that fell from the head turned into Medusa's two sons—Chrysaor (pronounced kree-SAY-ohr) and **Pegasus** (pronounced PEG-uh-suhs)—by the god **Poseidon** (pronounced poh-SYE-dun).

With the help of the magic sandals, Perseus flew off before the other Gorgons could catch him. When he reached Seriphos, he held up Medusa's head and turned Polydectes to stone. Perseus later gave the head to Athena, who mounted it on her shield.

Medusa in Context

Medusa can be seen as a reflection of the qualities that ancient Greeks felt were unappealing in women. She lived apart from men entirely and appeared to have no use for them, which was unlike the traditional image of a woman as servant and property of a man. She was also physically hideous, which the Greeks felt reflected an undesirable personality as well as a lack of beauty and grace. She even offered a fierce, direct gaze that may have seemed inappropriate or defiant if used by a normal woman.

Key Themes and Symbols

Medusa can be seen as a symbol of ugliness and solitude. She lives with her sisters and has few interactions with outsiders. The Gorgons may also represent the bonds of sisterhood, since they remain together and care for one another apart from the rest of the world. Medusa herself is unique among the Gorgons as a symbol of mortality; she is the only one who cannot live forever and is indeed slain by Perseus.

Medusa in Art, Literature, and Everyday Life

Medusa is the most popular of the Gorgons. She has appeared in art by Peter Paul Rubens, Pablo Picasso, and Leonardo da Vinci (though da Vinci's two paintings of Medusa have not survived). Perhaps the most famous images of Medusa are the headless portrait painted by Caravaggio in 1597, and the sixteenth century bronze statue of Perseus holding Medusa's head sculpted by Benvenuto Cellini. The story of Perseus and Medusa is retold in the 1981 film *Clash of the Titans*, in which Medusa is depicted as a grotesque woman with the lower body of a snake. The name Medusa has been borrowed for many other objects in modern life, including sea organisms, celestial bodies, ships, and even several roller coasters.

Read, Write, Think, Discuss

Corydon and the Island of Monsters (2005), by Tobias Druitt, is a tale of Corydon, a goat-legged shepherd boy taken captive by pirates who run a traveling freak show. There, Corydon meets Medusa, whose gaze does not hurt him, and the two escape the freak show, free the other captives, and make their way to Medusa's island home. Soon, however, Perseus and other glory-seeking **heroes** arrive to rid the island of its "monsters." The book is the first of a trilogy; Tobias Druitt is actually a pen name for the mother and son writing team of Diane Purkiss and Michael Downing.

SEE ALSO Danaë; Gorgons; Greek Mythology; Nymphs; Pegasus; Perseus

Melanesian Mythology

Melanesian Mythology in Context

Melanesia, an area in the southwest Pacific Ocean, consists of thousands of islands and a remarkable variety of cultures. These individual cultures possess different mythologies and deities (gods and goddesses). The main island groups of the region are New Guinea, New Caledonia, Vanuatu (formerly New Hebrides), New Britain, the Solomon Islands, the Admiralty Islands, the Trobriand Islands, and the Fiji Islands.

No single religion or mythology unifies Melanesia. Each island or community has its own distinct beliefs and its own collection of legends and mythological beings. Nevertheless, the mythologies of Melanesia do share certain basic elements and themes. For example, the names of the characters and the details of their stories differ from island to island, but the activities in which they are involved often have much in common.

A distinctive feature of many Melanesian cultures is the cargo cult, a religious movement created in response to European influence during colonial times. Cargo cults helped Melanesians explain the role of Europeans in the universe. When Europeans first arrived, the Melanesians were impressed by the huge amounts of material goods, or "cargo," they brought with them. The islanders believed that the Europeans must have acquired such wealth through strong magic, and they gradually developed cargo cults in an effort to gain knowledge of this magic for themselves. Religious in nature, cargo cults also had a political side, and they stressed resistance to foreign domination of their societies.

Members of the cargo cults believed that one day an ancestral spirit, tribal god, or hero would bring cargo to the people, leading to an age of prosperity, justice, and independence from foreign powers. To prepare for this day, the cults built structures representing docks for boats, runways for planes, and shelters for storing the cargo when it arrived. Such activities disrupted traditional economic practices and caused drastic changes in some parts of Melanesian society. Colonial authorities feared such changes and tried to put an end to the cults, but with little success.

This "henta-koi" is an example of a cargo cult good luck charm, used by the islanders of the Nicobar Islands near India. The wooden charm shows a white man dressed as sea captain and surrounded by European products such as mirrors, clocks, and umbrellas; it was designed to unlock the secrets of European wealth to the bearer.
WERNER FORMAN/ART RE-
SOURCE, NY.

Core Deities and Characters

Melanesian mythology has neither a supreme deity nor a distinct hierarchy, or ranked organization, of gods and goddesses. Instead, each cultural group possesses its own supernatural spirits, culture **heroes**, **tricksters**, and other beings that appear in local myths and stories.

Creator Gods and Heroes Most cultural groups have creation myths that explain or describe the origin of the world. Melanesians, however, believe that the world has always existed, so they have few stories about creation. Yet various figures do play roles in changing parts of the world and in the formation of islands and features of the landscape.

On the Banks Islands of Vanuatu, the first being in the world was Qat, a creator god and hero who fashioned islands and covered them with trees, animals, and plants. Qat also made humans by carving dolls from wood and then dancing and singing them to life. Then he created day and night so people could work and then sleep.

In the islands of Vanuatu and New Britain, a creator god made twin brothers, To-Kabinana and To-Karvuvu, by sprinkling the ground with his own blood. To-Kabinana became a creator hero who produced many good things, while To-Karvuvu was responsible for the evil and troubles in the world. In Papua New Guinea, the sky god Kambel made people and the moon. He also created the clouds, which pushed up the sky and separated it from the earth.

Tricksters and Other Spirits According to the Kiwai people of New Guinea, the trickster Sido could change his skin like a snake. He was killed by a powerful magician and then wandered the world seducing women and children. After losing his human wife, Sido transformed himself into a gigantic pig. Finally, he split himself open so that the pig's backbone and sides formed the house of death, the place where people go when they die.

Another mythological figure of New Guinea is Dudugera, known as the "leg child" because he sprang from a cut in his mother's leg. The people of his village mocked and bullied Dudugera, who one day told his mother to hide under a rock because he was going to become the **sun**. Dudugera soared into the sky and shot **fire** spears, which burned vegetation and killed many living things. To stop Dudugera from destroying everything, his mother threw mud or lime juice at his face, and it turned into clouds that hid the sun.

Marawa, the spider, is a friend of Qat. When Qat created humans Marawa tried to do the same, but his wooden figures turned into rotting corpses. That is how death came into the world. Tagaro, a trickster of Vanuatu, destroyed his evil brother Meragubutto by persuading him to enter a burning house to gain more magic and thus increase his power.

The mythologies of Melanesia include many spirits associated with nature and animals. The Adaro are sun spirits, part fish and part human, who use rainbows as bridges and come to earth during sun showers. The Bariaus are shy spirits that live in old tree trunks. The Kiwai of Papua New Guinea say that they are descended from Nuga, a half-human, half-crocodile creature created long ago from a piece of wood.

Major Myths

Throughout Melanesia some common mythological themes and characters appear. Many myths deal with two fundamental issues: where people came from and what happens after death. Certain characters, such as snakes, monsters, and **twins**, can be found in legends from numerous islands.

Myths of Origin Melanesians have several basic stories about how the first humans appeared. In some places these beings descended from the sky. The Ayom people of Papua New Guinea, for example, say that Tumbrenjak climbed down to earth on a rope to hunt and fish. When he tried to return to the sky, he found the rope cut. His wife threw down fruits and vegetables, including cucumbers that became women. The offspring of Tumbrenjak and these women became the ancestors of different cultural groups.

In other places, the first beings came from the sea or emerged from underground. Among the Trobriand islanders, the ancestors of each clan emerged from a particular spot in a grove of trees, or from a piece of coral, or from a rock. The Keraki of Papua New Guinea believe that the first humans emerged from a tree, while others say that they came from clay or sand, blood, or pieces of wood.

Many Melanesian myths explain the creation of the sea, an important feature in the lives of island peoples. A myth from Dobu Island in New Guinea says that when the sea was released, all the beautiful women were swept to the Trobriand Islands and the ugly women were carried inland on Dobu. People in southern Vanuatu have a myth in which a woman became angry with her son because he disobeyed her. In her fury she knocked down a wall that surrounded the water of the sea. The water broke free, scattering people and coconuts to other islands.

Magic Magic is an important aspect of the mythology and religion of Melanesia. According to a myth from the Trobriand Islands, a hero named Tudava taught the people various forms of magic, such as the secret knowledge needed to make plants grow abundantly in a garden. People use magical formulas to manipulate spirits, and most sacred rituals involve magic along with prayer and **sacrifice**. During ceremonies participants wear or carry carved wooden images of spirits said to contain the spirits' power.

Snakes, Monsters, and Twins Snakes appear in the myths of many Melanesian peoples as a symbol of fertility and power. In some myths they are said to control rain; in others, animals and humans emerge from their slaughtered bodies. Some snake-beings wander from place to place giving gifts to humans and teaching them how to grow crops or perform magic. The Arapesh of New Guinea believe that spirits called *marsalai* live in rocks and pools and sometimes take the form of snakes or lizards. The marsalai shaped different parts of the landscape and then became guardians of their territory.

Many Melanesian peoples believe in monstrous ogres that eat people. An ogre killer becomes a hero by slaying these monsters. Ogre killers often perform other great feats as well. According to a myth from Vanuatu, a terrible ogre killed everyone except a woman who hid under a tree. The woman gave birth to twin sons who destroyed the ogre and cut it into pieces, an act that enabled the people who had been eaten by the ogre to come to life again. The people reestablished their society and began to follow new rules of behavior. Twin brothers appear as central characters in many other Melanesian myths. These pairs often include one wise and one foolish brother, such as To-Kabinana and To-Karvuvu. Myths about twins may also represent the presence of both helpful and harmful forces in nature, such as nourishing rains and violent storms.

Afterlife People throughout Melanesia generally believe in an **afterlife**. Among the Kiwai of Papua New Guinea, the land of the dead is known as Adiri; in Vanuatu one of its names is Banoi. The god of the dead also has various names; in parts of New Guinea he is called Tumudurere.

In Vanuatu people say that humans have two souls—one goes to an afterlife while the other takes the form of an animal, plant, or object. The route taken by souls to the land of the dead is often well defined. The people of the Fiji Islands believe that this path is dangerous and only the greatest warriors can complete the journey. In other places, the success of the journey depends on whether the proper funeral rites have been carried out.

Souls that go to the afterlife often visit the land of the living as ghosts by taking on human or animal form. Ghosts sometimes help the living, but they can also frighten them and interfere with certain activities. Some places have special types of ghosts, such as beheaded men with wounds that glow in the dark, or the ghosts of unborn children.

Key Themes and Symbols

Supernatural beings, including ancestral spirits and spirits of nonhuman origin, play an important role in the lives of Melanesians. The islanders believe that ancestral spirits continue to influence the way people act in everyday life. Ancestor worship is a significant part of their religion.

Summoned through prayer and ritual, supernatural beings and forces can be controlled to a large extent by the use of magic, which is central to Melanesian religion. The presence and activities of ancestral spirits are revealed in dreams. Evidence of their effect on human society can be seen in the health, well-being, and prosperity of the people.

Music plays a key role in Melanesian religious rituals. Throughout the islands, the sounds of instruments such as drums and reed flutes are thought to be the voices of spirits and other supernatural beings. Today the use of instruments is usually restricted to men, but some myths tell how they originally belonged to women until men stole them or obtained them through trickery.

Closely related to the belief in spirits is the concept of mana, a supernatural power independent of any spirits or beings, yet linked to them. A characteristic of persons and objects as well as of spirits, mana can be either helpful or harmful. Anything uncommon or out of the ordinary—such as a weapon that has killed many animals or a great hero who defeats many foes—is said to possess mana.

Melanesian Mythology in Art, Literature, and Everyday Life

In some areas of Melanesia, mythology remains a powerful force in society, particularly where traditional religious systems and cult practices have been left relatively undisturbed. In other areas, traditional beliefs have been modified, usually as a result of modernization or the introduction of Christianity. Yet even where change has occurred, mythology continues to play an important role. It has helped Melanesians make sense of the changes in their society and in their relationship to the broader world by providing ways of understanding and interpreting events.

Read, Write, Think, Discuss

Cargo cults provide a unique opportunity to see mythology created as a direct result of one ethnic group's contact with an outside culture. These cults believe that, through rituals and magical thinking, they can obtain the material wealth of the outside culture and transform their lives. Compare the magical thinking of the cargo cults to modern consumer culture, in which people are encouraged to possess material things that, through the influence of clever advertising, they believe will transform their lives. What are the similarities? What are the differences?

SEE ALSO Afterlife; Animals in Mythology; Creation Stories; Micronesian Mythology; Polynesian Mythology; Twins

Mercury

See **Hermes.**

Merlin

Character Overview

In the legends about King **Arthur**, the king had the help and advice of a powerful wizard named Merlin. Indeed this magician, who arranged for Arthur's birth and for many aspects of his life, can be seen as the guiding force behind the **Arthurian legends**. Many stories about Merlin circulated in medieval times.

Some early legends claimed that Merlin was the son of a demon and of a human woman. Only half human, Merlin was mysterious and unpredictable, sometimes helping the human race but sometimes changing his shape and passing long periods as a bird, a cloud, or something else. He also had many relationships with women. By the thirteenth century, however, the influence of Christianity was reshaping the Arthurian legends, and Merlin became a more respectable figure—a wise old man who supplied moral and magical guidance.

In the legend of Vortigern (pronounced VOR-tuh-gurn), a legendary king of Britain, the king was trying to build a temple on Salisbury Plain, but it kept falling down. The young Merlin told the king of a vision in which he had seen a red dragon and a white dragon fighting in a pool under the temple's foundation. From this, he predicted that the red dragon of Wales (King Vortigern) would be defeated by the white dragon of Britain (King Uther Pendragon), which later happened. The

Nationality/Culture
Romano-British/Celtic

Pronunciation
MUR-lin

Alternate Names
Myrddin

Appears In
Nennius's *History of the Britons,* Geoffrey of Monmouth's *Prophecies of Merlin* and *Life of Merlin*

Lineage
Unknown

magician then built the temple himself, using his magic to bring standing stones from Ireland and arrange them on the plain in a single night. That, according to legend, was how Stonehenge was built.

Merlin became the ally of Uther (pronounced OO-ther) and used his magic to enable Uther to spend a night with another king's wife. The child born of that union was Arthur. Merlin predicted that he would be a great king who would one day unite all of Britain.

Entrusted with Arthur's upbringing, Merlin prepared the boy for kingship. Some accounts say that the wizard fashioned the magical sword Excalibur that proved that Arthur was the rightful king. According to other stories, Merlin also created the Round Table, around which Arthur's knights sat. Merlin was Arthur's helper and advisor in many things. Yet, even Merlin could not prevent the final crumbling of the knights' fellowship and the fall of Arthur, as recounted in every version of the Arthurian legends.

As for Merlin's own fate, accounts vary. Some say that he went mad after Arthur's defeat and wandered into the woods. Most versions of the magician's story, however, end with him being tricked by a witch named Nimuë (pronounced neem-OO-ay), also identified as the **Lady of the Lake**, with whom he had fallen in love. Nimuë did not really care for Merlin but simply wanted to learn his secrets. When she had learned enough, she trapped him in an underground cave from which he could never escape.

Merlin in Context

The figure of Merlin seems to be based on a magician named Myrddin, who appeared in the pre-Christian mythology of the Celtic people. The writings of Nennius, a Welsh storyteller who lived around 800 CE, include tales of a young magician named Ambrosius (pronounced am-BROH-zhuhs) who became an advisor to Vortigern.

Three hundred years later, British writer Geoffrey of Monmouth told a more elaborate story about the magician in his *History of the Kings of Britain* (1136). In this account, a sorcerer known as Merlin Ambrosius served as advisor to British king Uther Pendragon and, later, to his son Arthur. Geoffrey of Monmouth also wrote a work about Merlin that drew on old Celtic legends about a "wild man of the woods" with magical and fortune-telling powers. As Christianity spread throughout Britain, Merlin's role within the legend shifted. The re-casting of Merlin

as a fatherly advisor may reflect the influence of Christian ideals upon existing myths.

Key Themes and Symbols

An important theme in the myths of Merlin is prophecy, or the ability to see the future. When he meets with Vortigern, Merlin relates his vision of battling **dragons**, which suggests that Vortigern will be defeated by

Uther. Merlin later sees that Uther's son Arthur will unite Britain. Another theme found in the tales of Merlin and Arthur is the dangerous power of passion. For Arthur, **Guinevere**'s affair with the knight **Lancelot** causes the unity of **Camelot** to crumble. For Merlin, his love of Nimuë blinds him to her plan to imprison him after learning his secrets.

Merlin in Art, Literature, and Everyday Life

As an important character in the tales of King Arthur, Merlin has appeared in nearly every major adaptation of the Arthurian legends. This includes Sir Thomas Malory's *Le Morte d'Arthur* (1485), T. H. White's *The Once and Future King* (1958), and films such as *King Arthur* (2004). Merlin has also appeared in many other stories outside the traditional King Arthur myth, including Mark Twain's *A Connecticut Yankee in King Arthur's Court* (1889) and *That Hideous Strength* (1946) by C. S. Lewis. The wizard was also the subject of the Broadway musical *Merlin* that began and ended its run in 1983; the show was designed mainly as a showcase for magic tricks, and starred popular magician Doug Henning in the title role.

Read, Write, Think, Discuss

The Lost Years of Merlin (1996), by T. A. Barron, is a tale about Merlin's younger years. In the book, Merlin is initially known as Emrys, a seven-year-old boy who finds himself washed up on the beach at Wales with no memory at all. He eventually discovers that he has magical powers, and the story reveals how Merlin learns to use those considerable powers for good rather than evil.

SEE ALSO Arthur, King; Arthurian Legends

Mermaids

Character Overview

Mermaids and mermen are imaginary beings with the upper bodies of humans and the lower bodies of fish. Often mentioned in European

Nationality/Culture
Worldwide

Pronunciation
MUR-maydz

Alternate Names
None

Appears In
Various myths of the sea

Lineage
Varies

Portrayed as both lovely and dangerous, mermaids represent mankind's relationship to the sea. THE ART ARCHIVE/PRIVATE COLLECTION/MARC CHARMET.

legends, they also occur in the folklore of seagoing peoples from other regions of the world. The idea of a deity (god) or creature in which human features are combined with the body of a fish is very ancient. Babylonian (pronounced bab-uh-LOH-nee-uhn) texts mentioned a god named Oannes, who was part man and part fish and lived among humans. The Near Eastern god Dagon (pronounced DAH-gon) may have been portrayed as a merman, and the Syrian goddess Atargatis (pronounced ay-tar-GAY-tis) had the form of a mermaid. Ancient Greek and Roman sea gods and their attendants often appeared as human torsos rising from the waves with curved fish tails below. The Greeks called these beings Nereids (pronounced NEER-ee-idz) if they were female and tritons (pronounced TRY-tunz) if they were male. Japanese folklore features a mermaid called Ningyo (pronounced NEEN-gyoh), and **Polynesian mythology** includes a half-human and half-porpoise creator god called Vatea.

In European folklore, mermaids were associated with **sirens**, beautiful creatures whose singing lures sailors to their doom. Mermaids were commonly pictured as floating on top of the waves, singing, or combing their long hair while gazing into mirrors. Seeing a mermaid was considered bad luck, as mermaids often appeared before storms or other disasters and were believed to carry drowned men away to their kingdom at the bottom of the sea. Although encounters with mermaids and mermen often ended badly for humans, in some legends these sea creatures married human partners and took completely human form to live on land.

Mermaids in Context

Many sailors over the centuries believed mermaids to be real and have reported spotting mermaids while at sea. Christopher Columbus even reported sighting three mermaids near the Dominican Republic in 1493, though he was disappointed that they were not as pretty as popular depictions suggested. In truth, what Columbus and other sailors most likely saw were sea mammals known as manatees and dugongs. In fact, the name "dugong" is taken from a Malaysian term meaning "lady of the sea." Unlike most sea animals, these creatures have soft, rounded bodies; younger calves also have pale skin and are about the same length as a person. That these creatures were generally viewed as female is likely due to their pale skin, soft curves, and the fact that most sailors were men who did not have contact with women for weeks or months at a time.

Key Themes and Symbols

Although mermaids are usually portrayed as being lovely, they are also associated with danger. This reflects humankind's relationship with the sea, which can be either a beautiful and bountiful place or a realm of fear and disaster. Living in the ocean—a vast expanse barely explored by humans—mermaids also represented to sailors a whole unknown world that existed under the water. Mermaids may also represent the mysterious nature of women as viewed by men.

Mermaids in Art, Literature, and Everyday Life

Mermaids have appeared in many stories and other forms of art over the centuries. Perhaps the most popular story featuring a mermaid is the Hans Christian Andersen tale "The Little Mermaid" (1836), which was also the basis for the 1989 Disney animated film of the same name. Mermaids also appear in T. S. Eliot's 1915 poem "The Love Song of J. Alfred Prufrock," and in J. M. Barrie's 1904 play *Peter Pan*, later adapted into a novel and numerous films. More modern adaptations of classic mermaid stories include the 1984 film *Splash*, starring Daryl Hannah and Tom Hanks, and the 2006 film *Aquamarine*. A mermaid even appears prominently in the logo for the popular Starbucks coffee shop chain.

Read, Write, Think, Discuss

Using your library, the Internet, or other available resources, research the sea mammals known as dugongs and manatees. In what areas of the world are they found? What do they eat? Are they endangered? What risks do these creatures face from humans?

SEE ALSO Sirens

Mexican Mythology

Mexican Mythology in Context

Mexico's mythology, like its population, reflects a blend of Native American and Spanish influences. Most people in modern Mexico trace their ancestry to American Indians, to the Spanish who controlled Mexico for three centuries, or to both, in a mixed-ethnic heritage called mestizo (pronounced mes-TEE-zoh). In the same way, Mexican religion, myths, and legends are a blend of American Indian traditions and European influences, such as Christianity. The Maya believe, for example, that the *chacs*, ancient rain spirits, are controlled by Jesus Christ and accompanied in their movement across the skies by the Virgin Mary, his mother. Mexican mythology is thus a collection of diverse older beliefs that were creatively combined over the centuries to produce entirely new myths.

Even before the Europeans arrived, Mexico was a land of varied cultures. Peoples who shared the Nahua (pronounced NAH-wah) family of languages dominated the north, while Mayan languages and culture were widespread in the south. Migration, trade, and war brought the different people and cultures of Mexico into contact with one another.

These contacts led to a blending of different religions and mythologies. As the Aztecs of northern Mexico embarked on wars of conquest and built an empire in central Mexico, they absorbed the deities or gods of conquered peoples and made them a part of their own collection of recognized gods, also known as a pantheon. In turn, myths and religious practices from central Mexico filtered south to influence the Maya. The Aztec influence boosted the importance of the god **Quetzalcoatl** (pronounced keht-sahl-koh-AHT-l)—known as Kukulcan (pronounced koo-kool-KAHN) to the Maya—and of human **sacrifice** to the gods.

Spain conquered Mexico between 1519 and 1521 and governed it as a colony until 1821, when Mexico won its independence. During the three centuries of colonial rule, European beliefs strongly influenced the indigenous (native) cultures and mythologies. Spanish missionaries and priests worked to convert the native peoples to Christianity and to stamp out their previous non-Christian beliefs. At the same time, some of the missionaries collected information about native beliefs, customs, and myths. Father Bernardino de Sahagun published accounts of the Aztecs that remain valuable sources of traditional legends; Father Diego de Landa did the same for the Maya.

Roman Catholic Christianity did take hold in Mexico, and about ninety percent of Mexicans now practice it. Yet the old ways did not completely disappear. A few American Indian groups, especially the Huichol (pronounced wee-CHOHL) and the Tarahumara (pronounced tah-ruh-hoo-MAH-ruh), remained true to their older beliefs. Many others, however, combined Catholicism with surviving forms of pre-Christian beliefs and mythologies. For example, they identified Roman Catholic saints, whose feast days are scattered throughout the year, with the ancient gods, traditionally honored with agricultural festivals at specific times.

Some myths and legends of Mexico have grown out of the events of the country's history. Parts of **Aztec mythology**—such as the legend of how the ancient Aztecs founded their capital of Tenochtitlán (pronounced teh-nowch-TEE-tlan) on the site where they saw an eagle fighting a serpent—have become part of the national heritage of modern Mexico. The Spanish conquest, the fight for independence, and the Mexican Revolution of 1910–1920 have also produced legends that have helped shape Mexico's image of itself as a nation and a people.

The Black Legend

The term "Black Legend" refers to a centuries-old view of Spain and its people as particularly cruel, prejudiced, and greedy. Some of the literature that promoted the Black Legend came from European Protestants hostile to Catholic Spain. But part of the Black Legend emerged from the writings of Bartolomé de Las Casas, a Spanish bishop who served in Mexico and wrote a vivid account of the Spanish soldiers' brutality to the Indians. Although modern historical research has shown that other nations were guilty of similar cruelties, traces of the Black Legend linger as negative images of the Spanish element in Latin American culture.

Core Deities and Characters

Perhaps the most widely recognized and honored figure of Mexican religious mythology is the Virgin of Guadalupe (pronounced gwah-duh-LOO-pay). Tradition says that in 1531 the Virgin Mary appeared before a peasant named Juan Diego on Tepeyac, a hill to the north of Mexico City, and told him that she wished to have a church built there. When the bishop of Mexico asked Juan for proof of what he had seen, the Virgin appeared again to the peasant and instructed him to gather roses in his cloak and take them to the bishop. Juan unfolded the cloak before the bishop, and a miraculous image of the Virgin could be seen where the roses had been. Another tradition associated with the Virgin of Guadalupe says that a shrine to Tonántzin (pronounced toh-nawn-TSEEN), an Aztec **corn** goddess, once stood at Tepeyac and that the Virgin replaced Tonántzin as the goddess mother of the Mexican people. However, there is no clear evidence of pre-Christian worship at that site.

The Mexican people have long regarded a vision of the Virgin of Guadalupe as a sign of divine favor. They have credited her with ending an epidemic of disease in the 1700s, and later with inspiring movements toward independence and liberation for their country. Mexicans of all regions and all ethnic backgrounds are united in their devotion to the Virgin as an emblem of both religious faith and national pride.

Among the historical figures who have acquired legendary status in Mexico are Hernán Cortés (1485–1547), the conquistador (Spanish soldier) who overthrew the Aztecs and brought Mexico under Spanish rule. Another important figure is Malinche (pronounced mah-leen-CHAY), an American Indian woman who assisted Cortés as an interpreter of Indian languages. Malinche had a son by Cortés and later married one of his followers. In the past, Mexicans have condemned Malinche as a traitor, coining the term *malinchismo* to refer to favoring foreign things over those of one's own people or culture. In recent years, women writers and artists in Mexico have tried to create a more balanced image of Malinche.

Legends also cluster around Miguel Hidalgo y Costilla (1753–1811), a priest and leader of the independence movement who died before a firing squad; Francisco "Pancho" Villa (1878–1923), a bandit turned revolutionary general; and Emiliano Zapata (1879–1919), a peasant who fought for peasants' rights in the Mexican Revolution. It is said that Zapata is not really dead but only sleeping. One day, like King **Arthur** of British legend, he will return to help his people. Some speak of hearing the hoofbeats of his horse Lightning as he rides through their villages at night.

Major Myths

Myths and tales told in modern Mexico not only amuse and entertain but also preserve old traditions and offer lessons in good or wise behavior. Some stories reflect pre-Christian beliefs, mentioning Father Sun and Mother Moon, once regarded as deities. Legend says that eclipses—during which part or all of the **sun** or moon is hidden by shadow—are caused by evil creatures trying to devour the heavenly bodies. One version identifies the evil creatures as ants, which cover Father Sun or Mother Moon with their huge colonies.

Some Mexican myths explain features of the natural world. One story tells how the **basilisk** (pronounced BAS-uh-lisk), a type of lizard, acquired the crest on its head. The Lord of the Woods announced that he would give a special hat to the animal that won a race. Most of the animals refused to compete, protesting that Big Deer was bound to win. However, to the amusement of all, the little basilisk said that it would race on one condition: all the animals had to close their eyes at the start of the race. The Lord of the Woods agreed, and Big Deer and the basilisk took off toward the stone that was their goal. When Big Deer arrived, he slowed down, thinking that he must have passed the basilisk long before. But to his surprise, as he prepared to sit on the stone, he found the basilisk there before him. The Lord of the Woods awarded the hat to the basilisk because he knew that the little creature had cleverly grabbed Big Deer's tail at the starting point and ridden it to the stone.

Many apparently humorous Mexican tales contain criticisms of social injustice or of bad behavior by those in power. A legend about Pancho Villa, for example, says that he became a leader of men by selling his soul to the devil, who came accompanied by many kings, popes, generals, and cardinals of the church—all of whom had made similar deals. A myth about a hungry peasant tells of a poor man driven by desperation to steal a chicken and cook it. A stranger appeared and asked for some food. The peasant refused him. The stranger revealed that he was God, upon which the peasant declared that he would definitely not share with God, who favored the rich but was unkind to the poor. Another stranger appeared, asking for food. When this second stranger revealed that he was Death, the peasant gladly shared with him, explaining that Death was fair, taking the fat and thin, young and old, rich and poor equally.

Key Themes and Symbols

One recurring theme in Mexican mythology is death. The ancient belief that people's personalities and needs continue unchanged after death leads to the custom of burying possessions and useful objects with the dead. A related belief is the notion that the dead can harm the living unless ceremonies are performed to keep them from doing so. This theme is also seen in the Day of the Dead celebration each year.

Another theme common in Mexican mythology is fairness or equality for all. This is seen in the tale of God and Death visiting the peasant, as well as in the hero status awarded to outlaws such as Pancho Villa and revolutionaries like Zapata. These figures were viewed as fighters for the underprivileged and poor, while the government itself was often viewed with suspicion or scorn.

Mexican Mythology in Art, Literature, and Everyday Life

Several aspects of modern Mexican culture show the importance of myths in national life. Religious fiestas, or festivals, often combine pagan traditions with the worship of Christian saints. Mourning and funeral practices are also a blend of American Indian and Christian ideas.

On November 1 and 2, the people of Mexico celebrate a national holiday called the Day of the Dead. Images of death, such as skulls and skeletons, appear everywhere on toys, candies, breads, and masks; at the same time, families prepare altars with offerings for dead relatives, who are thought to visit the world of the living at that time.

Some of the best-known art of modern Mexico includes images drawn from American Indian, Christian, and revolutionary myth. The most noted painters of the Mexican School—José Clemente Orozco (1883–1949), Diego Rivera (1886–1957), and David Alfaro Siqueiros (1896–1974)—produced murals that glorified the Mexican past, the Indians and peasants, and revolutionary ideals. Rivera's painting *The Deliverance of the Peon* illustrates his use of mythic symbols: the figure of Christ being taken from the cross represents the peasants who gave their lives in the Mexican Revolution.

Read, Write, Think, Discuss

A blending of beliefs is common in regions that are conquered by people with a different cultural background from the native peoples. Using your library, the Internet, or other available resources, research a North American Indian group whose religious beliefs and myths were transformed after contact with Europeans. How does that example compare with the situation in Mexico? What are the similarities and differences?

SEE ALSO Aztec Mythology; Basilisk; Mayan Mythology

Micronesian Mythology

Micronesian Mythology in Context

Micronesia (pronounced mye-kroh-NEE-zhuh), an area in the southwest Pacific Ocean containing thousands of islands, has no single mythology. The various islands and island groups—including the Caroline Islands, Marshall Islands, Mariana Islands, and Gilbert Islands—each have their own collection of legends and mythological beings. Micronesia is part of a vast region known as Oceania (pronounced oh-shee-AN-ee-uh).

Europeans arrived in Micronesia in the 1520s and brought Christianity with them. As the new religion became established in many areas, traditional beliefs declined. In addition, the contact with European cultures led to changes in local myths and legends. Travelers and missionaries wrote down some of the original myths, but many were lost before they could be recorded. Although the myths and legends have changed over the years, reflecting developments in Micronesia, they remain an important part of the region's cultural heritage.

The Micronesian religions included spirits of dead ancestors (called Ani in the Caroline Islands) and numerous other spirits that performed specific functions and were associated with particular locations. Only certain people, such as priests, healers, and magicians, could communicate with these spirits. They usually did so through dreams and trances. Spirits might be called on for a variety of reasons, including the diagnosis and cure of illness, success in fishing, control of weather, courage in battle, and skill in navigation. To ensure the goodwill of the spirits, people often entertained them by dancing and singing. In return, the spirits provided information about the cause of individual misfortunes and prescribed cures and magical spells.

Myths were often used to teach members of a group about particular beliefs or skills. Myths about Aluluei (pronounced ah-LOO-loo-lay), a god of seafaring, included information useful for training navigators. In addition, legends told in the Marshall Islands dealt with forecasting weather and determining position at sea by observing natural phenomena. The Micronesians also had myths that expressed their beliefs about the earth and sky, the **afterlife**, and the roles of gods and culture **heroes**. The myths were passed from one generation to the next by professional storytellers.

Core Deities and Characters

Micronesian myths feature creator gods, demigods (half human, half god), **tricksters**, heroes, and ancestral spirits. Creation stories generally dealt with the origin of particular islands or groups of people. For this reason, there were numerous creation myths and a variety of creator deities.

Nareau, the Spider Lord of the Gilbert Islands, is one of the best-known creator gods. After emerging from an ancient place—consisting of darkness, endless space, or the sea—he created **heaven** and earth and two beings, Na Atibu and Nei Teukez. From these beings sprang many gods. One, also called Nareau and known as Young Spider, played an important part in separating the earth from the sky and in creating the stars, islands, trees, and creatures of the earth. Another creator deity was Loa, the supreme being of the Marshall Islands. From his leg emerged Wulleb and Limdunanij, the first man and woman.

One of Micronesia's mythological heroes was Motikitik, famous for his fishing feats. According to one myth, Motikitik was curious to know how his mother always managed to provide large quantities of food, so he stayed at home and spied on her. He heard his mother say a magic spell and watched her dive into the sea. Changing himself into a diving bird, Motikitik followed her and saw her gathering food. By discovering her secret, however, he caused her to die. During the next three days, Motikitik fished up many baskets of food. On the fourth day, he fished up an island, where he went to live with his two brothers.

Perhaps the most important trickster and culture hero in Micronesian mythology was Olifat (also called Olofat, Olofath, and Orofat). The son of the god Lugeilan and of a human woman, the mischievous Olifat was a contradictory figure torn between two worlds. He sometimes rose to heaven on a column of smoke and other times descended to earth on a bolt of lightning. He was often associated with **fire**. While in heaven, Olifat disturbed the gods by singing and making other noises. On earth, he played tricks on humans. Some tricks had unforeseen consequences, such as giving sharks sharp teeth and putting stingers on the tails of scorpions.

The Micronesians linked particular deities, spirits, and heroes with certain functions and skills. Aluluei, the god of seafaring, had numerous eyes that became the stars of the night sky used by sailors to navigate at sea. Bue, a culture hero of the Gilbert Islands, taught Micronesians how to sing and dance, build canoes and houses, and raise winds by magic. Naniumlap, the fertility god of the Caroline Islands, helped ensure that plants and animals grew and that women had children. Finally, Nei Tituaabine, the tree goddess of the Gilbert Islands, made sure that trees grew and bore fruit.

Major Myths

Despite the great variety of myths that existed on Micronesia's many islands, certain themes can be found throughout the region. Origin myths typically dealt with the creation of the earth and sky, gods, islands, heroes, features of the landscape, humans, and other creatures. The main event in many creation myths was the separation of the earth from the sky. Stories about the older Nareau, for example, told how he ordered Sand and Water to mate. Two of their offspring then produced many beings, including Riiki, the eel. Riiki pushed up the sky, and Nareau created the **sun**, moon, stars, rocks, and a great tree. The ancestors of humans sprang from the branches of this ancestral tree.

Myths about travels between the sky and the earth were also quite common. Stories about the trickster Olifat often described his journeys up to heaven and his descents to earth. In addition, a mythical child named Thilefial traveled to the sky to escape mistreatment on earth and then returned to earth to take revenge.

Micronesians believed that the gods made humans mortal—subject to death—and various myths dealt with death and the afterlife. According to one myth, when gods first created humans, men and women lived separately under two different trees. The guardian spirit Na Kaa warned them not to leave their particular trees, but once during his absence, the men and women gathered under the same tree. When Na Kaa returned, he told them that they had chosen the Tree of Death. This was how humans became mortal. When humans died, their souls journeyed either to a paradise (underwater or in the sky) or to a gloomy **underworld** realm whose gates were guarded by evil spirits.

The adventures of tricksters were a common feature in Micronesian myths. The trickster Olifat annoyed the gods, made fools of men, and sometimes caused human injury or death. Many stories about him tell how he changed his form to a bird, an animal, or an object to escape detection or punishment. Despite his often harmful behavior, Olifat sometimes helped humans who sought his advice about love and other personal matters. He is also credited with introducing the art of tattooing to the people of Micronesia.

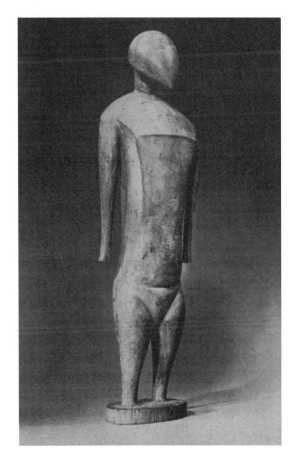

Micronesians worshiped ancestral spirits that were associated with particular purposes and places. Priests and healers communicated with these beings through dreams and trances. This wooden ancestral figure comes from the Caroline Islands. COPYRIGHT © 1999–2008 BY THE SMITHSONIAN INSTITUTION. ALL RIGHTS RESERVED.

Many Micronesian myths featured animal tricksters. The stories usually revolved around three main characters, such as a rat, a crab, and either a turtle or an octopus, and recounted the pranks they played on other creatures. The myths also helped explain the relationships among various animals.

Some evil characters in Micronesian myths were cannibal spirits or ogres. Usually characterized by their strength and stupidity, these creatures could be frightened away by loud noises and were terrified of fire. A well-known mythological hero was the ogre-killing child who sometimes saved entire villages by destroying the evil creatures.

Tales about Pälülop (pronounced pay-LOO-lop), a great canoe captain, and members of his family were popular in the Caroline Islands. The stories were complex, included a bewildering array of characters, and dealt with many different subjects. One story told how Pälülop's sons Big Rong and Little Rong became jealous of their younger brother Aluluei and killed him. Pälülop brought Aluluei back in spirit form and gave him lots of eyes that shone like stars to help the boy protect himself.

Another well-known myth involved a porpoise girl, a mermaid-like creature who came to land either to steal something or to watch people dance. While she was on land, a man hid her tail, preventing her from returning to the sea. The porpoise girl married the man and had children. Many years later she found her tail and returned to the sea after telling her children never to eat porpoise. Stories of this type, in which people learn not to eat certain foods, were often used to explain the origin of certain food taboos. In some versions of the myth, the girl came from the sky and the man hid her wings.

Key Themes and Symbols

The most common myths in Micronesian mythology are origin myths—stories that explain how things came to be. There are origin myths that explain the creation of the world, the creation of certain tribes and people, and the origins of certain practices or traditions. A common theme in eastern Micronesia was the use of a creator god's body to form the earth, sky, sun, moon, and other features. In the Gilbert Islands, the work of creation was shared by the Spider Lord, Nareau, and the younger Nareau (Young Spider). This represents the strong connection between the people, the gods, and the natural world.

The theme of an animal in human form who marries a mortal man and then leaves him to return to her home is also popular. This type of myth is not exclusive to Micronesia and can be found in stories from India dating back more than three thousand years. The presence of similar legends throughout Oceania suggests that a myth of this type may have originated in Asia and spread to the islands of the Pacific at a very early date.

Micronesian Mythology in Art, Literature, and Everyday Life

Micronesians include mythology in much of their art and daily life. Dance is an especially important part of most Micronesian cultures, with every member of a tribe frequently being required to show their dancing skills at ceremonies and celebrations. Music is equally important, and songs are viewed not as the creation of musicians but as gifts channeled from the gods and spirits. Many Micronesians also believe in magic and consult magicians regularly to help resolve personal or family issues.

Read, Write, Think, Discuss

Using your library, the Internet, or other available resources, locate Micronesia on a map of the Pacific Ocean. Where is it in relation to Melanesia and Polynesia? Are these different regions fairly distinct in their mythologies? What are some of the mythological themes they have in common?

SEE ALSO Afterlife; Animals in Mythology; Creation Stories; Melanesian Mythology; Polynesian Mythology

Midas

Character Overview

In Greek and **Roman mythology**, Midas was a king of Phrygia (pronounced FRIJ-ee-uh) fabled for having the "Midas touch"—the power to turn whatever he touched into gold.

Nationality/Culture
Greek/Roman

Pronunciation
MY-duhs

Alternate Names
None

Appears In
Ovid's *Metamorphoses*

Lineage
Son of King Gordias and Cybele

According to Greek and Roman mythology, Silenus (pronounced sye-LEE-nuhs), a companion of the god **Dionysus** (pronounced dye-uh-NYE-suhs), became drunk while visiting Phrygia. Silenus was captured and brought to Midas, who ordered that he be released and returned safely to Dionysus. The god gratefully granted Midas any wish as a reward. Midas asked that everything he touched turn to gold. Knowing the wish to be dangerous, Dionysus asked the king if he was sure that was what he wanted. Midas assured him that it was, and the god granted the wish.

At first Midas was overjoyed. He gathered great wealth simply by touching things. However, when he tried to eat, each mouthful of food turned to gold as it touched his lips. When he went to hug his daughter, she turned to gold as well. Midas finally begged the god to release him from his wish. Dionysus instructed him to bathe in the River Pactolus (pronounced pak-TOH-luhs). From that day forward Midas was cured, and the sands of the river turned to gold dust.

In another tale, Midas observed a music contest between the gods **Apollo** (pronounced uh-POL-oh) and **Pan**. Midas, who had become a follower of Pan, protested when Apollo was awarded the victory. The angry Apollo gave Midas the ears of a donkey as punishment for his inability to hear that Apollo was the superior musician. Midas wore a hat to hide the ears and made his barber swear never to tell anyone the embarrassing secret. Unable to keep the secret, the barber dug a hole in a meadow and whispered into it, "King Midas has the ears of an ass." Reeds later grew from the hole, and whenever a breeze blew through them, they whispered the secret to anyone who was nearby.

Midas in Context

The Pactolus River is a real river that was important to the people of Lydia, a kingdom that covered the entire western portion of Asia Minor (a region known as Turkey in modern times). Lydia was known as a wealthy kingdom, and much of its wealth came from the abundant gold that was found in the sands along the Pactolus. In fact, in the seventh century BCE, Lydia became the first culture to mint and use coins as currency. The myth of Midas can be seen as an "origin tale" that explains why gold is found in the sands of the Pactolus. The myth allowed the ancient Lydians to link the tales of the gods to their own environment. It also reflects the importance of gold in ancient cultures, where it was used mainly to create sacred or religious objects kept by rulers.

Key Themes and Symbols

One of the main themes of the myth of King Midas is greed. Midas wishes for great riches and believes at first that he has come up with a way to achieve that goal. However, his greed ultimately causes him to lose everything of true importance. In the story, gold at first represents wealth and the favor of the gods. In the end, especially after losing his daughter, gold symbolizes the high price Midas has paid for his greed.

Midas in Art, Literature, and Everyday Life

The myth of Midas has appeared in countless versions over the years. It remains especially popular in collections of children's stories. The Hand of Midas appears in the Disney animated film *Aladdin and the King of Thieves* (1995), a sequel to the 1992 hit film *Aladdin*. In the movie, the hand of Midas still possesses the ability to transform anything into gold by touch. In popular speech, saying someone has "the Midas touch" means that the person is very prosperous at any endeavor he or she attempts.

Read, Write, Think, Discuss

In the twenty-first century, there are many figures in the business and entertainment industry such as Microsoft founder Bill Gates and talk-show host Oprah Winfrey who have made fortunes worth millions and even billions of dollars. Do you think there is such a thing as having too much money? What might be some of the effects—social, emotional, and psychological—of being able to buy practically anything in the world you want?

SEE ALSO Apollo; Dionysus; Greek Mythology; Pan; Roman Mythology

Mimir

Character Overview

In **Norse mythology**, the giant Mimir was considered the wisest member of the group of gods known as the Aesir (pronounced AY-sur). He served

Nationality/Culture
Norse

Pronunciation
MEE-mir

Alternate Names
Mim

Appears In
The Eddas

Lineage
Unknown

as the guardian of the well of knowledge, located at the base of the world tree called **Yggdrasill** (pronounced IG-druh-sil).

Major Myths

During the war between the Aesir and another group of gods called the Vanir (pronounced VAH-nir), the Vanir took Mimir and a companion, named Hoenir (pronounced HUH-nir), as hostages. Hoenir was treated as a chieftain by the Vanir, but without the wise Mimir he could not speak well. The Vanir felt cheated and cut off Mimir's head. They sent it back to **Odin** (pronounced OH-din), the father of the gods, who kept it alive in a shrine near the base of Yggdrasill.

The well of knowledge sprang from the spot where Mimir's head was kept. Seeking wisdom, Odin rode to the well to drink its waters. However, Mimir allowed him to do so only after Odin left one of his eyes in the well. From then on, when Odin wished to learn secrets from the well, he asked questions to Mimir's head, which gave him the answers.

Mimir in Context

The myth of Mimir reflects Norse attitudes about drawing resources from nature and transforming them into something useful, rather than simply hoarding resources as wealth. In this case, the well of Mimir is a natural source of knowledge that serves no purpose until someone drinks from it. Odin uses this knowledge to gain insight into the fates of the gods. Mimir does serve as a guardian of the well, but only to ensure that those who do drink from the well earn their knowledge through **sacrifice**. This contrasts with Norse depictions of the Vanir and other less heroic figures, such as Fafnir, who are depicted as greedy creatures, more concerned with possessing treasures than actually using them in a positive way.

Key Themes and Symbols

In Norse mythology, Mimir represents knowledge and wisdom. This is emphasized by the fact that only his head survives after he is kidnapped by the Vanir. The head is a traditional symbol of knowledge in many cultures, and, in the myth, Odin continues to seek guidance from the head. Mimir is also portrayed as a protector because he guards the well of knowledge and keeps the unworthy from drinking out of it. The fact that Mimir demands Odin's eye as a sacrifice before he can drink from the well indicates that there is a price to be paid to gain knowledge, but that it is worth it.

Mimir in Art, Literature, and Everyday Life

Mimir appears in the *Prose Edda* and the *Poetic Edda*, most notably the *Gylfaginning* and *Voluspa*. Though Norse mythology has become increasingly well known since the nineteenth century, Mimir only seldom makes appearances. He is perhaps best known from the Richard Wagner opera cycle *The Ring of the Nibelung*, which combines Norse and German myths into an epic tale about the gods. "Mimir" is also the name of a class of disembodied skulls found in *Dungeons and Dragons* role-playing games that provide knowledge to the player, much like the mythical Mimir provided knowledge to Odin.

Read, Write, Think, Discuss

The Sea of Trolls (2004), by Nancy Farmer, is a fantasy novel set in the realm of Norse and Saxon myth. It tells the tale of a young apprentice bard named Jack who accidentally causes the half-troll Queen Frith to lose her hair during a performance at the royal court. She threatens to sacrifice Jack's sister unless he fixes the problem, so Jack embarks on a quest to find Mimir's well; by drinking from the well, he hopes to learn a spell that will replace the Queen's hair. Along the way, Jack has countless adventures and meets creatures that are both humorous and frightening.

SEE ALSO Giants; Norse Mythology; Odin; Yggdrasill

Minerva

See **Athena.**

Minos, King

See **Minotaur.**

Minotaur

Nationality/Culture
Greek

Pronunciation
MIN-uh-tawr

Alternate Names
Asterion

Appears In
Plutarch's *Life of Theseus*,
Ovid's *Heroides*, Hygi-
nus's *Fabulae*

Lineage
Son of the Cretan bull and
Pasiphaë

Character Overview

In **Greek mythology**, the Minotaur was a monstrous creature with the head of a bull on a man's body. Like many other mythological monsters, the Minotaur had a ravenous appetite for human flesh. He was eventually slain by a worthy hero with the help of a resourceful heroine.

The Minotaur—which means "Minos's bull"—was born in the palace of King Minos (pronounced MEYE-nuhs) of Crete (pronounced KREET), a large island south of Greece. Some time earlier, the sea god **Poseidon** (pronounced poh-SYE-dun) had sent Minos a pure-white bull to be sacrificed in his honor. When the king saw the magnificent creature, however, he refused to kill it. This angered Poseidon, who arranged for Minos's wife, Pasiphaë (pronounced pa-SIF-ah-ee), to fall in love with the bull. The offspring of their unnatural mating was the Minotaur. The king imprisoned the Minotaur in the Labyrinth (pronounced LAB-uh-rinth), a maze built by a craftsman at his court named **Daedalus** (pronounced DED-uh-lus).

In later years, after the people of the Greek city of Athens killed one of Minos's sons, the Cretan king called down a plague on their city. Only by agreeing to send seven young men and seven young women to Crete every year could the Athenians obtain relief. These youths and maidens were sent into the Cretan Labyrinth, where the Minotaur devoured them.

Theseus (pronounced THEE-see-uhs) of Athens was determined to end the slaughter of young people. He volunteered to go to Crete as one of the sacrificial victims, vowing to slay the Minotaur. When the ship carrying the Athenians reached Crete, **Ariadne** (pronounced ar-ee-AD-nee), daughter of Minos and Pasiphaë, fell in love with Theseus. She gave him a plan of the Labyrinth that she had obtained from Daedalus, as well as a ball of string. He was to tie one end of the string to the exit as he went in and then follow the string to find his way out. Deep in the Labyrinth, Theseus met the bellowing, bloodthirsty Minotaur and killed it with a blow from his fist. He and the other Athenians then fled Crete, taking Ariadne with them.

A monstrous creature in Greek mythology, the Minotaur had the head of a bull and the body of a man. This vase painting dating from the 500s BCE shows Theseus killing the Minotaur. ERICH LESSING/ART RESOURCE, NY.

The Minotaur in Context

Some scholars suggest that the myth of the Minotaur arose out of ancient rituals in which a priest or king donned a bull mask before performing sacrifices. The Labyrinth may have represented the ancient palace at Knossos on Crete, which was a sprawling complex of chambers and hallways. In addition, the tale reflects ancient Greek ideas about women and infidelity. Unlike many male characters in Greek mythology, Pasiphaë does not seek to love the bull, but is forced to do so through the magic of the gods. This reflects the much lower incidence of female infidelity in ancient Greece. However, the child she bears is hideous and must be hidden from the outside world, which also reflects the enormous stigma—social disapproval—that was attached to wives who were unfaithful.

The Minotaur, World War II, and Art

The myth of the Minotaur captured the imagination of many artists during the period of the Second World War. Henri Matisse, Max Ernst, Giorgio de Chirico, and Victor Brauner all created artistic versions of the myth. Among writers, André Gide, Jorge Luis Borges, James Joyce, T. S. Eliot, and Ezra Pound also found the myth central to their dark vision of humanity during and after the war. But it was Pablo Picasso who delved most deeply into the myth of the Minotaur in his paintings and sketches. Picasso used the beast to depict the loss of balance between the natural and human worlds. The Minotaur, once confined to a dark and secret labyrinth, has escaped in Picasso's paintings and appears lost and disoriented as he makes his way through the human world. Picasso thus expresses what many were feeling during the terrible years of the Second World War and its aftermath.

Key Themes and Symbols

As with many Greek myths, one of the central themes of the myth of the Minotaur is vengeance. Poseidon seeks vengeance upon Minos for his failure to offer an intended **sacrifice** (the white bull); this leads to the Minotaur's birth. King Minos later seeks vengeance upon the people of Athens for killing his beloved son. This leads to the offering of Athenian sacrifices as payment, and ultimately to the Minotaur's death at the hands of Theseus.

The Minotaur in Art, Literature, and Everyday Life

The Minotaur is such a visually distinctive character that he has remained popular in art and culture throughout the centuries. He is nearly always depicted as having the head of a bull and the body of a man, though some sources describe him as having an ox's body and a man's head. The Minotaur has appeared in Dante's *Inferno*, as well as in works by Ted Hughes and C. S. Lewis. In the film version of the C. S. Lewis novel *The Lion, the Witch, and the Wardrobe* (2005), General Otmin is a Minotaur who leads the White Witch's evil army. "The House of Asterion," a short story by Jorge Luis Borges, tells the tale of the Minotaur from his own point of view rather than from the perspective of the hero Theseus. The artist most closely associated with the Minotaur, however, is Pablo Picasso, who created many works of art centered around the mythical creature.

Read, Write, Think, Discuss

The Minotaur is somewhat unique among mythical Greek characters because he has the head of an animal; most mythical Greek hybrids have animal body parts combined with human heads. What do you think this says about the "humanness" of the Minotaur in the eyes of the ancient Greeks? Why do you think other cultures, such as the Egyptians, have many gods and goddesses with animal heads, while the Greeks did not?

SEE ALSO Ariadne; Daedalus; Greek Mythology; Theseus

Mithras

Character Overview

Mithras—also called Mithra—was a god of ancient **Persian mythology** associated with the **sun**. He became a major figure in the religion known as Zoroastrianism, which originated in ancient Persia and was connected with the supreme Zoroastrian god **Ahura Mazda** (pronounced ah-HOO-ruh MAHZ-duh). In early forms of Zoroastrianism, Ahura Mazda created Mithras as a god of justice and light. Mentions of this incarnation of Mithras date to 1500 BCE. Later, Mithras came to be seen by some as a version of Ahura Mazda himself. A cult devoted to Mithras spread into the Mediterranean world in the first few centuries of the common era, where for a time it rivaled Christianity as the fastest-growing new religion. It is unclear whether the practices associated with the Mithras cult are connected with Zoroastrian worship of Mithras.

Major Myths

According to earliest Zoroastrian legends, Mithras was born from the earth, emerging from a broken rock with a torch in one hand and a sword in the other. He worked for Ahura Mazda by battling demons, sorcerers, and other evildoers. He also judged the deeds of the dead and it was believed he could bring worthy humans back to life at the time of the end of the world.

Hundreds of years later, in ancient Greece and Rome, the worship of Mithras focused on his role as god of war, so soldiers in particular were

Nationality/Culture
Persian

Pronunciation
MITH-rahs

Alternate Names
Mithra, Mitra, Meher

Appears In
The Avesta; the Vedas

Lineage
None

drawn to the Mithras cult. The legend most associated with this phase of Mithras worship tells of Mithras slaying a great bull whose body and blood became the source of all life on earth. Animal sacrifices were central to his worship, which took place in caves or cavelike buildings in honor of the god's birth from the earth. Little concrete information about the Greek and Roman form of Mithras-worship survives. Most descriptions of how the religion was practiced in Greece and Rome come from later Christian writers and date to the third and fourth centuries CE, when Mithras-worship was at its peak. It seems most likely that it was an all-male cult with various levels, or ranks, and that rising through the ranks of the cult required special training and initiation. The Roman army carried the religion to Britain, Germany, and other outposts of the Holy Roman Empire.

Mithras in Context

The legends surrounding the Greek and Roman version of Mithras bear much in common with some elements of Christianity. For example, like Jesus Christ, Mithras was said to be born on December 25, to have performed miracles, to have the power to "save" human souls at the end of the world, and to have eaten a last supper with twelve followers. After Christianity became the official religion of the Roman Empire in the 300s, worship of Mithras was suppressed, along with other pagan beliefs. It is unclear whether the Mithras cult borrowed from Christianity or vice versa as both religions were widespread in the fourth century CE.

Key Themes and Symbols

Mithras is born with a sword and a torch. These two objects represent his roles as the god of war and the god of light. The "light" he represents is both literal and figurative: like the Greek god **Apollo** (pronounced uh-POL-oh), Mithras is a sun god. Mithras represents the light of truth and justice. Mithras himself came to represent strength, bravery, and manliness, which made him an appealing god for soldiers.

Mithras in Art, Literature, and Everyday Life

At the turn of the twentieth century, an influential book on the Mithras cult was published: Franz Cumont's *Texts and Illustrated Monuments Related to the Mysteries of Mithra*. Cumont argued that the worship of Mithras by the Romans had its origins in a similar religion practiced by the ancient Zoroastrians, although there is little evidence to support this idea. The Mithras of the Zoroastrians is hardly mentioned outside the Avesta and the Vedas, and there is no archeological evidence in modern Iran (the area that was ancient Persia) of the caves devoted to later Mithras-worship.

Hundreds of the ancient caves and cavelike structures in which the Roman Mithras cult was practiced survive today in Italy, Germany, and Britain. Three Mithras-worship caves have been excavated along Hadrian's wall (built by Roman Emperor Hadrian) in northern Britain. One sculpture discovered there is of Mithras emerging from an egg, surrounded by the twelve signs of the zodiac.

Read, Write, Think, Discuss

Several writers have speculated about a connection between the Mithras cult of the first few centuries CE and another secret society that still exists today: the Freemasons. Because it is a secret society, and because it has boasted among its members some of the most famous men in Western history, the Freemasons have been the subject of much wild speculation and rumor. Using your library and the Internet, write a report about the origins and functions of the Freemasons. Evaluate your sources carefully. Only include information that seems reliable and verifiable, and only use sources that seem trustworthy and unbiased.

SEE ALSO Ahura Mazda; Apollo

Mordred

Nationality/Culture
Romano-British/Celtic

Pronunciation
MAWR-dred

Alternate Names
Modred, Medraut (Welsh)

Appears In
Geoffrey of Monmouth's *History of the Kings of Britain*, Thomas Malory's *Le Morte d'Arthur*

Lineage
Son of King Arthur and Morgause

Character Overview

Mordred was the illegitimate son of King **Arthur** and his half-sister Morgause (pronounced mor-GAWZ). Mordred is best remembered for his betrayal of Arthur and for launching the battle that led to Arthur's demise. He appears in even the earliest versions of Arthurian legend, though the specifics of his life vary widely.

According to legend, Morgause and Arthur shared the same mother, though they did not know it. Mordred was conceived when the two had an affair, and was raised by his mother and her husband, King Lot, along with her other children. Another of her sons, Gawain (pronounced gah-WAYN), was admired for his bravery and became a knight of King Arthur's Round Table. Mordred used the connections of his brother Gawain to secure himself a position as one of Arthur's trusted knights as well. Though Mordred developed a reputation for womanizing and treachery, Arthur—who by then knew himself to be Mordred's uncle, but not his father—left Mordred in charge of his kingdom while he ventured on a campaign against Roman forces.

Mordred immediately seized control of Arthur's kingdom and attempted to take Arthur's wife **Guinevere** (pronounced GWEN-uh-veer) as his own. Guinevere fled to the Tower of London, and Arthur immediately returned to reclaim his throne. Mordred and Arthur's armies clashed in battle at Camlann, where Arthur killed Mordred—but not before being mortally wounded by him. According to legend, Arthur did not die but was taken from the battlefield to recover on the island of Avalon, where he still remains. Arthur's battle against Mordred marks the fall of **Camelot**, and with it the end of the Knights of the Round Table.

Mordred in Context

Although Mordred is almost universally viewed as a villain by those familiar with basic Arthurian legend, many lesser known sources tell a different story. Considering the early references to Mordred in several Welsh texts, Mordred may have been an historical figure from Welsh nobility. In fact, he is portrayed as courteous and brave in some early writings—quite the opposite of the Mordred of legend. The first mention of his presence at the Battle of Camlann merely indicates that he fought there and does not state that he fought against Arthur. In fact, some sources suggest that the battle was brought about by a dispute between Queen Guinevere and her sister.

Key Themes and Symbols

A central theme in the myth of Mordred is the vengeance of the illegitimate son. Though Arthur had an affair with a woman he did not know to be his sister, and later believed himself to be Mordred's uncle, the legends suggest that the final clash between the two was fated to occur. Mordred represents all of Arthur's secret flaws, unseen by most of the Knights of the Round Table, but which ultimately played an important part in the failure of his seemingly perfect kingdom.

Mordred in Art, Literature, and Everyday Life

Mordred is a key figure in nearly all versions of Arthurian legend. He is present even in the earliest documented portions of the myth, found in *The Annals of Wales*, and in Geoffrey of Monmouth's *History of the Kings of Britain*. Mordred is also found in Thomas Malory's *Le Morte d'Arthur* and in newer works such as *The Once and Future King* by T. H. White and *The Mists of Avalon* by Marion Zimmer Bradley.

Read, Write, Think, Discuss

The Winter Prince (2003) by Elizabeth Wein offers a fresh vision of Arthurian legend from the point of view of a young Medraut (Mordred). Medraut is a gifted boy who uses his powers of healing to help his sickly younger brother, Lleu, who is destined to become the next king—

something Medraut, the illegitimate son of King Artos (Arthur), cannot do. When his cunning mother Morgause attempts to pit the boys against each other for her own wicked ends, the two brothers seem destined to either grow closer through understanding, or destroy each other through envy.

SEE ALSO Arthur, King; Arthurian Legends

Morgan Le Fay

See **Arthur, King; Arthurian Legends.**

Muses

Nationality/Culture
Greek

Pronunciation
MYOO-siz

Alternate Names
Camenae (Roman)

Appears In
Hesiod's *Theogony*,
Homer's *Iliad*

Lineage
Daughters of Zeus and
Mnemosyne

Character Overview

In **Greek mythology**, the Muses were sister goddesses of music, dance, poetry, and other artistic and intellectual pursuits. Poets and other artists often called on them for inspiration. **Zeus** (pronounced ZOOS), the king of the gods, was the father of the Muses. Their mother was Mnemosyne (pronounced nee-MOSS-uh-nee), goddess of memory. In his role as god of music, poetry, and dance, **Apollo** (pronounced uh-POL-oh) was sometimes said to be their leader. The Muses also figured in **Roman mythology**, although the Romans usually associated them with the four goddesses known as the Camenae (pronounced kuh-MEE-nee).

Major Myths

The Muses lived on two sacred Greek mountain peaks, Olympus (pronounced oh-LIM-puhs) and Helicon (pronounced HEL-i-kon). Originally they were three in number—Melete (pronounced MEL-i-tee, meaning Practice), Mneme (pronounced NEE-mee, meaning Memory), and Aoede (pronounced ay-EE-dee, meaning Song)—but the Greek poet Hesiod named nine Muses in his *Theogony* (*Birth of the Gods*). Ancient writers, particularly the Romans, often linked individual Muses with specific arts and sciences, but they did not agree on the functions of particular Muses. One widely recognized list identified Calliope (pronounced kuh-LYE-uh-pee) with heroic and epic poetry, Erato (pronounced AIR-uh-toh) with lyric and love poetry, Polyhymnia (pronounced pol-ee-HIM-nee-uh) with sacred songs and pantomime, Melpomene (pronounced mel-POM-uh-nee) with tragedy, Thalia (pronounced thuh-LYE-uh) with comedy, Euterpe (pronounced yoo-TUR-pee) with music played on instruments, Terpsichore (pronounced turp-SIK-uh-ree) with dancing, Clio (pronounced KLEE-oh) with history, and Urania (pronounced yoo-RAY-nee-uh) with astronomy.

In myths, the Muses often punished or rewarded mortals. Hesiod claimed that they gave him knowledge and inspired him. The *Odyssey* tells of Demodocus (pronounced dee-MOH-duh-kuhs), a man who was blinded and then given the gift of song by one of the Muses, who claimed that song was even more precious than sight. Although the Muses could be generous, they resented mortals who questioned their supremacy in the arts. The *Iliad* mentions Thamyris (pronounced THAH-mi-ruhs), a poet who challenged the Muses. They made him blind and took away his ability to sing. Another myth tells of the Pierides (pronounced pye-AIR-uh-deez), nine sisters who lived in Macedonia (pronounced mas-uh-DOHN-ee-uh), north of Greece. The Pierides challenged the Muses to a contest. The Muses won and then turned their challengers into chattering birds. Some of the Muses had famous offspring. Calliope, for example, was the mother of the great musician **Orpheus** (pronounced OR-fee-uhs), and Clio was the mother of the beautiful Hyacinthus (pronounced high-uh-SIN-thuhs).

The Muses in Context

Poets in ancient Greece often expressed the idea that the Muses were responsible for the works that the poets had created. This may have served a specific purpose: it informed readers and listeners that the work fit within established traditional formats. At one time, for example, all traditional books—regardless of subject matter—were written with a poetic structure. Crediting the Muses as the originators of a work also reflected how ancient Greeks viewed their cultural knowledge as something that did not belong solely to the person writing it down or saying it, but to all Greeks. In addition, this may have indicated that a

work was derived from a historical source, passed down from other poets or storytellers.

Key Themes and Symbols

The Muses represent creativity and the arts, with each one representing a different aspect of these things. One of the main themes of the stories of the Muses is divine inspiration—the idea that artists somehow receive their ideas, insights, and talents from a source greater than themselves. This is illustrated when others challenge the Muses to a contest of skills;

since the Muses are the source of all great art, they always defeat their challengers.

The Muses in Art, Literature, and Everyday Life

The Muses appear frequently in ancient art and poetry, often in acknowledgement for helping to create the work itself. The Muses have been painted by artists such as Gustave Moreau and Johannes Vermeer. They have been called upon by writers from Homer and Virgil to William Shakespeare and Geoffrey Chaucer. The Muses have also appeared several times in movies. The 1980 musical film *Xanadu* features Olivia Newton-John as Terpsichore, a Muse who enters the modern world and falls in love with a commercial artist, played by Michael Beck. In the 1999 Albert Brooks film *The Muse*, Sharon Stone plays a woman named Sarah who may or may not be an actual Muse from Greek mythology. Three of the Muses also appear as narrating characters in the 1997 animated Disney film *Hercules*.

The word *museum* is taken from the Muses. It means "place of the Muses" and was first used for the museum of ancient Alexandria, Egypt, a center of scholarship and learning. The word "music" is also taken from these goddesses, and means "art of the Muses." Interestingly, the Greek word for Muse may come from an older Indo-European word meaning "to think," and even today to "muse" over something means to think deeply about it, or to meditate upon it.

Read, Write, Think, Discuss

Myths of the Muses are linked to ideas about inspiration and creativity in the arts and sciences, and place great importance upon the mind and thought processes. What do the myths of the Muses tell us about the way the ancient Greeks thought about the arts and sciences? Did they divide the arts and sciences into categories, such as emotional versus rational, like many Western cultures do? Using your library, the Internet, or other available resources, trace the development of one subject, such as history or astronomy, to identify its origins and learn how opinions about it have changed over the centuries. What were some of the social and cultural factors that may have influenced the changes?

SEE ALSO Apollo; Greek Mythology

Mwindo

Nationality/Culture
African/Nyangan

Pronunciation
MWEE-n-doh

Alternate Names
None

Appears In
Nyangan oral mythology

Lineage
Son of Shemwindo and Nyamwindo

Character Overview

In the mythology of the Nyanga people of central Africa, Mwindo was a hero with supernatural powers who had many adventures. His story is told in the epic of Mwindo. Mwindo was the son of Shemwindo (pronounced shay-MWEE-n-doh), a powerful chief who had seven wives. Shemwindo heard a prophecy, or prediction, that he would be removed from his throne by his son. To prevent this, Shemwindo decreed that his wives should bear only female children, and that he would kill any male child they produced. Six of his wives gave birth to females. Then his favorite wife, Nyamwindo (pronounced nee-ah-MWEE-n-doh), had a boy. The child emerged from her middle finger and could walk and talk immediately. His appearance was like that of a Pygmy, one of several culture groups within Africa whose average height is less than five feet tall. Nyamwindo named her child Mwindo. When Shemwindo found out about Mwindo, he tried to kill the boy with his spear. But Mwindo used magic to protect himself and to throw off his father's aim. Shemwindo then buried the child alive, but Mwindo escaped. Next the father sealed his son in a drum and threw him into a river to drown. Again, Mwindo used his magic powers to travel beneath the water.

Mwindo decided to visit his aunt Iyangura (pronounced ee-yong-GOO-rah). Iyangura's husband tried to stop him by setting traps. But with the help of animal spirits, Mwindo escaped the traps and met his aunt. A guard called upon Master Lightning to strike Mwindo down, but Mwindo's magic made the lightning bolts miss.

Later Mwindo led his uncles to his father's village, intending to punish Shemwindo. They killed all of the villagers and destroyed the village. Shemwindo fled to the **underworld**, or land of the dead, followed by Mwindo. There Mwindo met with the ruler of the underworld, Muisa, who promised to reveal Shemwindo's hiding place if Mwindo performed some tasks for him. Mwindo did so, but twice Muisa tried to kill Mwindo, and twice Mwindo used a magic scepter (a club-like staff) to save himself. Finally, Mwindo tracked down his father. Shemwindo apologized for trying to kill Mwindo and agreed to share his kingdom with his son. Mwindo then rebuilt the village and restored all the villagers to life.

Later Mwindo killed a dragon that was a friend of Master Lightning. As punishment, Mwindo was taken up to the sky, where he had to endure blazing heat from the **sun** and terrible cold and rain. Mwindo endured this for a year, and, after he promised never to kill another living thing, the spirits of the sky let him return to earth. From then on, Mwindo ruled his kingdom in peace, instructing his people to live in harmony, to avoid jealousy and hatred, to accept every child, and to be kind to the sick.

Mwindo in Context

The story of Mwindo reflects the attitudes of the Nyanga people toward the Pygmy people, who live in the same region. The Pygmy people are closely associated with Nyangan tribal chiefs, hunting for them and even providing them with wives. The Pygmies, however, remain an independent group outside the Nyanga tribe. It is believed that Pygmies greatly influenced the way the Nyanga people hunt, gather food, and perform religious ceremonies. The story of Mwindo can be seen as a celebration of the Pygmy people through a hero who is still considered a member of the Nyanga. This positive attitude toward a Pygmy group is rather unusual, since many Pygmy groups face prejudice and persecution in other parts of Africa.

Key Themes and Symbols

One of the main themes in the epic of Mwindo is the attempt to change fate. Shemwindo thinks he can avoid losing his throne to a son by preventing his wives from having sons. He even tries to kill his son Mwindo several times in an effort to prevent the prophecy from coming true. Ultimately, Shemwindo fails and agrees to share his throne with his son.

In the tale of Mwindo, Nyamwindo gives birth to Mwindo through her finger. This represents Mwindo's magical nature, as well as his small size. The scepter that saves Mwindo's life in the underworld represents tribal authority; scepters are usually associated with leaders, and this suggests Mwindo's rightful place as leader of the Nyanga people.

Mwindo in Art, Literature, and Everyday Life

The story of Mwindo was passed orally within the Nyanga tribe, and performances of the tale by a skilled storyteller are events that sometimes last days. The myth was first recorded by anthropologist Daniel Biebuyck, and an English translation was published in 1969. The tale has also been retold in the children's book *The Magic Flyswatter: A Superhero Tale of Africa* (2008) by Aaron Shepard.

Read, Write, Think, Discuss

There are many Pygmy groups throughout Africa, and anthropologists have written extensively about them. These groups represent a lifestyle based on hunting and gathering, which is how all of our first ancestors lived. Using your library, the Internet, or other available resources, research the hunting and gathering groups that remain. In what regions of the world do they now live? How would you describe those regions? Choose one group and trace its history to a pre-contact period (a period before it came into contact with Europeans). Contrast what the group's day-to-day life is like today with what it was like in the pre-contact period. What were some of the important changes that occurred in the group? Do you think the group is better or worse off today?

SEE ALSO African Mythology; Dragons; Heroes

N

 Character

 Deity

 Myth

 Theme

 Culture

Nationality/Culture
Hindu/Buddhist

Pronunciation
NAH-gahz

Alternate Names
Nagis, Naginis (female)

Appears In
The Vedas, the *Mahabharata*

Lineage
Children of Kadru and Kasyapa

Nagas

Character Overview

Nagas are a race of serpent creatures in Hindu and Buddhist mythology. Female Nagas are called Nagis or Naginis. Usually depicted as human above the waist and snake below the waist, Nagas can also change shape to appear fully human or snake. Nagas and Nagis are known for their strength, supernatural wisdom, and good looks. When Nagis take human form, they can marry mortal men, and some Indian groups claim descent from them.

According to legend, Nagas are children of Kadru, the granddaughter of the god **Brahma** (pronounced BRAH-muh), and her husband Kasyapa (pronounced kahsh-YUH-puh). Nagas lived on earth at first, but their numbers became so great that Brahma sent them to live under the sea. They reside in magnificent jeweled palaces and rule as kings at the bottom of rivers and lakes and in the underground realm called Patala (pronounced PAH-tuh-lah).

Like humans, Nagas show wisdom and concern for others, but also show cowardice and injustice. Nagas are immortal, or able to live forever, and are potentially dangerous. Some are demons; others seem friendly and are worshipped as gods. Nagas also serve as protectors and guardians of treasure—both material riches and spiritual wealth.

In Buddhism, one famous Naga named Mucalinda spreads his cobra hood to shelter Buddha (pronounced BOO-duh) while he meditates. When the god **Vishnu** (pronounced VISH-noo) sleeps, he is protected by Shesha, king of the Nagas. Shesha is said to have many heads—as many as a thousand—that support the planets and shelter Vishnu beneath them. As servants of the god **Indra** (pronounced IN-druh), Nagas oversee the distribution of rain. Sometimes they withhold the rain until forced to release it by the eagle god Garuda (pronounced GUH-ruh-duh).

Nagas in Context

In Hindu culture, snakes and serpents do not have the negative associations they have throughout Western culture. This may be due to the greater exposure to snakes that people in India have, with many species of snakes thriving throughout the region thanks to the tropical and sub-tropical environment and monsoon weather. The ***Mahabharata*** even contains a tale about snake **sacrifice** that, according to the text, will remove any fear of snakes from a listener once it has been heard.

Key Themes and Symbols

In many respects, Nagas symbolize humankind's relationship with nature. Their attitude toward humans is directly related to how humans treat the environment in which the Nagas live, especially lakes and rivers. In relation to Vishnu and Buddha, Nagas represent protection and shelter.

Nagas in Art, Literature, and Everyday Life

Nagas are mentioned in the Hindu epic the *Mahabharata* and are considered to be the ancestors of certain groups of Indian people. One area in northeastern India is known as Nagaland, and its many tribes are collectively known as Nagas. In Western culture, a race of serpentine beings appeared in the Warcraft video game universe and in *Dungeons and Dragons* role-playing games, and Marvel Comics features a snake person villain called Naga who was introduced in the *Sub-Mariner* comic series in 1969. In the Harry Potter series of books by J. K. Rowling, Nagini is the name of the serpent servant and companion of the evil Lord Voldemort, Harry's arch-enemy.

Nagas are semi-divine serpent creatures in Hindu and Buddhist mythology. They can take human or serpent shape, sometimes appearing as human from the waist up and snake below the waist.
SCALA/ART RESOURCE, NY.

Read, Write, Think, Discuss

Nagas are often associated with a specific type of snake, usually the Indian cobra. Using your library, the Internet, or other available resources, research the Indian cobra. Why is it considered important in

Indian culture? How dangerous is it? Are Indian cobras endangered, and if so, what measures are being taken to protect the species?

SEE ALSO Brahma; Buddhism and Mythology; Hinduism and Mythology; Indra; Serpents and Snakes

Nala and Damayanti

Nationality/Culture
Hindu

Pronunciation
NAHL-ah and dah-muh-YAN-tee

Alternate Names
None

Appears In
The *Mahabharata*, the *Naiadhiyacarita*

Lineage
Daughter of King Bhima (Damayanti)

Character Overview

In Hindu mythology, Nala and Damayanti were lovers who overcame various obstacles to marry and live happily. Their story appears in the Hindu epic called the ***Mahabharata***, and in the *Naiadhiyacarita*, a poem written by the poet Shriharsha.

According to legend, Nala was the young, handsome, and skillful king of Nishadha (pronounced NEE-shuh-duh) in central India. Damayanti, said to be the most beautiful girl in the world, was the daughter of King Bhima of Vidarbha (pronounced VEE-dahr-buh), a neighboring country. One day Nala captured a swan. In return for freedom, the swan flew to Vidarbha and praised the virtues of Nala to Damayanti. After hearing about him, Damayanti hoped that he would fall in love with her.

Soon after, Damayanti's father decided to find a suitable husband for his daughter and invited many princes to his palace. Several of the gods also sought Damayanti's hand in marriage. On the way to the palace, the gods met Nala and told him to serve as messenger and announce their intentions to Damayanti. When he arrived at the palace, Damayanti marveled at Nala's good looks. Nala relayed the message from the gods, but Damayanti told him that she wanted only him and vowed to wed him or die.

On the day that Damayanti was supposed to choose her future husband, the royal court was full of men. Among them were the gods, who each appeared as the handsome Nala. Unable to distinguish among them, Damayanti announced that she had pledged herself to Nala and began to pray. As she prayed, the gods assumed their own forms. Damayanti chose Nala, and the two were married.

Angered that Damayanti had married a mortal, the demon Kali (pronounced KAH-lee) vowed to take revenge and tricked Nala into gambling away the royal treasury. Having lost everything, Nala advised his wife to leave him, but she refused. Kali lured Nala away from Damayanti, and Nala wandered through the world. During his travels, a Naga (pronounced NAH-gah), or serpent god, bit Nala and changed him into a dwarf named Bahuka, the chariot driver of King Rituparna of Ayodhya (pronounced ah-YOH-dee-uh).

Uncertain whether Nala was alive, Damayanti announced that she would marry again within a day. She did this as a test to draw Nala out of hiding. Rituparna sped with Bahuka to claim her. When they arrived, Damayanti did not recognize the dwarf as Nala. Yet she suspected that the man was Nala because only he could reach her so quickly. After she questioned him, Bahuka changed back into Nala. The two lovers were reunited and lived together in Nishadha. Nala, having learned great gambling skills from Rituparna, used this talent to reclaim everything else that he had lost.

Nala and Damayanti in Context

The tale of Nala and Damayanti reflects traditional Hindu marriage and courtship practices. The type of ceremony conducted in the myth is a traditional *swayamvara*, where several male suitors are gathered together, and the potential bride—along with her family—is able to choose a husband from the available suitors. The marriage usually happens immediately following her selection. This is an alternative to arranged marriages, in which the bride has little say over who will become her husband; in a *swayamvara*, the bride can even ask the suitors to prove themselves through a challenge. The *swayamvara* reflects the small amount of control females have during the marriage process. Although it allows for more freedom than an arranged marriage, the bride is still bound by the family's decision regarding the time for her to marry, and her choice is limited to the suitors who happen to attend.

Key Themes and Symbols

The main theme of this tale is the enduring power of love. Damayanti never gives up her love for her husband, even after he loses everything and disappears. She is even able to recognize him when his appearance has changed into that of a dwarf. Jealousy is also an important theme in this myth. The gods all wish to marry Damayanti, and even take the form of Nala in an attempt to trick her. The demon Kali is so jealous after the marriage that he destroys Nala's life.

Nala and Damayanti in Art, Literature, and Everyday Life

The tale of Nala and Damayanti is found in the *Mahabharata*, one of the two major epics in Hindu literature. The tale is one of the few Hindu myths that can be classified as a romantic tale, and is therefore quite popular. It has been adapted to film several times for Indian cinema, including Kemparaj Urs's musical drama *Nala Damayanti* (1957). In English literature, many adaptations have appeared as part of translated texts of the *Mahabharata*, and as stand-alone retellings of the myth. In the early nineteenth century, for example, the English historian Henry Hart Milman wrote a version of the poem.

Read, Write, Think, Discuss

In India, the *swayamvara*—in which a potential bride chooses a husband from a group of suitors—is still held today, though some details of the event have changed. How do these differ from other modern dating practices, such as online matchmaking services and blind dates? How are they similar? Do you think one technique is more likely to result in an ideal match? If so, which technique, and why?

SEE ALSO Hinduism and Mythology; Indra; *Mahabharata, The*; Nagas

Narcissus

Character Overview

Narcissus was the son of the river god Cephissus (pronounced seh-FYE-suhs) and the nymph (female nature deity) Liriope (pronounced luh-RYE-uh-pee). He was a handsome Greek youth whose beauty ultimately led to his death. A prophet named Tiresias (pronounced ty-REE-see-

Nationality/Culture
Greek

Pronunciation
nar-SIS-us

Alternate Names
None

Appears In
Ovid's *Metamorphoses*, Pausanias's *Description of Greece*

Lineage
Son of Cephissus and Leiriope

uhs), who could see the plans of the gods, told Liriope that her son would enjoy a long life as long as he never knew himself or saw his reflection. Although Liriope did not understand the prediction at the time, its meaning eventually became clear.

Narcissus was so handsome that both women and men fell in love with him, but he rejected all of them. One of his admirers was the nymph **Echo** (pronounced EK-oh), who had been cursed by **Hera** (pronounced HAIR-uh) to repeat only the last words spoken to her. Ameinias (pronounced uh-MYE-nee-uhs), another admirer, was so devastated when Narcissus rejected him that he killed himself. Before doing so, however, Ameinias called on the gods to punish Narcissus. They caused the beautiful youth to gaze into a pond at his reflection. He fell in love with his own image and drowned trying to touch it. In other accounts of the story, Narcissus killed himself out of sorrow and frustration. The gods then changed him into the flower that bears his name.

Narcissus in Context

The earliest forms of the myth of Narcissus focus on his rejection of an older male admirer. It has been suggested that this myth was meant to warn young boys about the dangers of rejecting male companions. In ancient Greece, relationships between adolescent boys and older men were common among the wealthy classes, and were considered normal, healthy, and masculine. Men and boys often exercised and performed athletics in the nude together, and soldiers fighting together often formed bonds as couples. These relationships existed in addition to traditional male-female marriages.

Key Themes and Symbols

An important theme in the myth of Narcissus is vanity. Narcissus is aware of his own beauty and rejects everyone who wishes to become his partner, considering them unsuitable. This vanity leads to a punishment that matches his personality: only a vain person could fall in love with his own reflection as Narcissus does. Narcissus can be seen as a symbol of beauty that cannot be possessed; no one is ever worthy of his love, except himself.

Narcissus in Art, Literature, and Everyday Life

As a symbol of beauty, Narcissus has long been a popular figure in art and literature. Some artists who have painted depictions of Narcissus include Caravaggio, Nicolas Poussin, and John William Waterhouse. Salvador Dali's painting *The Metamorphosis of Narcissus* (1937) is a clever double-image that shows a water-gazing Narcissus becoming transformed into a hand holding a flower.

The name of Narcissus appears in contemporary life. The term "narcissist" refers to someone who is vain or overly self-absorbed, as was Narcissus. Narcissus is also the name of a genus of flowering plants known also as daffodils.

Read, Write, Think, Discuss

Some critics of modern society proclaim that people are becoming increasingly narcissistic, or concerned only with themselves, especially with their physical appearance. Using your library, the Internet, or other available resources, research sites that seem to speak to people's concern with their physical appearance. What are some of the "ideal beauty" images these sites try to project? Are these ideal images attainable by most people? What effect do you think a narcissistic attitude has on society as a whole?

SEE ALSO Echo; Greek Mythology

Native American Mythology

Native American Mythology in Context

The Native American peoples of North America do not share a single, unified body of mythology. The many different tribal groups each developed their own stories about the creation of the world, the appearance of the first people, the place of humans in the universe, and the lives and deeds of gods and **heroes**. Yet, despite the immense variety of Native American mythologies, certain mythic themes, characters, and stories can be found in many of the cultures. Underlying all the myths is the idea that spiritual forces can be sensed throughout the natural world—including clouds, wind, plants, and animals—which they shape and sustain. Many stories explain how the actions of gods, heroes, and ancestors gave the earth its present form.

According to the mythologies of most Native American cultures, people originated in the places where their ancestors traditionally lived. Some tales speak of ancient migrations. Native Americans are descended from hunting and gathering peoples of northeastern Asia who migrated across the Bering Sea into North America during the most recent Ice Age. During that Ice Age, which ended around 8000 BCE, the level of the oceans was much lower, and a bridge of land linked Siberia and Alaska. Some groups may also have reached Alaska from Siberia by boat or by walking on ice. Over thousands of years, the population of North America grew and diversified into the peoples and cultures that Europeans encountered when they began to colonize the continent in the 1500s CE.

Before the arrival of Europeans and the spread of European influence, most Native Americans did not use written languages. As a result, many myths and legends were passed from generation to generation in oral form, usually by special storytellers who sometimes used objects such as stone carvings, shells, rugs, or pottery to illustrate the tales. Mythology, religion, history, and ritual were not separate things for Native American peoples. They were strands woven together in the various tales and stories that defined people's identity and gave order and meaning to their lives. The most serious of these were myths about how the gods created and ordered the universe, and about the origins of important things, such as humans, landforms, food, and death.

Certain myths could not be told lightly. They formed the basis of sacred rituals, including ceremonies in which participants acted out traditional sacred stories. Many Native Americans believed that some myths could be told only at certain times, often during winter nights. A dire fate—such as an attack by snakes—awaited those who told the stories at the wrong time. Other myths resembled folktales. They could be told for fun or to teach a lesson about proper behavior, and those who told them were free to change or add elements to the basic story. Many such tales involved **tricksters**.

Core Deities and Characters

Native American mythology contains a great many gods, tricksters, heroes, and other mythical beings. The creator gods and heroes usually establish or restore order. Characters such as tricksters and animals can have either positive or negative qualities. Sometimes they are helpful and entertaining; at other times, they are unpredictable, deceptive, or violent. Mythic figures do not always fall into just one category. A trickster may act as a culture hero, a culture hero may be an animal, an animal may be a creator figure, and a creator may also have a capacity for destruction.

Creators, Gods, and Spirits Many Native American mythologies have a high deity—sometimes referred to as the Great Spirit—who is responsible for bringing the universe or the world into existence. Often, however, the Great Spirit merely begins the process of creation and then disappears or removes itself to **heaven**, leaving other gods to complete the detailed work of creation and to oversee the day-to-day running of the world. In many Native American mythologies, Father Sky and Mother Earth, or Mother Corn, are important creative forces. The high god of the Pawnee people, Tirawa (pronounced TEER-uh-wuh), gave duties and powers to the Sun and Moon, the Morning Star and Evening

Star, the Star of Death, and the four stars that support the sky. The Lakota people believe that the **sun**, sky, earth, wind, and many other elements of the natural, human, and spiritual worlds are all aspects of one supreme being, **Wakan Tanka** (pronounced WAH-kuhn TAHN-kuh). The secondary gods are often embodiments of natural forces, such as the wind. In the mythology of the Iroquois people, for example, the thunder god Hunin is a mighty warrior who shoots arrows of **fire** and is married to the rainbow goddess.

Not all creators are universally good. Napi (pronounced NAW-pee), the creator god of the Blackfoot people in the Plains region, appears as both a wise sky god in **creation stories** and as a trickster in his actions toward humans. The character Coyote is a trickster in some tales, and in others is a creator whose actions benefit humankind.

Kachinas (pronounced kuh-CHEE-nuhz), spirits of the dead who link the human and spiritual worlds, play an important role in the mythologies of the Pueblo peoples of the American Southwest, including the Zuni and Hopi. In Hopi mythology, the creator deity is a female being called **Spider Woman**. Among the Zuni, the supreme creator is Awonawilona (pronounced uh-woh-nuh-wee-LOH-nuh), the sun god. The mythology of the Navajo Indians—who live in the same area as the Hopi and Zuni but are not a Pueblo people—focuses on four female deities called **Changing Woman**, White Shell Woman, Spider Woman, and First Woman.

Culture Heroes and Transformers Central to many Native American myths is the culture hero who makes the world a suitable place for humans and teaches people how to live. Such a character might form the earth and sky, create people and animals, or kill monsters or turn them into stones. These figures might also release animals that evil spirits have imprisoned, establish social structures for humans, or teach people crafts, arts, and ceremonies.

In the mythologies of some Indian groups of the Northeast, the culture hero **Gluskap** (pronounced GLOOS-kahb) creates humans, returns from death to defeat evil, and protects people from natural and magical disasters. In Navajo mythology, warrior **twins** named Monster Slayer and Child of Water—sons of Sun and of Water, respectively—play a similar role. The myths of some California Indians tell of the Attajen, who teaches the first people how to make rain and how to fill the earth with plants and animals, and of Chinigchinich (pronounced chi-NICH-nich), who teaches the wise men how to perform ceremonial dances that will summon him when they have need of help in the future.

Tricksters Tricksters appear in nearly all Native American mythologies, but they generally have a greater place in the folklore of hunter-gatherer peoples than of settled agricultural groups, possibly because people who lived on wild resources were more keenly aware of the uncertain nature of life. The trickster, who is almost always male, represents uncertainty. He loves to upset things and spread confusion.

Sometimes the trickster's acts are comic pranks, but they often have a cruel side as well. They might involve sexual trickery, as when the trickster disguises himself as a woman so that he can marry a man or marries his own daughters while in disguise. A trickster can also be a devilish figure who eats babies or leads other creatures to harm themselves. His behavior often stems from impatience or from uncontrollable appetites.

Occasionally, the trickster ends up being tricked himself. The Eye-Juggler story, for example, tells how the trickster saw birds tossing their own eyes into the air and then putting them back in their heads. He tried to do the same thing, but once he had taken out his eyes, he could not put them back.

The trickster appears as a culture hero when his pranks—such as stealing fire or the sun—benefit humans. Stories from the Northwest Coast region tell how a distant chief had stolen all the light, leaving the earth in darkness. The trickster Raven flew to the chief's land and turned himself into a tiny seed in water, which the chief's daughter swallowed. In time the girl gave birth to the chief's grandson, who was really Raven in disguise. The boy begged the chief to give him the stars and moon as toys, and when the chief gave them to him, the boy released them into the sky. Finally the young boy tricked the old man out of his dearest possession, the sun. He then turned back into Raven and flew away, taking the sun with him.

Animals Tricksters are often animals. Common trickster figures in Native American mythology include Rabbit in the Eastern regions, Coyote and Spider in the Plains and the Southwest regions, and Raven in the Pacific Northwest. Although animals appear in many myths and legends, they seldom have purely animal characteristics. They talk and interact with people and often change between human and animal form.

According to tradition, in the "myth age"—before people and animals became fixed in their present forms—animals could change their appearance whenever they wished.

Some stories tell of an Animal Wife or Animal Husband, as when a human marries a deer who is disguised as a person. Often the animal spouse is a bear. Many Native American cultures regarded bears as close relatives of people or as people wearing bear coats. A myth from the Northwest Coast region tells of Rhpisunt, a chief's daughter who met two young men while gathering berries. She went with them to the home of the bear chief and married his son. Some time later, Rhpisunt's brothers found their sister in the den of her bear husband and took her and her twin cubs back to their home village. Under the cubs' bear coats were two fine boys, who lived with the people until Rhpisunt died. They then returned to bear life. However, Rhpisunt's family never forgot their kinship with the bears, who brought them good luck in the hunt.

Native American groups of the Northwest Coast of the United States and Canada create carved and painted logs of wood called totem poles. The animals and spirits on these poles often come from Native American myths and folktales.
© BOHEMIAN NOMAD PIC-TUREMAKERS/CORBIS.

Major Myths

Despite the great number and variety of Native American myths and legends, certain themes and subjects occur again and again. One of the key concepts of Native American mythology is creation, the steps by which the world and everything in it took on their present forms.

Creation Native American creation stories fall into several broad categories. In one of the oldest and most widespread myths, found everywhere but in the Southwest and on the Arctic coast, the earth is covered by an ancient sea. A water creature—such as a duck, muskrat, or turtle—plunges to the depths of the sea and returns with a lump of mud that becomes the earth, which is often supported on the back of a turtle. This Earth Diver myth also exists in northern Europe and Asia, which suggests that the Native American versions may be survivals of ancient myths shared with distant Asian ancestors.

The creation myth of the Iroquois peoples combines elements of the Earth Diver story with the image of a creator who descends from the heavens. Creation begins when a sky goddess named Ataensic plummets through a hole in the floor of heaven. This Woman Who Fell from the Sky lands in the primeval sea. To support her and give her room to move about, the animals dive deep into the sea for bits of earth. The goddess spreads this earth on Great Turtle's back to create the land, and the daughter she bears there becomes known as Earth Woman.

The Navajo and Pueblo peoples, as well as some Plains groups, have a different image of creation, one in which life emerges from the earth like a sprouting plant rising from the soil. The Navajo emergence myth tells how insects climbed up from their First or Red World to the Second or Blue World, the realm of birds. When the Second World became too crowded, the insects and birds flew up to the Third or Yellow World, where they found animals and people. All lived together until food became scarce. Then the people, animals, birds, and insects flew up again into the Fourth or Black and White World of day and night. They found people created by the gods already living there, and these people taught the newcomers how to farm and live in their new world.

The Hopi emergence myth centers on Spider Woman, a powerful earth goddess and creator who is the mother of life. Together with Tawa, the sun god, Spider Woman sang the First Magic Song. This song brought the earth, light, and life into being. She then shaped and wove Tawa's thoughts into solid form, creating birds, fish, and other creatures. After people were created, Tawa rose into the sky, but Spider Woman moved among humans, dividing them into groups, leading them to their homelands, and teaching them how to live and worship the gods. Spider Woman then disappeared from the people's sight, drawn back down into the earth in a whirlpool of sand.

Death A number of Native American myths explain how death came into the world, usually to prevent the earth from becoming overcrowded. The Shoshone people say that long ago Wolf and Coyote got into an argument. Wolf said that people could be brought back to life after they died. Coyote argued that if people returned from death, there would soon be too many of them. Wolf agreed that Coyote was right, but then he arranged for Coyote's son to be the first to die. Coyote asked Wolf to bring his son back to life. However, Wolf reminded Coyote that he had insisted on death, and so his son must remain dead.

Pairs and Opposites A number of Native American mythologies feature paired or opposing characters or qualities as a recurring theme. Twins or sets of brothers appear in many myths and legends. For example, in Iroquois mythology, Earth Woman gives birth to the twin brothers Good Twin and Evil Twin. Good Twin creates light, forests, and food plants, while Evil Twin creates impassable mountains, mosquitoes, and a toad that drinks all the water. After a long struggle, Good Twin finally kills Evil Twin. However, Evil Twin's soul and creations survive to make life difficult for the people that Good Twin brings into being.

The main heroes of Navajo myth are the warrior twins Monster Slayer and Child of Water. Monster Slayer is associated with bright light, and Child of Water with rain clouds. While traveling to see Sun, the warrior twins notice smoke rising from a hole in the ground. Climbing down, they find themselves in the home of Spider Woman. She warns them of dangers they will face on their travels and gives them magic feathers for protection. After many adventures, the brothers reach the house of Sun, who tests them by trying to spear them, boil them, and poison them. With the help of their magic feathers and a friendly caterpillar that provides magic stones to protect them from the poison, the twins survive these ordeals. Sun finally recognizes them as his sons and gives them weapons to use to protect the Navajo people.

Key Themes and Symbols

Scholars have divided North America into different regions based on patterns of Native American mythology. Although each region contains many different peoples and languages, some elements of mythology are shared across the region, and some themes are particularly important in each region.

In the eastern part of the Arctic region, the myths of the Inuit or Eskimo people focus on **Sedna**, a deity known as the mistress or mother of sea animals. In the western Arctic, tales about Igaluk, the moon god, and trickster stories are common. The peoples of the subarctic region of inland Alaska and western Canada have myths about tricksters and heroes who transform the world into its present state. Such characters also play an important role in the Coast-Plateau region of the Pacific

Northwest. Stories about the origins of groups called clans, found in many regions, are widespread among peoples of the northwest coast from Puget Sound to southern Alaska.

In addition to trickster and "transformer" myths, the California region produced various myths about animals and about the deities who started the process of creation. The Great Basin region, located east of California, has a number of myths about female heroes and about gods who die and are reborn. Myths about a "dying god" also appear in the Midwest region, which stretches into central Canada. Clan and trickster myths are important in the Midwest as well.

Between the Great Basin and the Midwest is the Plains region, where legends of heroes and tricksters predominate. Such tales appear also in the Southeast region, along with stories about councils of animals. Myths from the Northeast cluster around culture heroes.

Stories about dying gods appear among peoples of the Southwest, such as the Hohokam, as well. The tales are similar to Aztec and Mayan legends from South and Central America. Myths about migrations, heroes who rid the world of monsters, and the origins of humans within the earth are also important in the Southwest.

Native American Mythology in Art, Literature, and Everyday Life

Although many early European explorers noted the beliefs of the Native Americans they met, Americans and Europeans did not begin recording and collecting Indian myths in earnest until after the 1820s. By that time, many Indian societies had already been disrupted and some of the ancient traditions lost. Between the 1880s and the 1930s, scholars made great efforts to record the words of Native Americans who still knew traditional myths, legends, and folktales. Modern scholars, both Indian and non-Indian, are still studying those texts, as well as gathering old lore and exploring new interpretations of familiar myths.

Today Native American myths and legends occupy a significant place in the study of world mythology. More importantly, they remain a living spiritual foundation for Native Americans who practice their traditional religions. The stories help explain the origins of ceremonies and customs, provide tribal and clan histories, and inspire Native American artworks, such as the sand paintings of the Navajo and the totems and other carved wooden objects of the Northwest Coast peoples.

Read, Write, Think, Discuss

Many Native American myths are not just stories that are told aloud. They are incorporated into songs, rituals, and other aspects of daily life. Research your own culture for myths that still hold meaning for members of your group. How are these myths expressed? How are they passed on from generation to generation?

SEE ALSO Animals in Mythology; Corn; Creation Stories; Fire; Heroes; Tricksters; Twins

Neptune
See **Poseidon.**

Nibelungenlied, The

Myth Overview

The *Nibelungenlied* is a thirteenth-century German epic poem that combines tales of chivalry with more ancient Germanic folktales. Based on old Norse legends, the *Nibelungenlied* tells the story of Siegfried, a German prince. The Nibelungs of the poem's title were originally evil dwarves who had a magical but cursed treasure of gold. The dwarfs known as the Nibelungs lived in Nibelheim, an underground land of darkness or mist. Many stories about their treasure appear in Norse and Germanic mythology. The *Nibelungenlied* combines a number of these myths with tales of legendary rulers, princes, princesses, and **heroes**. Some of these stories may have been based on events of an earlier age. In time, people who possessed the gold were also identified as Nibelungs.

The story begins in the city of Worms on the Rhine River, where Princess Kriemhild (pronounced KREEM-hilt) of Burgundy has a vision in which two eagles attack and kill a falcon. Her mother, a skilled interpreter of dreams, explains that this means that Kriemhild's future husband will be attacked. Meanwhile, in the town of Xanten farther west on the Rhine, Prince Siegfried (pronounced SIG-freed) hears of

Nationality/Culture
German

Pronunciation
NEE-buh-loong-uhn-leet

Alternate Names
The Song of the Nibelungs

Appears In
None

Kriemhild's great beauty and decides to woo her. When Siegfried arrives in Worms, he is recognized in the court as a great hero, famous for slaying a dragon and defeating two brothers, Nibelung and Schilbung, for their treasure—the Nibelungen treasure. Kriemhild notices the prince while gazing from her window and falls in love with him.

Siegfried wins the favor of Kriemhild's brother, King Gunther (pronounced GOON-tur) of Burgundy, when he helps the Burgundians defeat their enemies in Saxony and Denmark. After meeting Kriemhild at a victory tournament, Siegfried asks for her hand in marriage. Gunther agrees, on one condition. He asks Siegfried to help him win the hand of **Brunhilde** (pronounced BROON-hilt) of Iceland, a queen of outstanding strength and beauty who has vowed to marry only a man who can match her athletic skills.

Disguised as Gunther's servant, Siegfried accompanies the king on his quest. When they arrive in Iceland, Brunhilde warns Gunther that he and his men will all die if he does not match her skills. Gunther becomes fearful when he sees the spear he must hurl, a spear that can barely be lifted by twelve men. But Siegfried reassures the king, telling him to pretend to lift and throw the spear. Meanwhile, Siegfried puts on a magic cloak that makes him invisible and hurls the great spear farther than Brunhilde can. He also throws an enormous stone and bests the queen as well. Defeated, Brunhilde agrees to marry Gunther.

The adventurers return to the Rhine, where in a double wedding ceremony Gunther marries Brunhilde and Siegfried marries Kriemhild. However, Brunhilde wonders why the king's sister is marrying Siegfried, a mere vassal. Later that night, she questions Gunther about the apparent mismatch and refuses to sleep with him until he explains. When Gunther refuses to answer, she angrily picks her husband up and hangs him from a peg on the wall.

When Siegfried hears what has happened, he again uses his magic cloak to make himself invisible. The next evening, he follows Gunther and Brunhilde to their room and wrestles with Brunhilde in the dark. Believing that it is her husband who is overpowering her, Brunhilde submits to Gunther, and in doing so she loses her miraculous strength. Before leaving their room, Siegfried takes Brunhilde's belt and gold ring. These he gives to his wife after explaining what happened. Siegfried then returns to his own country with Kriemhild.

After many years, Siegfried and Kriemhild visit Gunther and Brunhilde. During a ceremonial feast, the two women quarrel. Brunhilde ridicules Kriemhild for marrying a mere vassal, and in retaliation, Kriemhild suggests Brunhilde has been unfaithful to her husband and allowed Siegfried to sleep with her. She produces Brunhilde's belt and ring as proof. Siegfried denies the charge, but the matter is not settled. Brunhilde persuades Gunther's friend Hagen that Siegfried has wronged her, and Hagen promises to avenge her.

Siegfried had become invulnerable—unable to be harmed—after he bathed in the blood of a dragon during a previous adventure. However, Hagen discovers that one spot between the hero's shoulders is vulnerable. While out hunting one day, Hagen thrusts a spear through that spot, killing Siegfried. At her husband's funeral, Kriemhild discovers the identity of Siegfried's murderer and curses Hagen.

Kriemhild stays on in Burgundy. Three years after Siegfried's death, Hagen suggests to Gunther that Kriemhild should be persuaded to bring Siegfried's Nibelungen treasure to Burgundy. When the treasure arrives, Hagen sinks it in the Rhine, hoping to recover it for himself and Gunther one day.

In time, Kriemhild marries King Etzel of Hungary, who agrees to help her avenge Siegfried's death. After several years, Etzel invites the Burgundians to Hungary. Guided by Hagen, they reach the banks of the Danube River but find no ships to carry them across. Hagen meets three swan maidens and forces them to help him. After telling Hagen about a ferryman, they warn him that only one person from his group, a priest, will return home.

Hagen tricks the ferryman into bringing his boat ashore and then kills him. Then while ferrying the Burgundians across the river, Hagen throws the priest overboard, hoping to prove the swan maidens wrong. But when the priest swims safely to shore, Hagen knows that their prediction will come true.

When the Burgundians arrive in Hungary, Kriemhild demands her treasure, but Hagen tells her it will remain at the bottom of the Rhine. Vicious fighting later breaks out between the Hungarians and Burgundians. Hagen kills the child of Etzel and Kriemhild, and Kriemhild promises a reward to anyone who captures and brings Hagen to her.

After more fighting, Hagen and Gunther are captured and taken to Kriemhild. Once again she asks Hagen to reveal the location of the treasure. Again Hagen refuses, explaining that he promised never to reveal the secret while his lord was alive. Insane with fury, Kriemhild

Kriemhild identified her husband Siegfried's murderer at his funeral. KUNSTHAUS, ZURICH, SWITZERLAND/PHOTO © HELD COLLECTION/THE BRIDGEMAN ART LIBRARY.

orders the execution of Gunther, her own brother, and then carries Gunther's head to Hagen as proof that his lord is dead. When Hagen still refuses to reveal the hiding place, she cuts off his head with a sword that belonged to Siegfried. In the end, a hero named Hildebrand (pronounced HIL-duh-brand), outraged at Kriemhild's actions, kills the queen.

The *Nibelungenlied* in Context

The actual text of the *Nibelungenlied* probably dates to the turn of the thirteenth century, but the stories were likely recounted orally since the fifth or sixth century. Many of the elements of the *Nibelungenlied* also appear in other Northern European folklore. Because the epic poem deals with values and events that pre-date the arrival of Christianity in Western Europe, it has attracted many readers seeking to pinpoint a "true" German collective identity. Though many scholars rate the *Nibelungenlied* as a less important work of literature than the Greek poems the ***Iliad*** and the ***Odyssey***, it nonetheless has come to be seen as a defining national epic. Though popular throughout German history, the characters and images of the *Nibelungenlied* were infamously put to use for propaganda purposes by the Nazi Party before and during World War II, with the heroic Siegfried (symbolizing Germany) often shown stabbed in the back by his treacherous enemies.

Key Themes and Symbols

Though based on legendary characters, the *Nibelungenlied* expresses ideals of heroism and chivalry that were very important in the period in which the work was written. Moreover, while the roots of the Nibelungen legends are found in pre-Christian Scandinavia, the *Nibelungenlied* presents a Christian view of European courtly life and traditions. The work also strongly illustrates the Germanic ideas of fate and loyalty to the chief or king.

One of the main themes of the *Nibelungenlied* is revenge. Brunhilde seeks revenge on Siegfried after she discovers he was the one to whom she submitted on the night after her wedding. After Siegfried is killed, Kriemhild seeks revenge against Hagen, the man who killed him. In the myth, treasure—specifically, the Nibelungen gold that Siegfried has acquired—represents power. Gunther and Hagen fear it, knowing that Kriemhild could use the wealth to mount an army against them; they hide it in the Rhine, hoping to claim it someday when it can no longer be used to harm them.

The *Nibelungenlied* in Art, Literature, and Everyday Life

The *Nibelungenlied* had a tremendous impact on later Germanic art and literature. Most notably, it provided the characters for a series of operas, *Der Ring des Nibelungen* (*The Ring of the Nibelung*), written by German composer Richard Wagner between 1853 and 1873. Many adaptations have been made of this work and of the original poem, including two films by Fritz Lang in 1924 and a 2004 miniseries titled *Sword of Xanten*.

U•X•L Encyclopedia of World Mythology

The story of the Nibelung was even parodied in one of the most famous animated cartoon short films of all time, "What's Opera, Doc?" (1957) starring Bugs Bunny and Elmer Fudd.

Read, Write, Think, Discuss

The *Nibelungenlied* was clearly one inspiration for J. R. R. Tolkien's classic Middle-earth books, *The Lord of the Rings* and *The Hobbit*. In these books, the ultimate treasure is a gold ring that possesses great powers. Also similar to the myth, the character of Bilbo—like Siegfried—aids in battling a dragon and takes some of its treasure. Tolkien's world of Middle-earth features many other elements common to German and Norse myth, including elves and dwarves.

SEE ALSO Brunhilde; Dwarfs and Elves; Heroes; Norse Mythology; Sigurd

Nationality/Culture
Christian

Pronunciation
saynt NIK-uh-luhs

Alternate Names
Santa Claus

Appears In
Christian mythology, tales of Christmas

Lineage
Unknown

Nicholas, St.

Character Overview

One of the most popular saints in Christianity, St. Nicholas is the patron (guardian) of children, unmarried women, sailors, and merchants, as well as the patron saint of Russia. He has long been associated with winter, and is the model for the myth of Santa Claus.

Little is known for certain about the life of St. Nicholas. According to tradition, he was born in the seaport of Patara in Asia Minor (present-day Turkey) and became bishop of Myra in the fourth century CE. He was persecuted and imprisoned for his Christian faith.

After his death around 350 CE, St. Nicholas was buried in the church at Myra. In about 1087, his relics—holy artifacts associated with him, including his remains—were moved to Bari, Italy, which became a popular pilgrimage site in the Middle Ages. The church of San Nicola in Bari remains the main shrine to St. Nicholas.

St. Nicholas had a reputation for kindness and generosity, especially to the poor, and these traits became the basis for various legends. According to one story, St. Nicholas helped three poverty-stricken girls

escape a life on the streets by giving them bags of gold to serve as dowries (the property and money a woman brings to her future husband). In another tale, he miraculously brought back to life three young children who had been chopped up by an evil butcher and put in a barrel to cure and be sold as ham. In yet another legend, St. Nicholas saved the lives of three drowning sailors by stopping a violent storm that threatened to overwhelm them.

St. Nicholas in Context

During the Middle Ages, devotion to St. Nicholas spread throughout Europe, and it became customary to give gifts to children on the saint's feast day, December 6. The people of Holland called him Sinte Klaas, and when Dutch settlers came to North America, they brought the traditions associated with him to the New World.

When the English took over the Dutch colony of New Netherland, they adopted the tradition of Sinte Klaas. But to avoid celebrating the feast day of a Catholic saint, English Protestants transformed him into a non-religious figure based on both Sinte Klaas and the Germanic god **Thor**, a figure also associated with winter. In addition, they moved the feast day from December 6 to Christmas Day, December 25. The name Sinte Klaas was eventually transformed into Santa Claus, the jolly figure who brings gifts to children on Christmas Eve.

Key Themes and Symbols

St. Nicholas is a symbol of generosity, as shown by the giving of gifts in his honor. He is also closely associated with the guardianship of children, as illustrated in the tale about him saving a group of children from being eaten. More generally, those who St. Nicholas protects can be classified as helpless. St. Nicholas is often associated with money, as in the story of the three girls without a dowry, and has been adopted as a symbol for pawnbrokers; the three bags of gold given by St. Nicholas as dowries are traditionally shown as three gold balls on pawnshop signs.

St. Nicholas in Art, Literature, and Everyday Life

St. Nicholas, in the form of Santa Claus, is one of the most recognized figures in the world. The physical appearance of Santa Claus was first described in Clement Moore's 1822 poem "The Night Before Christmas," and his image has remained the same to this day. He is usually depicted with a thick white beard, and wearing a red suit and hat.

Santa Claus appears in countless stories, songs, television shows and movies. Some notable appearances include: the C. S. Lewis fantasy novel *The Lion, the Witch, and the Wardrobe* (1950); the film *Miracle on 34th Street* (1947); the animated television classic *Santa Claus is Comin' to Town* (1970), inspired by a 1934 Eddie Cantor song; the 1994 film *The Santa Clause* and its sequels, starring Tim Allen; and the 2004 film *The*

Polar Express, based on a 1985 Caldecott Medal–winning book by Chris Van Allsburg.

Read, Write, Think, Discuss

Santa Claus is a unique mythical character in modern society. Although very few adults believe he exists, nearly all children up to a certain age believe in his existence. What purpose does the myth of Santa Claus serve in contemporary Western societies? Do you think a belief in Santa Claus and other mythical figures is healthy and helpful for young children?

SEE ALSO Thor

Noah

Character Overview

In the book of Genesis in the Bible, Noah was the hero chosen by God to survive a great flood on earth. According to the monotheistic religions of the Middle East, Noah and his family survived the flood in an ark he had built by God's instruction. He also saved the earth's animals by bringing two of every kind with him onto the ark. The biblical story was probably based on similar accounts of a flood in myths from Mesopotamia (pronounced mess-uh-puh-TAY-mee-uh).

According to the story in Genesis, the human race had become so wicked that God was sorry he ever created it. He decided to wash away all the creatures of the earth in a great flood. However, God saw that Noah was a righteous man, so he decided to save him. God told Noah of his plans and instructed him to build a great ark in which he could ride out the storm with his wife and children. Then he commanded Noah to find male and female specimens of every type of animal on the earth and bring them into the ark, and also to gather plants and seeds. Noah followed God's instructions and entered the ark as the rain began to fall.

It rained for forty days and forty nights, until the waters covered even the tops of the highest mountains. After the rain ended, Noah released a raven and a dove to find out whether there was any dry land on earth. Both birds returned, indicating that water still covered the planet.

Nationality/Culture
Judeo-Christian

Pronunciation
NOH-uh

Alternate Names
None

Appears In
The Book of Genesis

Lineage
Son of Lamech

Seven days later, Noah sent the dove out again. This time it returned with an olive branch, which meant that dry land had finally appeared. According to later Jewish legend, the ark came to rest on the top of Mount Ararat (in what is now Turkey), and Noah and his family emerged with all the animals.

Noah built an altar and made a **sacrifice** to God. God then made a covenant, or agreement, with Noah, promising never again to destroy the earth with a flood. He placed a rainbow in the sky as a reminder of this covenant.

Noah in Context

Since all other humans were destroyed in the flood, biblical scholars took this to mean that all living people were descended from the sons of Noah. In this sense, the myth is a second creation myth for Christians. In medieval times, it was accepted that each of Noah's three sons populated one of the known continents: Japheth in Europe, Shem in Asia, and Ham in Africa. Ham, shortly after the flood, had been cursed by Noah for his disrespect, and his sons were doomed to act as servants for the others. Since Ham's sons were thought to be the ancestors of all Africans, some Europeans used this myth as a justification for the enslavement of African people. It was even believed by some that the darker skin of Africans must have resulted from Ham's wickedness, since Noah's descendants would all otherwise have had the same skin color.

Key Themes and Symbols

In Christian tradition, Noah is a symbol for virtue and righteousness. This explains why God warned him of the coming flood, and why God tasked him with saving all the species in the world. In later times, many viewed the Ark as a symbol of the body of Christ or the church; this corresponds to the fact that the Ark is the only protection against God's wrath. The olive branch that the dove brings back to Noah is a symbol of salvation and the restoration of peace, since it shows that the catastrophe is over. The rainbow represents harmony with nature as God's promise to never again bring a flood to destroy the earth.

Noah in Art, Literature, and Everyday Life

Noah is one of the best-known characters in the book of Genesis. He has appeared in paintings by Michelangelo, Jacopo Bassano, and Giovanni

Turkish Earthquakes and the Flood

There is geological evidence that in ancient times the Bosphorus (the strait by Istanbul, Turkey, that joins the Sea of Marmara with the Black Sea) was once blocked up. The Black Sea had a water level below that of the other nearby bodies of water—the Aegean Sea and the Sea of Marmara. Evidence suggests that at some point many thousands of years in the past, a violent earthquake shook loose the rock and earth blocking the Bosphorus, allowing the water from the Aegean and the Sea of Marmara to inundate the communities surrounding the coast of the Black Sea. Indeed, archaeologists have found the remains of sunken cities deep in the Black Sea along the Turkish coast. This cataclysm may be the source of the story of the "great flood."

Bellini, among others. His tale is frequently offered on its own as an example of the benefits of living a virtuous life. In modern times, the Disney animated film *Fantasia 2000* contains a sequence retelling the myth of Noah with Donald Duck filling the role, while the 2007 comedy *Evan Almighty* casts Steve Carell as a modern-day version of Noah.

Read, Write, Think, Discuss

The trials of Noah are remarkably similar to those of Utnapishtim from the ancient epic *Gilgamesh*. Compare the two. What events are common to both stories? In what ways are they different? Do you think this suggests that both stories come from the same source? Why or why not?

SEE ALSO Floods; Gilgamesh; Semitic Mythology

Norse Mythology

Norse Mythology in Context

Norse mythology comes from the Scandinavian countries of the northernmost part of Europe: Sweden, Norway, Denmark, and Iceland. The mythology of this region mirrors the weather, which is grim and shadowed by long, sunless winters. Yet the darkness is laced with gleams of grandeur and sparks of humor. The myths depict a universe in which gods and **giants** battle among themselves in a grand-scale conflict fated to end in the destruction of the world.

Norse mythology developed from the myths and legends of northern peoples who spoke Germanic languages. It shares many features with the mythology of pre-Christian Germanic groups. When some of these groups spread into England and Scandinavia, they carried their myths with them. As they converted to Christianity, their traditional beliefs faded. But Christianity did not take hold in Scandinavia until a later date, and the Norse version of Germanic mythology remained vigorous through the Viking era, from about 750 to 1050 CE. Modern knowledge of Norse mythology stems from medieval texts, most of them written in Iceland. Descendants of Norse colonists in that country maintained a strong interest in their heritage even after becoming Christian.

A major source of information about Norse mythology is a book called the *Poetic Edda*, sometimes known as the *Elder Edda*. It consists of mythological and heroic poems, including *Voluspa*, an overview of Norse mythology from the creation to the final destructive battle of the world known as **Ragnarok** (pronounced RAHG-nuh-rok). The unknown author who compiled the *Poetic Edda* in Iceland around 1270 drew on materials dating from between 800 and 1100.

Around 1222, an Icelandic poet and chieftain named Snorri Sturluson (pronounced STUR-luh-suhn) wrote the *Prose Edda*, or *Younger Edda*, which interprets traditional Icelandic poetry for the audiences of Snorri's time. Part of the *Prose Edda* describes a visit by Gylfi (pronounced GIL-fee), a Swedish king, to the home of the gods in Asgard (pronounced AHS-gahrd). There the king questioned the gods about their history, adventures, and fate.

Norse mythology is known from other Scandinavian texts as well. Many Norse poems refer to mythic events or figures. In the early 1200s, Icelanders started writing family sagas about their ancestors and heroic sagas about their legendary **heroes**. Many of these sagas contain references to mythological subjects. Also in the 1200s, a Danish scholar named Saxo Grammaticus (pronounced gruh-MAT-i-kuhs) wrote a history of the Danish people that begins with an account of their pre-Christian gods and ancient heroes. Works by earlier Roman and medieval historians also include information about Germanic and Norse myths. In 98 CE, for example, the Roman historian Tacitus (pronounced

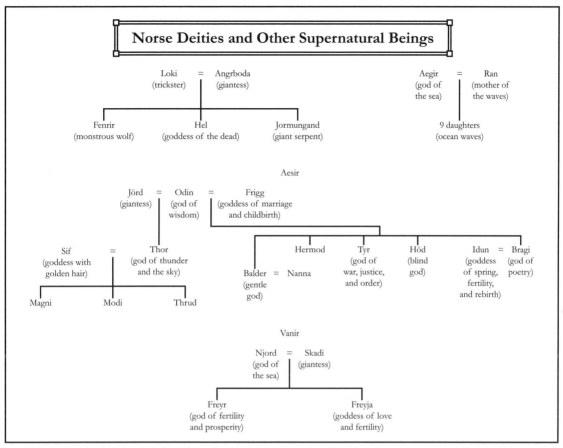

Norse Deities and Other Supernatural Beings

Loki (trickster) = Angrboda (giantess)
- Fenrir (monstrous wolf)
- Hel (goddess of the dead)
- Jormungand (giant serpent)

Aegir (god of the sea) = Ran (mother of the waves)
- 9 daughters (ocean waves)

Aesir

Jörd (giantess) = Odin (god of wisdom) = Frigg (goddess of marriage and childbirth)
- Balder (gentle god) = Nanna
- Hermod
- Tyr (god of war, justice, and order)
- Höd (blind god)
- Idun (goddess of spring, fertility, and rebirth) = Bragi (god of poetry)

Sif (goddess with golden hair) = Thor (god of thunder and the sky)
- Magni
- Modi
- Thrud

Vanir

Njord (god of the sea) = Skadi (giantess)
- Freyr (god of fertility and prosperity)
- Freyja (goddess of love and fertility)

ILLUSTRATION BY ANAXOS, INC./CENGAGE LEARNING, GALE.

TAS-i-tuhs) wrote *Germania*, a description of the Germanic tribes that mentions some of their religious beliefs and customs.

Core Deities and Characters

Like the Greek gods, the Norse gods and goddesses have all the characteristics of larger-than-life human beings. Unlike the Greek gods, however, they seldom interact with human beings. The world of Norse mythology includes two groups of gods, the Aesir (pronounced AY-sur) and the Vanir (pronounced VAH-nir), as well as giants, **trolls**, elves, dwarves, and heroic human warriors.

The Aesir The Aesir were gods of war and of the sky. Chief among them was **Odin** (pronounced OH-din), god of battle, wisdom, and poetry.

The Vikings regarded him as the ruler of the deities and the creator of humans. The mighty **Thor**, warrior god of thunder, ranked as the second most important Norse deity. Tiwaz (pronounced TEE-wahz)—an early Germanic sky god who became **Tyr** (pronounced TEER) in Norse mythology—appears in some accounts as a son of Odin. **Balder** (pronounced BAWL-der), also Odin's son, was a gentle, beloved god. After his murder, he descended to the **underworld**, or land of the dead, to await return after a new world had been created. **Loki** (pronounced LOH-kee), a cunning trickster, sometimes helped the other gods, but more often caused trouble because of his spiteful, destructive nature. The sky goddess **Frigg** (pronounced FRIG) was Odin's wife and the goddess of marriage, children, and households.

The Vanir The Vanir were associated with the earth, fertility, and prosperity. In the beginning, the Aesir and Vanir waged war against each other, perhaps reflecting an actual historical conflict between two cultures, tribes, or belief systems. Realizing that neither side could win, the two groups of gods made peace and together fought their common enemy, the giants. To ensure a lasting peace, some of the Vanir came to Asgard, the home of the Aesir, as hostages. Among them was Njord (pronounced NYORD), the patron of the sea and seafaring. His twin children, **Freyr** (pronounced FRAY) and **Freyja** (pronounced FRAY-uh), were the most important Vanir and represented love, sexuality, and fertility. The giants' desire to capture Freyja was one cause of strife between the gods and the giants.

Other Mythological and Legendary Beings The supernatural beings who inhabited the Norse mythic world included elves, creatures related to humans; and dwarves, skilled crafts workers who made many of the finest treasures of gods and humans. The most powerful and dreaded mythological beings were the giants, huge beings associated with ice, snow, and paralyzing cold. They were descended from **Ymir** (pronounced EE-mir), the frost giant, who was killed by Odin and his brothers. Although the giants were generally enemies of the gods, many marriages took place between deities and giants. Both the mother and the wife of Freyr, for example, were giantesses.

Although human beings appear rarely in Norse myths about the gods, Norse literature is filled with legends of heroic warriors, kings, and ancestors. The most important is the *Volsunga Saga*, written around

Norse Deities and Other Supernatural Beings

Balder: Odin's son, a gentle and handsome god.

Bragi: god of poetry and music.

Fenrir: monstrous wolf, child of Loki.

Freyja: goddess of love and fertility, twin of Freyr.

Freyr: god of fertility and prosperity, twin of Freyja.

Frigg: wife of Odin, goddess of the sky, marriage, and childbirth.

Heimdall: god who guards Asgard, the home of the gods.

Hel: goddess of the dead, child of Loki.

Idun: goddess of fertility, spring, and rebirth.

Jormungand: giant serpent.

Loki: trickster figure, companion to the gods.

Mimir: giant who guards the well of knowledge.

Njord: sea god, father of Freyr and Freyja.

Odin: god of wisdom, battle, and poetry, and ruler of the gods.

Thor: god of the sky and thunder, associated with the weather, crops, and warriors.

Tyr: god of war, justice, and order.

Valkyries: female spirits, servants of Odin.

Ymir: frost giant whose body was used to form the world.

1300. The Norse version of the German epic known as the *Nibelungenlied* (pronounced NEE-buh-loong-uhn-leet), it tells the story of **Sigurd** (pronounced SI-gurd), a hero who slays a dragon, acquires a magical ring, and awakens a sleeping beauty named **Brunhilde** (pronounced BROON-hilt). Like **Beowulf**, another Germanic hero, Sigurd triumphs over the forces of evil by slaying a monster.

Major Myths

Creation Various accounts of the creation of the world and of human beings appear in Norse mythology. All begin in Ginnungagap (pronounced GIN-oon-gah-GAHP), a deep empty space between realms of heat and ice. Frost formed and became a giant, Ymir. A cosmic cow named Audhumla (pronounced OWD-hoom-lah) also appeared. Licking the cliffs of ice, she revealed a man who had three grandsons. One of them was Odin. With his two brothers, Odin killed the frost giant Ymir and formed the earth from his body, the seas and rivers from his blood, and the sky from his skull, which was held suspended above the earth by four strong dwarfs.

The *Voluspa* says that Odin and his brothers made the first man and first woman out of an ash tree and an elm tree. They gave the humans life, intelligence, and beauty. A poem called "The Lay of Vafthrudnir" (pronounced vahft-HROOD-nir), however, says that the first man and first woman grew out of Ymir's armpits before he was killed.

Once they had killed Ymir, Odin and the other gods created an orderly universe in three levels. Although journeys between the different levels of the universe were possible, they were difficult and dangerous, even for the gods. The top or heavenly level contained Asgard, the home of the Aesir; Vanaheim (pronounced VAN-uh-haym), the home of the Vanir; and Alfheim (pronounced AHLF-haym), the place where the light or good elves lived. **Valhalla** (pronounced val-HAL-uh), the hall where Odin gathered the souls of warriors who had died in battle, was also located on this level.

Connected to the upper level by the rainbow bridge, Bifrost (pronounced BIV-rost) was the middle or earthly level. It contained Midgard, the world of men; Jotunheim (pronounced YAW-toon-heym), the land of the giants; Svartalfaheim (pronounced SVART-ahlf-haym), the land of the dark elves; and Nidavellir (pronounced NEED-uh-vel-ir), the land of the dwarfs. A huge serpent called Jormungand (pronounced YAWR-moon-gahnd) encircled the middle world. The bottom level consisted of the underworld of Niflheim (pronounced NIV-uhl-heym), also known as **Hel** after Loki's daughter Hel, who ruled there.

Running through this universe from bottom to top, holding it all together and linking the three worlds of **heaven**, earth, and underworld, was a great ash tree called **Yggdrasill** (pronounced IG-druh-sil). Its branches spread over the heavens, and its roots stretched into all three worlds. Springs rose from these roots. One, the Well of Urd, was guarded by the Norns, the three goddesses of fate. A serpent or dragon named Nidhogg (pronounced NEED-hawg) gnawed endlessly at the Yggdrasill's roots, and an eagle perched on its topmost branch. Goats, deer, and other animals ate the tree's shoots and lived in it, and a squirrel named Ratatosk (pronounced RAT-uh-tawsk) ran up and down its trunk, carrying messages and insults between the eagle and Nidhogg.

Good Against Evil Myths describe the gods' interactions with one another and with the giants. One story, for example, tells how Loki helped a frost giant kidnap **Idun** (pronounced EE-thoon), the goddess who tended the golden apples that kept the gods young. Without the magic apples the gods began to age, and they demanded that Loki rescue Idun. Donning a feathered cloak, he flew to Jotunheim, changed the goddess into a nut, and brought her back to Asgard. The giant took the form of an eagle and pursued Loki. But the gods lit a **fire** on the walls of Asgard that burned the giant's wings, causing him to drop to the ground, where the gods killed him. The giant's daughter was furious. However, Loki the jokester made her laugh, and she made peace with the gods.

Another myth tells of **Fenrir**, a wolf who was one of several monstrous children that Loki fathered. Fenrir grew up in Asgard among the gods, but he was so fierce that only Odin's son Tyr (pronounced TEER) could feed him. Fearing what Fenrir might do, the gods tried to chain him down. The wolf, however, broke every metal chain as though it were made of glass. Odin ordered the dwarfs to produce an unbreakable chain. The suspicious Fenrir would not let the gods put it around his neck until Tyr placed his hand in the wolf's mouth. Once he discovered that he could not break this new chain, the enraged Fenrir bit Tyr's hand off. The gods left Fenrir bound on a distant island, from which his howls could be heard. When the final battle of Ragnarok approached, he would break free.

Ragnarok The twilight of the gods and end of the earth began when Loki used trickery to kill Balder, whose death was a sign that the orderly universe was falling apart. The gods chained Loki to a rock, but eventually he would break loose and lead the giants in a last bitter battle against the gods and the greatest heroes from Valhalla. Then, the bridge Bifrost will shatter, cutting Midgard off from Asgard, and all monsters will run free. Fenrir will kill Odin, while Thor will perish in the process of slaying the serpent Jormungand. In the end, all worlds will be consumed by fire and flood. One man and one woman will survive, sheltered in the World Tree Yggdrasill, to become the parents of a new human race.

Key Themes and Symbols

Bravery in the face of a harsh fate is one of the main themes of Norse mythology. Even the gods were ruled by an unalterable fate that doomed everything to eventual destruction. A hero who strove to accept his

One story from Norse mythology tells of Sigurd, a hero who used a special sword to slay the dragon Fafnir. When Sigurd roasted and ate the beast's heart, he was able to understand the language of the birds. They warned him that he was going to be killed. WERNER FORMAN/ART RESOURCE, NY.

destiny with reckless courage, honor, and generosity might win lasting fame, regarded as the only true life after death.

The battle between good and evil is another important theme. The gods represented order in the universe, but their enemies, the giants, tried constantly to return to the state of formless chaos, or disorder that had existed before the creation. Although the gods sometimes displayed treachery, cowardice, or cruelty, in general they stood for virtue.

The natural world is an important theme in Norse mythology as well. Rather than focusing on magical elements unrelated to nature, many aspects of Norse myth arise directly from the environment. Cold and ice are found throughout Norse mythology, as one might expect in such a frigid region. The ancient formlessness before creation contains fire and ice, and the creator Ymir is made completely of ice. The base of the world is a giant tree, and the bridge that connects Asgard to Midgard is a rainbow.

Norse Mythology in Art, Literature, and Everyday Life

Norse mythology inspired the stirring poems and sagas that were written down during the late Middle Ages, and it has inspired more recent artists as well. German composer Richard Wagner used the legend of Sigurd as the basis for his cycle of four operas, known collectively as *Der Ring des Nibelungen* (*The Ring of the Nibelung*). Some modern writers of fantasy have drawn on Norse stories and creations such as elves and dwarfs in their work. The best known of these is J. R. R. Tolkien, whose *Lord of the Rings* features many themes from Norse mythology, such as dragon slaying and enchanted rings. High-spirited and muscular Thor, the subject of many of the most popular myths, has even been the subject of a comic-book series called *The Mighty Thor*, which features many other Norse gods as heroes and villains.

Read, Write, Think, Discuss

Using your library, the Internet, or other available resources, research the Norse culture. During what time period did it flourish? What was the greatest geographic extent of Norse culture in Europe? What is the difference between the Norse and the Vikings?

SEE ALSO Balder; *Beowulf*; Dwarfs and Elves; Fenrir; Freyja; Freyr; Frigg; Heimdall; Hel; Idun; Loki; Mimir; *Nibelungenlied, The*; Odin; Ragnarok; Sigurd; Thor; Trolls; Tyr; Valhalla; Valkyries; Yggdrasill; Ymir

Nut

Character Overview

In **Egyptian mythology**, Nut was the sky goddess and the mother goddess of ancient Egypt. She was the twin sister and wife of the earth

Nationality/Culture
Egyptian

Pronunciation
NOOT

Alternate Names
None

Appears In
The Book of the Dead

Lineage
Daughter of Shu and Tefnut

god Geb (pronounced GEB). Nut was said to swallow the **sun** each night and give birth to it anew each morning. She was also regarded as an important deity, or god, related to the **afterlife**.

Major Myths

Nut and Geb, children of the god Shu (pronounced SHOO, meaning "air") and goddess Tefnut (pronounced TEF-noot, meaning "moisture"), were born locked together in a tight embrace. The sun god **Ra** ordered Shu to separate them, so Shu held his daughter high above the earth, creating room between Nut and Geb for other creatures to live. In another version of the myth, Ra climbed onto Nut's back and asked her to lift him into the heavens. As Nut rose higher, she became dizzy, but four gods steadied her legs, and Shu held up the middle of her body. In this way, Nut's body became the sky, and Ra attached stars to her.

Angered by the marriage of Nut and Geb, Ra decreed that Nut could not bear children during any month of the year. **Thoth** (pronounced TOHT), the god of wisdom, took pity on Nut and played a game with the moon—the regulator of time—that allowed him to create five extra days in the year. Because these days were not covered by Ra's decree, Nut was able to give birth to five children: **Osiris** (pronounced oh-SYE-ris), **Isis** (pronounced EYE-sis), **Set** (pronounced SET), Nephthys (pronounced NEF-this), and **Horus** (pronounced HOHR-uhs).

Nut's body divided the cosmos and helped keep the forces of chaos, or disorder, from breaking through the sky and overwhelming the earth. During the day, Ra sailed along Nut's body in a boat. When he reached her mouth, she swallowed him, bringing on the night. After traveling through Nut's body at night, Ra emerged again at dawn and brought on the day. In some myths, Nut plays an important role in the **underworld**, or land of the dead, providing fresh air for the souls of the dead.

Nut in Context

For ancient Egyptians, Nut served as an explanation for where the sun went at night. Although Egyptians understood the cycles of the sun, moon, and seasons, they did not know that the earth was round and that heavenly bodies traveled around each other in orbit. The idea that an enormous goddess consumed the sun at one end of the sky, and then gave birth to it at the other, may have seemed as likely an explanation as any for how the sun got back across the sky without being seen. Astronomers have also noted that the Milky Way, the galaxy in which we live, was probably visible as a faint glowing arch in the Egyptian night sky—similar to ancient depictions of Nut as a starry woman arched across the sky from horizon to horizon.

Key Themes and Symbols

Nut represented many things to ancient Egyptians. She was a protector and provider, often depicted as a cow—a symbol of nourishment. An important theme in the myths of Nut is death and rebirth. Every night, she consumed Ra by swallowing him, and then gave birth to him again every morning. In this way, the ancient Egyptians viewed each day as a cycle of death and rebirth. In much the same way, Nut transported Ra from death to new life, and was also regarded as an escort or vehicle for humans at death, accompanying the dead to the unknown world of the afterlife. She was sometimes symbolized as a ladder that allowed souls to ascend to the sky.

Nut in Art, Literature, and Everyday Life

Egyptian artists often portrayed Nut as a woman holding a pot of water on her head, an indication of her role as the provider of rain. She was also shown as a woman arched over the earth god Geb, with her fingers and toes touching the horizon. Typically, her body was painted blue and covered with stars to resemble the night sky. Nut was often painted on the insides of coffins, since she was considered an escort and protector for the dead. Although Nut was important to the ancient Egyptians, she was seldom worshipped in the same way as many other gods and is not very well-known in modern times, except to those who study ancient Egyptian culture.

Read, Write, Think, Discuss

An important theme in many non-Western myths is birth, death, and rebirth. The myths of Nut emphasize this theme in stories of Nut and Ra, which portray life as an ongoing cycle. While many non-Western cultures incorporate this notion of cycles in their understanding of life, Western societies tend to view life as linear: birth and death, rather than birth, death, and rebirth. Using your library, the Internet, or other available resources, find examples of societies with cyclical and linear views of life. How are their cyclical and linear views expressed through their religious beliefs and ideas about the afterlife? Can you find any historical evidence that Western societies once held cyclical views of life?

SEE ALSO Egyptian Mythology; Isis; Osiris; Ra; Thoth

Nymphs

Character Overview

In **Greek mythology**, nymphs were minor female deities, or goddesses, associated with nature. Typically pictured as beautiful girls or young women, they could live for a very long time but were not immortal (able to live forever). Most nymphs were the daughters of **Zeus** (pronounced ZOOS), the leader of the gods, or of other gods. They generally had gentle natures and acted with kindness toward humans. Some stories, however, tell of nymphs who lured unsuspecting mortals to their deaths.

Different kinds of nymphs were associated with particular parts of the natural world. The Oceanids (pronounced oh-SEE-uh-nidz) were sea nymphs, daughters of the sea god Oceanus (pronounced oh-SEE-uh-nuhs). One of the Oceanids married the sea god Nereus (pronounced NEER-ee-uhs) and their daughters became the Nereids (pronounced NEER-ee-idz), nymphs who lived in both freshwater and saltwater. Another group of water nymphs, the Naiads, were freshwater spirits associated with fountains, streams, rivers, and other forms of running water. Forest nymphs were divided into Dryads (pronounced DRYE-adz), originally linked specifically with oak trees but later known as nymphs of woods and forests in general, and the Hamadryads (pronounced ham-uh-DRYE-adz), who dwelled inside particular trees and perished when the trees died. Other types of nymphs included the mountain nymphs known as Oreads (pronounced OR-ee-adz), the nymphs of ash trees called Meliae (pronounced MEE-lee-ee), and Limoniads (pronounced lee-MOH-nee-adz), or meadow nymphs.

Nationality/Culture
Greek/Roman

Pronunciation
NIMFS

Alternate Names
Oceanids, Nereids, Dryads, Naiads

Appears In
Ovid's *Metamorphoses*, Pausanias's *Description of Greece*

Lineage
Varies

Nymphs rarely had a central role in Greek myths. Usually they played supporting parts as the companions of gods and **satyrs** (creatures that are half human and half goat). The goddess **Artemis** (pronounced AHR-tuh-miss), for example, often had nymphs attending her when she went hunting. Nymphs also became the lovers or wives of gods or **heroes**. The Dryad **Eurydice** (pronounced yoo-RID-uh-see) married the poet and musician **Orpheus** (pronounced OR-fee-uhs). After Eurydice died from a snakebite, Orpheus tried to retrieve her from the **underworld**, or land of the dead, but failed to meet the conditions set for her return.

Another nymph who gained mythic status as a wife was Oenone (pronounced ee-NOH-nee). Married to Paris, prince of Troy, Oenone predicted that if Paris left on a journey to Greece, the trip would be disastrous for Troy. During that trip, Paris eloped with **Helen**, the wife of the Spartan king, setting in motion the events that led to the Trojan War and the eventual destruction of Troy. When Paris lay wounded from fighting, Oenone refused to help him, even though she had the gift of healing. Eventually she relented and rushed to Troy to save her husband, but she arrived too late. Upon discovering that Paris had died, Oenone killed herself.

Nymphs in Context

In contrast to the most famous gods of the Greek and Roman pantheons (or collections of recognized gods), nymphs were generally associated with very specific locations. Small communities each had their own groups of nymphs that were recognized, and just as certain gods were linked with professions, these nymphs were an important part of the community's identity. For the ancient Greeks, physical beauty was extremely important; it was considered to be a reflection of a person's mind and spirit. If a community was associated with a group of beautiful goddesses, that community would surely enjoy a special reputation among travelers. This purpose had little to do with the larger body of Greek or **Roman mythology**, and because of that, myths about nymphs continued in more remote Greek communities well into the twentieth century—nearly two thousand years after most Greek mythology had fallen out of fashion.

Key Themes and Symbols

Above all, nymphs were considered symbols of beauty and femininity. This is illustrated by the number of gods and men that fall in love with them on sight or have love affairs with them, including **Odysseus** (pronounced oh-DIS-ee-uhs) and Orpheus. Another theme present in the tales of nymphs is the close association of females with nature. All nymphs are said to be female and all represent different aspects of nature, such as trees, streams, mountains, and meadows. The nymphs themselves are symbolized by these objects. A hamadrya, for example, is said to live in a specific tree, and, if that tree is harmed, the nymph perishes also. In this way, it can be said that nymphs symbolize the beauty and fragile state of the natural world.

Nymphs in Art, Literature, and Everyday Life

Though the idea of nymphs in general has endured in art and literature, only a few specific nymphs have remained well-known. Eurydice is perhaps the most famous, appearing in paintings, operas, and even films. **Echo** was another nymph famous for her love of the vain **Narcissus** (pronounced nar-SIS-us), a myth often captured in art and literature. The **Muses** are also nymphs and are popular in their own right as the goddesses who inspire creativity. More often, however, nymphs are portrayed less specifically, with many authors and artists depicting nameless nymphs of a certain type, such as dryads or nereids. Dryads have remained the best known of the nymphs and have appeared in literary works such as C. S. Lewis's *The Chronicles of Narnia* and the poems of Sylvia Plath. They have also appeared in numerous video games, including the *Warcraft*, *Dungeon Siege*, and *Castlevania* series, and are considered a race in the collectible card game *Magic: The Gathering*. Nereids have also appeared as characters in many video games, and in modern times the term "nereid" is commonly used to represent all nymphs, regardless of their origins.

Read, Write, Think, Discuss

In ancient times, it was believed that a person who cut down a tree that housed a nymph would be punished by the gods. In modern times, some environmentalists chain themselves to trees or take up residence in long-lived trees in an effort to protect them from destruction by lumber or construction crews. Do you think the myths of tree-dwelling nymphs may have been an ancient form of environmentalism? Why or why not?

SEE ALSO Echo; Eurydice

O

Odin

Character Overview

Odin was the ruler of the Aesir (pronounced AY-sur), a group of deities, or gods, in **Norse mythology**. Sometimes called Allfather, Odin played a central role in myths about the creation and destruction of the world. He was the god of battle and also of wisdom, magic, and poetry. His name means "fury" or "frenzy," the quality of fierce inspiration that guided warriors and poets alike. The god probably originated in the myths of early Germanic peoples, who called him Wodanaz. Odin was married to **Frigg** (pronounced FRIG), the guardian of marriage.

Major Myths

Odin spanned the history of the Norse mythic world from its creation to its destruction. Before the world existed, he and his two younger brothers, Vili and Ve, killed the frost giant **Ymir** (pronounced EE-mir). They used Ymir's bones, blood, and flesh to form the universe. Odin arranged the heavens for the gods, the middle world for humans and dwarfs, and the **underworld** for the dead. He then created the first man and woman from an ash tree and an elm tree. Among the deities said to have been Odin's children were **Balder** (pronounced BAWL-der) and **Thor**. Odin—the favorite deity of princes, nobles, and warriors—came to be seen as the supreme Norse god, the one to whom the other deities

 Character

 Deity

 Myth

 Theme

 Culture

Nationality/Culture
Norse

Pronunciation
OH-din

Alternate Names
Wotan (German)

Appears In
The Eddas

Lineage
Son of Bestla and Borr

turned for help and advice. He ruled them from his palace **Valhalla** (pronounced val-HAL-uh) in the heavenly realm called Asgard (pronounced AHS-gahrd). As the god of war, Odin watched over warriors who fell in battle. **Valkyries**, female deities who served Odin, carried the bravest of the warriors straight to Valhalla. There Odin feasted them and prepared them for **Ragnarok** (pronounced RAHG-nuh-rok), the final battle in which the gods were doomed to perish.

Odin was credited with great wisdom, including knowledge of magic and the ability to see the future. He paid a high price for this gift, however, giving one of his eyes in exchange for a drink from the well of **Mimir** (pronounced MEE-mir). The waters of this well, which seeped from among the roots of the enormous tree known as **Yggdrasill** (pronounced IG-druh-sil) that supported the world, contained great wisdom. Another myth says that Odin stabbed himself with his magical spear, called Gungnir (pronounced GOONG-nir), and hung from Yggdrasill for nine days and nights in a living death. This self-**sacrifice** gave him knowledge of the runes, the Norse symbols used for writing and fortune-telling. Yet, although Odin was wise, he could also be sly and treacherous. It was not unusual, for example, for him to break his word or to turn people against each other to start conflicts.

Odin had the power to change his appearance, and this shape-shifting played a part in the myth that explains Odin's connection with poetry. The wisest being who ever lived was Kvasir (pronounced VAHS-eer), whom the gods had formed from their own saliva. Dwarves killed Kvasir and mixed his blood with honey to form a potion that granted wisdom and the gift of poetry. A giant hid the potion in the middle of a mountain and set his daughter to guard it. Odin changed himself into a snake and slithered through a tiny hole in the mountain. Taking the form of a handsome giant, he charmed the daughter into letting him drink the potion. Once Odin had swallowed it, he changed into an eagle and flew to Asgard, where he vomited the potion into three sacred vats. A few drops of the potion fell to the earth during his flight and became the inspiration for human poets.

Another myth reveals Odin as both a treacherous figure and the enforcer of divine justice. He observed two young princes, Agnar and Geirrod (pronounced GEHR-rod). On Odin's advice, Geirrod sent Agnar out to sea in a boat and then reported that his brother had drowned. After Geirrod grew up and became king, he was tested when a man named Grimnir appeared in his court. Fearing that the man was a sorcerer, Geirrod had him tortured. The king's son, however, showed pity on Grimnir and helped him. After predicting that Geirrod would kill himself with his own sword, Grimnir revealed that he was Odin. The king grabbed his sword to attack him but tripped and stabbed himself. Odin then set the kindly son on the throne.

Odin liked to wander the earth in the form of an old man wearing a blue cloak and a wide-brimmed hat that hid his one-eyed face. Often he was accompanied by wolves and ravens, flesh eaters that haunt battlefields. His ravens Hugin (pronounced HYOO-gin, meaning "thought") and Munin (pronounced MYOO-nin, meaning "memory") traveled around the world and the underworld each day, returning to tell their knowledge-loving master what they had seen. Odin occasionally rode an eight-legged horse named Sleipnir (pronounced SLAYP-nir), who could travel at great speed through the air and across water.

Odin in Context

The worship of Odin flourished across much of northern Europe and gained strength in the eighth and ninth centuries CE, the age of the Vikings. These Norse warriors and raiders, especially the fearsome fighters called the Berserks, regarded Odin as their special protector. As warriors, they were drawn to his battle-scarred exterior and no-nonsense nature. The increasing popularity of Odin also reflected the increase in warlike behavior among the Norse people. The ceremonies in honor of Odin sometimes included human sacrifice, with victims dying by the spear or by **fire**. Ritual hangings were especially important in the worship of Odin, who was sometimes called the Lord of the Gallows or the Hanging God because of his own mythic hanging on the tree Yggdrasill. When the Vikings raided Nantes, a town in northwestern France, in 842, they hanged many of the inhabitants, perhaps as an offering to Odin.

Key Themes and Symbols

One of the main themes found in the myths of Odin is sacrifice. For example, Odin gives up one of his eyes in order to drink from Mimir's well of wisdom. Odin's missing eye can be viewed as a symbol of his ability to see beyond normal sight. Another theme found in the myths of Odin is the inability to escape destiny—the notion that future events have already been determined and cannot be changed. Odin gains the

ability to see the future and knows that he and the other gods of the Aesir will die at Ragnarok, but nothing he can do will change that fate.

Odin in Art, Literature, and Everyday Life

Odin is one of the best-known gods of Norse mythology. He appeared under the name Wotan in the opera cycle known as *Der Ring des Nibelungen* (*The Ring of the Nibelung*), written by German composer Richard Wagner in the late nineteenth century. Odin has appeared more recently as a character in the Marvel Comics Universe, and as a character in the *Sandman* series by author Neil Gaiman. The name of the fourth day of the week, Wednesday, comes from Woden's-day, the god's Old English name.

Read, Write, Think, Discuss

In modern times, human sacrifice is almost universally condemned as a barbaric practice that violates basic human rights. Soldiers fighting in wars, however, often end up killing enemies, much like the Vikings did, though it is not considered human sacrifice. Do you think there is a basic difference between killing an enemy in modern warfare and the sacrifice of an enemy in ancient combat? Explain your position.

SEE ALSO Frigg; Mimir; Norse Mythology; Ragnarok; Thor; Valhalla; Yggdrasill; Ymir

Odysseus

Character Overview

In **Greek mythology**, Odysseus was a celebrated hero, best known for his role in the Trojan War and for his ten-year journey home after the war. Odysseus (known as Ulysses to the Romans) appears as the central character in the ***Odyssey***, an epic poem by the ancient Greek poet Homer, and he also plays a role in the ***Iliad***, Homer's other major epic.

Early Life Odysseus was generally said to be the son of Anticlea (pronounced an-tuh-KLEE-uh) and of King Laertes (pronounced lay-UR-teez) of Ithaca (pronounced ITH-uh-kuh). However, some stories maintain that his father was **Sisyphus** (pronounced SIZ-ee-fuhs), founder of the city of Corinth and a cunning man who outwitted the god **Hades** (pronounced HAY-deez). This version says that Sisyphus seduced Anticlea before her marriage to Laertes and that Odysseus inherited his cleverness from Sisyphus.

Educated by the centaur Chiron—a half-human, half-horse creature—Odysseus began to display great strength and courage at an early age. While out hunting with his uncles and his grandfather, the young hero

Nationality/Culture
Greek

Pronunciation
oh-DIS-ee-uhs

Alternate Names
Ulysses (Roman)

Appears In
Homer's *Iliad*, Homer's *Odyssey*

Lineage
Son of Laertes and Anticlea

saved the adults by killing a wild boar. Before the creature died, however, it wounded Odysseus on the leg with its sharp tusk, leaving a permanent scar.

When Odysseus reached manhood, King Laertes stepped aside and let his son rule Ithaca. Around the same time, Odysseus began thinking of marriage. Like other young rulers and **heroes** in Greece, he desired **Helen**, the beautiful daughter of King Tyndareus (pronounced tin-DAIR-ee-uhs) of Sparta. But Ithaca was a poor kingdom, and Odysseus had little hope of winning her. Nevertheless, he went to Sparta as a suitor.

While in Sparta, Odysseus displayed some of the cunning for which he became famous. Crowds of men had come to Sparta to seek the hand of Helen, and King Tyndareus feared what might happen when he chose one of them to marry his daughter. Odysseus advised the king to make all the suitors swear an oath to protect Helen and the man she married. The suitors agreed and thus accepted Menelaus (pronounced men-uh-LAY-uhs) when he was chosen to be Helen's husband. To show his gratitude, Tyndareus helped Odysseus win the hand of his niece **Penelope** (pronounced puh-NEL-uh-pee), with whom the young hero had fallen in love. The couple returned to Ithaca, and Penelope bore Odysseus a son named Telemachus (pronounced tuh-LEM-uh-kuhs).

The Trojan War When the Trojan War began, Odysseus tried to avoid participating. An oracle, or person through whom the gods communicated with humans, had told him that if he went to war, he would be away for twenty years and would return a beggar. So Odysseus pretended to be mad and sowed his fields with salt instead of seeds. When officials came to fetch him, they suspected a trick so they placed the infant Telemachus in the field. Odysseus stopped the plow to avoid killing the child, something a madman would not have done.

According to the *Iliad*, Odysseus's role in the Trojan War was mainly as an advisor and speaker rather than as a warrior. He helped discover the whereabouts of **Achilles** (pronounced uh-KILL-eez) and he convinced the great hero to join the war. He tricked Clytemnestra (pronounced klye-tem-NES-truh), wife of **Agamemnon** (pronounced ag-uh-MEM-non), into sending her daughter Iphigenia (pronounced if-uh-juh-NEYE-uh) to be sacrificed to the goddess **Artemis** (pronounced AHR-tuh-miss) so that the Greek ships would have good winds for their voyage to Troy. When a go-between was needed to settle quarrels

It was the idea of the cunning Odysseus to conquer the Trojans by sending them a large wooden horse as a gift, in which was hidden Greek soldiers who were able to open the city gates of Troy to the Greek army. © HERITAGE-IMAGES/THE IMAGE WORKS.

between Agamemnon and Achilles, Odysseus stepped in. He also spied on the Trojans and discovered their plans.

Renowned for his eloquent and persuasive speaking, Odysseus was called upon many times to give advice. Although he fought bravely, he preferred strategy to heroics. When the Greeks captured the Trojan prophet Helenus, who could see the future, and asked what they must do to capture Troy, it was Odysseus who accomplished the three tasks that were set. He persuaded Neoptolemus (pronounced nee-op-TOL-uh-muhs), the son of Achilles, to join the Greeks in battle. He used trickery to get Philoctetes (pronounced fil-uhk-TEE-teez), keeper of the bow and arrows of **Heracles** (pronounced HAIR-uh-kleez), to join the fighting. He also used cunning to sneak into Troy and steal the Palladium (pronounced puh-LAY-dee-um), a statue of **Athena** (pronounced uh-THEE-nuh) believed to protect the city and bring it good fortune. Finally, Odysseus came up with the idea of pretending to sail away from Troy, leaving behind an enormous wooden horse as a gift to the Trojans—inside of which Greek soldiers were hidden. This trick enabled the Greeks to enter Troy at night and defeat the Trojans.

The Journey Home After the fall of Troy, Odysseus set sail for Ithaca, but his voyage took ten long years because he angered the sea god **Poseidon** (pronounced poh-SYE-dun). His journey and adventures, described fully in the *Odyssey*, took the hero to many wondrous and dangerous places. Along the way, he lost all his companions and the treasure he had taken from Troy. Arriving home at last after an absence of twenty years, Odysseus had to defeat rivals trying to take possession of his wife and his kingdom. Then he had to prove his identity to his wife, Penelope.

There are several different accounts of Odysseus's final years. Some stories say that he was accidentally killed by Telegonus (pronounced tuh-LEG-uh-nus), his son by the enchantress **Circe** (pronounced SUR-see). Other tales say he married Callidice (pronounced kuh-LID-uh-see), the queen of Thesprotia (pronounced thes-PROH-shuh), and ruled there for a time while Penelope was still alive. Still other versions of the story report that Odysseus was forced into exile by relatives of the rivals he killed upon his return to Ithaca.

Odysseus in Context

One notable aspect of Odysseus in his adventures is that he has romantic relationships with many women throughout his journey. At the same time, the whole purpose of his journey is to return home to his wife, Penelope. While Odysseus enjoys the company of numerous women, Penelope is busy fending off the many suitors who wish to marry her and take over the kingdom of Ithaca. This reflects a double standard common in ancient Greek culture and myth: male characters are often shown being unfaithful to their wives, but the wives are expected to remain true. In many cases, Odysseus appears to fall victim to magical powers of attraction or seduction, which suggests that he is not to blame for his affairs.

Another important aspect of Odysseus is how the character was treated differently by Greek and Roman writers. In the works of the ancient Greek poet Homer, he was a hero who helped defeat the Trojans through his cunning. To the Romans, who claimed that they were descended from the noble Trojans, Odysseus was deceitful and cowardly, choosing to resort to trickery instead of facing a fair fight. This reflects the Greek celebration of ingenuity, while also showing the Roman tendency to solve matters through physical might.

Key Themes and Symbols

Odysseus has stood as an enduring symbol of cleverness and mental power over the physical: although he is shown to be strong, he very often escapes trouble through his shrewdness rather than through brute force. Two important examples of his cleverness include his invention of the Trojan horse, which ended a bloody ten-year war in a single night, and his escape from the blinded Polyphemus, where he and his men hide underneath the giant's sheep as they are put out to pasture.

Another important theme in the tales of Odysseus is endurance: although his journey takes ten years—after spending another ten years fighting against Troy—he does not lose sight of his goal to return home to his wife and kingdom. Penelope also shows endurance, fending off men who seek her hand in marriage for twenty years while her husband is away. Equally important as a theme is the danger of temptation. Odysseus is tempted by the lotus-eaters and by Circe; many of his men fall victim to both, in the latter case being turned into animals. Odysseus resists Circe's charms and saves his crew; he later resists temptation again when she asks him to remain with her, choosing instead to continue the difficult journey home. Odysseus also recognizes the dangerous tempta-tion of the **Sirens**, and acts to protect his men from their songs—though he himself succumbs to temptation and listens to the Sirens while tied to the mast of his ship.

Odysseus in Art, Literature, and Everyday Life

The tale of Odysseus is best known from the epic poems the *Iliad* and, more importantly, the *Odyssey*, both by Homer. Another ancient Greek epic, the *Telegony*, was said to chronicle the later years of Odysseus's life, but this work appears to have been lost. The *Odyssey* has been adapted countless times over the centuries, inspiring novels, poems, symphonies, and songs. A partial retelling of Odysseus's adventures even occurs in Virgil's **Aeneid**, a Roman work modeled after Homer's epics. Odysseus also appears in Dante's *Inferno* as one of the damned souls in **hell**, and has been the subject of many sequels to the original tale, including Alfred, Lord Tennyson's *Ulysses* (1842), and *The Odyssey: A Modern Sequel* (1938) by Nikos Kazantzakis. The tale of Odysseus has also loosely inspired many other works, including James Joyce's landmark novel *Ulysses* (1922), and the 2000 Coen brothers' film *O Brother, Where Art Thou?*

Read, Write, Think, Discuss

Odysseus in the Serpent Maze by Jane Yolen and Robert J. Harris (2002) is an adventure tale that takes place long before the *Iliad* or the *Odyssey*. In this novel, Odysseus is a thirteen-year-old prince who becomes shipwrecked far from home along with his friend, Mentor. The two meet up with Helen of Troy and Odysseus's future wife Penelope. Before they can return home, they must face off against bloodthirsty pirates and a monstrous serpent with one hundred heads. Yolen and Harris base their tale on existing fragments of the early life of Odysseus, as well as an in-depth knowledge of ancient Greek culture.

SEE ALSO Achilles; Circe; Greek Mythology; Helen of Troy; *Iliad, The*; *Odyssey, The*; Penelope

Odyssey, The

Nationality/Culture
Greek

Pronunciation
AH-dis-ee

Alternate Names
None

Appears In
Homer's *Odyssey*

Myth Overview

One of the great epic poems of ancient Greece, the *Odyssey* tells the story of the struggles and triumphs of the hero **Odysseus** (pronounced oh-DIS-ee-uhs) as he made his way home after the Trojan War. Pursued by the sea god **Poseidon**, but aided both by his own cunning and by the goddess **Athena**, Odysseus overcame countless obstacles during his long journey home. Along the way, he lost his ships, his crew, and the riches he had gained at Troy. The *Odyssey* is believed to be the work of the Greek poet Homer, who also composed the ***Iliad***.

The story actually opens in the middle of his journey, with Odysseus stranded on Ogygia (pronounced oh-GIG-ee-uh), the island home of the enchantress Calypso (pronounced kuh-LIP-soh). Almost ten years had passed since the end of the Trojan War. All the other Greek **heroes** were either dead or safely back in their homelands. Only Odysseus had yet to return home. Calypso was holding the hero captive, hoping that her beauty and offer of immortality—the ability to live forever—would make him forget his wife, **Penelope** (pronounced puh-NEL-uh-pee), and marry her instead.

Finally the gods took pity on Odysseus. The goddess Athena (pronounced uh-THEE-nuh) encouraged Odysseus's son Telemachus (pronounced tuh-LEM-uh-kuhs) to go on a quest in search of his father. The young man traveled to Pylos and then to Sparta, where he met **Helen** and Menelaus (pronounced men-uh-LAY-uhs), the king and queen. Telemachus was proud when he learned of his father's fame. Meanwhile **Zeus** (pronounced ZOOS), the leader of the gods, sent **Hermes** (pronounced HUR-meez) to command Calypso to let the hero leave. She reluctantly agreed, and Odysseus sailed from the island on a raft. While the hero was at sea, the sea god Poseidon (pronounced poh-SYE-dun) sent a great storm that destroyed the raft. Saved by a sea goddess, Odysseus finally reached the land of the Phaeacians (pronounced fee-AY-shunz). The Phaeacians welcomed the stranger and treated him as an honored guest. In return, Odysseus revealed his name and told the Phaeacians about the adventures he had had since leaving Troy many years before.

Odysseus's Tale When the Trojan War ended, Odysseus set sail for his homeland of Ithaca (pronounced ITH-uh-kuh) with a number of companions in several ships. They first stopped in the land of the Cicones (pronounced SI-kuh-neez). After sacking the city of Ismara, they were driven off and suffered significant losses. Next they arrived at the land of the lotus-eaters, so named because the people there ate the honey-sweet fruit from the lotus plant. This fruit acted like a drug, and when some of the Greeks ate it, they lost all desire to return home. Odysseus had to drag them to the ships and tie them down before he could set sail again.

The Greeks next arrived at the land of the **Cyclopes** (pronounced sigh-KLOH-peez), a race of one-eyed savage **giants**. When Odysseus and some of his men went into a large cave, the Cyclops Polyphemus (pronounced pol-uh-FEE-muhs) trapped them inside by rolling a huge stone across the entrance. Polyphemus, a son of Poseidon, proceeded to kill and eat several of Odysseus's men, and the survivors lost nearly all hope of escaping. Odysseus came up with a plan. After blinding Polyphemus with a stake, he and his men escaped the cave by clinging to the undersides of the giant's sheep as they were let out to graze. The Greeks ran to their ships and set sail. Polyphemus hurled rocks at them and called on Poseidon to take revenge against Odysseus.

The Greeks landed next on the island of Aeolus (pronounced EE-uh-luhs), the keeper of the winds. Aeolus listened eagerly to Odysseus's tales of the Trojan War and gave the hero a bag containing all the storm winds. With these winds, Odysseus would be able to sail safely and quickly to Ithaca. After setting sail, however, his men became curious about the bag. Thinking that it might contain gold and jewels, they opened it and released the winds. The winds tossed the ships about and blew them back to the island of Aeolus. Aeolus refused to help Odysseus again and ordered the ships to leave.

After sailing for some time, Odysseus came to the land of the Laestrygonians (pronounced les-tri-GOH-nee-uhnz), a race of cannibal giants. The giants destroyed all but one of his ships and ate many of his men. Barely escaping these dreadful creatures, Odysseus and his surviving companions traveled on to the island of **Circe** (pronounced SUR-see), a powerful enchantress. Circe cast a spell on some of Odysseus's men and turned them into pigs. Protected by a magical herb given to him by Hermes, Odysseus forced the enchantress to reverse her spell, and his men resumed their human form. Circe then invited Odysseus and his men to remain as her guests.

The Greeks stayed with Circe for a year. She told Odysseus that he must visit the **underworld**, or land of the dead, and consult the blind prophet Tiresias (pronounced ty-REE-see-uhs), who could see the secrets of the gods, before returning to his homeland. Reluctantly and full of dread, Odysseus went to the kingdom of the dead. While there, he met his dead mother, Anticlea (pronounced an-tuh-KLEE-uh), and the spirits of **Agamemnon** (pronounced ag-uh-MEM-non), **Achilles** (pronounced uh-KILL-eez), and other Greek heroes. Tiresias told Odysseus what to expect and do during the rest of his journey and after he returned home to Ithaca.

After leaving the underworld, Odysseus went back to Circe's island for a short stay. Before he set sail again, the enchantress warned him about some of the dangers he still faced and advised him how to survive them. The first of these dangers was the **Sirens**, sea **nymphs** who lured sailors to their deaths with their beautiful singing. Odysseus ordered his men to plug their ears with wax so they would not hear the Sirens' song. Wanting to hear their songs himself, he had his men tie him to the ship's mast so he could not be lured away.

Odysseus and his men next faced the monsters Scylla (pronounced SIL-uh) and Charybdis (pronounced kuh-RIB-dis), who guarded a narrow channel through which their ship had to pass. Odysseus barely escaped the monsters and he lost some of his men to them. The survivors reached the island of Helios (pronounced HEE-lee-ohs) with its herds of sacred sheep and cattle. Both Tiresias and Circe had warned Odysseus not to harm any of these animals, but his men ignored the warning and killed some of them as a **sacrifice** and for food. When Helios complained to the gods, Zeus sent a storm that destroyed Odysseus's ship and drowned all his remaining companions. Alone, the hero reached the island of the enchantress Calypso, the point at which the *Odyssey* began.

Return to Ithaca After hearing the story of Odysseus's adventures, the Phaeacians gave him a ship, and he set sail for Ithaca. This time Poseidon put aside his anger and allowed Odysseus to reach home, but he punished the Phaeacians for helping him. In Ithaca, the goddess Athena appeared before Odysseus and reassured him that his wife, Penelope, had been faithful. She had resisted the attentions of many suitors who desired both her and his kingdom and were occupying his house. Disguised as a beggar by Athena, Odysseus stayed with a loyal swineherd while the goddess went to fetch his son Telemachus from Sparta.

When Telemachus returned, Odysseus revealed himself to his son, and together they plotted the undoing of Penelope's suitors. Still disguised as a beggar, Odysseus went to the palace and walked among the suitors. Later that night, Penelope asked to speak with the beggar, whom she did not recognize as her husband. She asked what he knew of Odysseus and told him how she had fended off the suitors. She had refused to marry until she finished weaving a shroud for Odysseus's father, Laertes (pronounced lay-UR-teez). She would weave the shroud by day and then unravel her work at night. This worked until her trick was discovered. While they were talking, an old nurse came in to wash

the beggar's feet. Recognizing a scar on his leg, she knew him to be Odysseus, but he swore her to secrecy.

Penelope announced to the suitors that she would marry the man who could string the bow of Odysseus and shoot an arrow through twelve axes placed in a row. The suitors all failed. Telemachus then demanded that the beggar be allowed to try. The beggar accomplished the feat. Then throwing off his disguise, he and Telemachus fought and killed all the suitors. At first Penelope could not believe that this man was truly her long-absent husband. Only when Odysseus revealed a secret that only they knew—that their bed was carved from a tree and remained rooted in the ground—did she acknowledge and embrace him.

On the day following this reunion, Odysseus visited his father, Laertes, and learned that the families of the dead suitors were planning to attack. When the battle was about to begin, Athena frightened the attackers away. She then assured Odysseus that his reign would be long and would bring lasting peace to Ithaca. The *Odyssey* ends with this promise of peace and happiness.

The *Odyssey* in Context

It would be nearly impossible to overstate the importance of the *Odyssey* to Greek literature and culture—and by extension Western literature and culture in general. The *Iliad* and *Odyssey* both served a fundamental role in shaping their political and cultural lives. The framers of Greece's famous governmental systems (the foundation of our modern democracy) used Homer's epics as precedent and support in much the same way a lawyer today would appeal to Supreme Court rulings in trying to argue a case. The events and language of the poems permeate subsequent ancient Greek literature, from the dialogs of Socrates to the plays of Euripides, and continue to echo strongly in today's literature.

Ancient Rome gradually seized control of Greece between the second and first centuries BCE, and in the process appropriated much of what they found valuable about Greek culture. The great poems of Homer were considered chief among Greece's cultural gems. In writing his own national epic for Rome, the poet Virgil plainly admitted he was attempting to recreate the glory Homer's work. As Rome's military and political dominance spread north across Europe all the way to England, Greek culture (in Roman "packaging") spread, too, and the *Iliad* and the *Odyssey* won more admirers. Countless artists, writers, philosophers, and politicians of the past two thousand years of Western history have acknowledged their debt to Homer, including such famous figures as the Italian artist Michelangelo, English poet John Milton, American politician Thomas Jefferson, American writer Ralph Waldo Emerson, and English writer James Joyce. Eminent eighteenth-century Irish author Samuel Johnson summed up the influence of Homer's work thus: "Nation after nation, century after century, has been able to do little more than transpose Homer's incidents, new-name his characters, and paraphrase his sentiments."

Key Themes and Symbols

A key theme in the tale of Odysseus is cleverness. Although he is shown to be strong, Odysseus very often escapes trouble through shrewdness rather than brute force, as when he devises a plan to escape from the Cyclops Polyphemus by hiding under the giant's sheep as they are put out to graze. Another important theme in the tales of Odysseus is determination: although his journey takes ten years, he does not lose sight of his goal to return home to his wife and kingdom. His wife Penelope represents faithfulness, since she never gives up hope that her husband will return. The best symbol of their love is their bed, which Odysseus describes as a final test to prove his identity. The bed represents their marriage, a living and enduring thing with roots that give it strength even though they may not be seen.

The *Odyssey* in Art, Literature, and Everyday Life

The *Odyssey* has been adapted in many forms since its first appearance. The Roman poet Virgil even borrowed from the *Odyssey* in his own epic, the ***Aeneid***. The *Odyssey* has also inspired many modern works, including James Joyce's landmark novel *Ulysses* (1922), and the 2000 Coen brothers' film *O Brother, Where Art Thou?* The term "odyssey" has even come to mean a great adventure that takes a long time and includes many different locations, such as in Stanley Kubrick's *2001: A Space Odyssey*.

Read, Write, Think, Discuss

Odysseus embodies a spirit of adventure and travel, and the *Odyssey* takes him to the farthest reaches of the ancient world. In modern times, the entire globe is connected through communication systems, such as telephones and the Internet. It is a simple task to see an image of Mount Fuji or the Eiffel Tower without having to travel to Japan or France. Do you think this ability to connect with faraway places leads to an increase or decrease in a person's spirit of adventure and desire to travel? Why? Similarly, do you think the *Odyssey* inspired ancient audiences to travel, or do you think the terrifying stories would have the opposite effect and cause people to prefer the safety of their homes?

SEE ALSO Athena; Circe; Cyclopes; Greek Mythology; *Iliad, The*; Odysseus; Penelope; Poseidon; Sirens

Oedipus

Character Overview

Oedipus was a tragic hero of **Greek mythology**, a king doomed to a dire fate because he unknowingly killed his father and married his mother. His story is the tale of someone who, because he did not know his true identity, followed the wrong path in life. Once he had set foot on that path, his best qualities could not save him from the results of actions that violated the laws of gods and men.

Oedipus was born to King Laius (pronounced LAY-uhs) and Queen Jocasta (pronounced joh-KAS-tuh) of Thebes (pronounced THEEBZ). The oracle at **Delphi** (pronounced DEL-fye), who could communicate directly with the gods, told Laius and Jocasta that their child would grow up to murder Laius and marry Jocasta. Horrified, the king fastened the infant's feet together with a large pin and left him on a mountainside to die.

However, shepherds found the baby—who became known as Oedipus, or "swollen foot"—and took him to the city of Corinth. There King Polybus (pronounced POL-uh-buhs) and Queen Merope (pronounced MER-uh-pee) adopted him and raised him to think that he was their own son. When Oedipus was grown, however, someone told him that he was not the son of Polybus. Oedipus went to Delphi to ask the oracle about his parentage. The answer he received was: "You are the man fated to murder his father and marry his mother."

Like Laius and Jocasta, Oedipus was determined to avoid the fate predicted for him. Believing that the oracle had said he was fated to kill Polybus and marry Merope, he vowed never to return to Corinth. Instead, he headed toward Thebes.

Along the way, Oedipus came to a narrow road between cliffs. There he met an older man in a chariot coming the other way. The two quarreled over who should give way, and Oedipus killed the stranger and went on to Thebes. He found the city in great distress. He learned that a monster called the **Sphinx** was terrorizing the Thebans by devouring them when they failed to answer its riddle, and that King Laius had been murdered on his way to seek help from the Delphic oracle. The riddle of the Sphinx was: "What walks on four legs in the morning, two at noon,

Nationality/Culture
Greek

Pronunciation
ED-uh-puhs

Alternate Names
None

Appears In
Seneca's *Oedipus*, Sophocles' *Oedipus the King*

Lineage
Son of Laius and Jocasta

and three in the evening?" Oedipus gave the correct answer: "A human being, who crawls as an infant, walks erect in maturity, and leans on a staff in old age." With this answer, Oedipus not only defeated the Sphinx, which killed itself in rage, but won the throne of the dead king and the hand in marriage of the king's widow, Jocasta.

Oedipus and Jocasta lived happily for a time and had two sons and two daughters. Then a dreadful plague came upon Thebes. A prophet declared that the plague would not end until the Thebans drove out Laius's murderer, who was within the city. A messenger then arrived from Corinth, announcing the death of King Polybus and asking Oedipus to return and rule the Corinthians. Oedipus told Jocasta what the oracle had predicted for him and expressed relief that the danger of his murdering Polybus was past. Jocasta told him not to fear oracles, for the oracle had said that her first husband would be killed by his own son, and instead he had been murdered by a stranger on the road to Delphi.

Suddenly Oedipus remembered that fatal encounter on the road and knew that he had met and killed his real father, Laius. At the same time, Jocasta realized that the scars on Oedipus's feet marked him as the baby whose feet Laius had pinned together so long ago. Faced with the fact that she had married her own son and the murderer of Laius, she hanged herself. Oedipus seized a pin from her dress and blinded himself with it.

Some accounts say that Oedipus was banished at once from Thebes, while others relate that he lived a miserable existence there, despised by all, until his children grew up. Eventually he was driven into exile, accompanied by his two daughters, **Antigone** (pronounced an-TIG-uh-nee) and Ismene (pronounced is-MEE-nee). After years of lonely wandering, he arrived in Athens, where he found refuge in a grove of trees called Colonus. By this time, warring factions in Thebes wanted him to return to that city, believing that his body would bring it luck. Oedipus, however, died at Colonus, and the presence of his grave there was said to bring good fortune to Athens.

Oedipus in Context

The tale of Oedipus reflects and reinforces ancient Greek traditions and values in more than one way. First, the myth emphasizes the importance of following traditions related to family members. The idea of killing a relative was shocking to ancient Greeks and was considered so serious that it was beyond the scope of punishment by human laws. Similarly,

When Oedipus found out that he had killed his father and married his mother—and was therefore responsible for the plague in the city he ruled—he blinded himself. This painting by Ernest Hillemacher shows him walking blind among the victims of the plague with his daughter. THE ART ARCHIVE/MUSÉE DES BEAUX ARTS ORLÉANS/ALFREDO DAGLI ORTI/THE PICTURE DESK, INC.

marrying one's own parent went against the most basic marriage traditions in Greek culture (and most other cultures). By showing how these unspeakable acts led to a tragic end for Oedipus, the myth reinforced these traditions among the ancient Greeks who knew the tale.

The myth also reflects cultural beliefs about destiny, or the idea that future events in a person's life are already determined and cannot be changed. For the ancient Greeks, who consulted with messengers of the gods regularly, this was a widely accepted notion. The abundance of such stories in Greek myth—as opposed to stories where characters successfully defy the gods and change their destinies—indicates that the ideas of freedom and free will were much more limited in scope than they are in modern society. Stories like the myth of Oedipus would instead encourage citizens to accept their destiny, whatever it may be.

Key Themes and Symbols

The story of Oedipus contains two enduring themes of Greek myth and drama: the flawed nature of humanity, and an individual's powerlessness against the course of destiny. Laius and Oedipus are both flawed because of their arrogance or overconfidence. Not only do they both believe they can defy the predictions of the oracles, but neither is willing to grant the other first passage when they meet on the road between the cliffs. This results in Oedipus killing Laius, therefore fulfilling the first part of the prophecy. This inability to escape destiny is also shown in Oedipus's flight from Corinth; Oedipus believes he is safe from the prediction of the oracle, even though his actions directly result in the prediction coming true. The fact that Oedipus blinds himself is symbolic of the arrogance that blinded him to the destiny he thought he could escape.

Oedipus in Art, Literature, and Everyday Life

The best-known account of the myth of Oedipus is preserved in *Oedipus the King* and *Oedipus at Colonus*, two dramas by the ancient Greek playwright Sophocles. Most versions of the story have followed the pattern that Sophocles set down, although an earlier version, mentioned by Homer in the Greek epics the ***Iliad*** and the ***Odyssey***, says that after Oedipus's identity was revealed, Jocasta hanged herself. Oedipus, however, continued to rule Thebes, died in battle, and was buried with honor.

The story of Oedipus has inspired artists and thinkers since ancient times. The Roman philosopher Seneca wrote a tragedy entitled *Oedipus* that influenced writers such as England's John Dryden and Alexander Pope and France's Voltaire and Pierre Corneille. Later artistic treatments of the Oedipus story include a translation of Sophocles' work by Irish poet William Butler Yeats; a play entitled *The Infernal Machine* by Jean Cocteau of France; music by Russian composer Igor Stravinsky; and the movie *Oedipus Rex* by Italian filmmaker Pier Paolo Pasolini. Sigmund Freud, one of the founders of modern psychiatry, used the term *Oedipus complex* to refer to a psychological state in which a boy or man experiences hostility toward his father due to an inappropriate attraction or bond to his mother.

King Midas Turns His Daughter to Gold

King Midas found that his greedy wish to have everything he touched turn to gold backfired when he accidentally turned his own daughter to gold. *See* Midas.

HIP/Art Resource, NY.

The Snake Legend of the Hopi People

For many centuries, Native Americans have passed their myths from generation to generation through oral stories and artistic representations. *See* Native American Mythology.

© Tom Bean/Corbis.

Nereids Playing in the Waves

Nereids were a type of nymph that lived in the ocean. *See* Nymphs.

Erich Lessing/Art Resource, NY.

Odin Coming to Drink from the Fountain of Mimir

Mimir was a giant in Norse mythology who guarded the well of knowledge. The god Odin came to the well in order to gain wisdom by drinking its waters. *See* Mimir.

© Mary Evans Picture Library/The Image Works.

Noah Makes a Sacrifice after the Flood

According to the Bible, God sent a flood to destroy the world, saving Noah, his family, and two of every kind of animal in a large boat called an ark. After the flood waters went down, Noah made a sacrifice to God, and God promised that he would never destroy the world with a flood again, sending a rainbow as a seal of that promise. *See* Noah.

Pan Chasing the Nymph Syrinx

In Greek mythology the satyr Pan attempted to catch the nymph Syrinx, who prayed to the gods to save her from his attentions. The gods responded by turning her into a group of reeds, which Pan used to make a set of pipes as a musical instrument. *See* Pan.

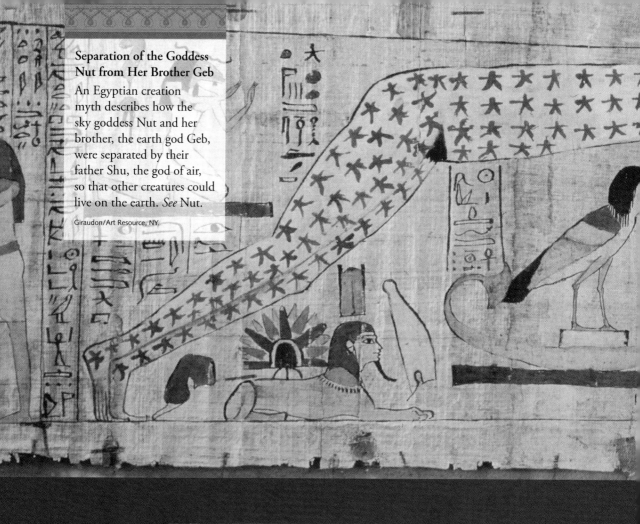

Separation of the Goddess Nut from Her Brother Geb

An Egyptian creation myth describes how the sky goddess Nut and her brother, the earth god Geb, were separated by their father Shu, the god of air, so that other creatures could live on the earth. *See* Nut.

The Marriage of Nala and Damayanti

In Hindu mythology, Nala and Damayanti were lovers who overcame many obstacles to marry and live happily together. *See* Nala and Damayanti.

The Marriage of Draupadi to the Five Pandava Brothers
According to the Hindu epic *The Mahabharata*, the princess Draupadi married all five Pandava brothers. *See Mahabharata, The.*

Hermod Pleading for the Return of Balder from Hel

The untimely death of the god Balder was a significant story in the Norse mythology. *See* Norse Mythology.

Read, Write, Think, Discuss

Oedipus commits two unspeakable acts—killing his father and marrying his mother—without knowing he has done either one. In modern law, if a person commits a crime without knowing that it was illegal, the person can still be held accountable for committing the crime. At the same time, many laws differ from state to state or even city to city, with some cities still carrying old laws that might seem silly to modern visitors (in Gainesville, Georgia, for example, it is technically illegal to eat chicken with a fork). Do you think not knowing about a law is ever a valid defense for breaking that law? Why or why not?

SEE ALSO Antigone; Greek Mythology; Sphinx

Oisin

Character Overview

In **Celtic mythology**, Oisin (or Ossian) was a great warrior poet and the son of **Finn**, leader of a warrior band known as the Fianna (pronounced FEE-uh-nuh). Legend says that an enchanter had changed Finn's lover, the goddess Sadb (pronounced SAWV), into a deer. One day while looking for Sadb, Finn came upon Oisin. He realized the boy was his son after Oisin told him that his mother was a gentle deer. Finn raised Oisin and trained him to be a warrior, but Oisin also inherited his mother's gift of eloquent speech. He became a great poet as well as one of the fiercest warriors of the Fianna.

As a man, Oisin met Niamh (pronounced NEE-uhv), daughter of the sea god Manannan Mac **Lir** (pronounced muh-NAH-nahn mak leer). She invited him to visit her father's kingdom of Tir Na Nog, the Land of Ever Young. After what seemed like a few years, Oisin grew lonely for home and asked if he might visit Ireland. Niamh agreed and sent him back on horseback, warning him not to touch the ground or he would never be able to return to Tir Na Nog. However, Oisin slipped out of his saddle while helping some men lift a stone. When he fell to the ground, he instantly became a blind, white-haired old man. He discovered that three hundred years had passed since he left Ireland, and

Nationality/Culture
Irish/Celtic

Pronunciation
uh-SHEEN

Alternate Names
Ossian

Appears In
The Fenian Cycle

Lineage
Son of Finn and Sadb

when he touched the ground, all those years caught up with him. He never saw his beloved Niamh or Tir Na Nog again.

Oisin in Context

The character of Oisin, despite playing an active part in several fantastic adventures, was traditionally regarded as an actual historical figure in

Irish culture. He is the narrator and alleged author of many poems and ballads. Although there is little evidence that Oisin is based on a real person, this reflects Celtic and Irish beliefs that the gods and other races of beings frequently interacted with humans. It also reflects the notion in Irish culture that the Irish people are directly descended from figures with mythical roots such as Oisin.

Key Themes and Symbols

One theme found in the tales of Oisin is the danger of disobeying the gods. Although he does not intend to disobey Niamh, his carelessness results in his losing his eternal youth. Oisin also represents eloquence of speech and song, which he inherited from his goddess mother. Oisin, whose name actually means "little deer," is sometimes associated with deer.

Oisin in Art, Literature, and Everyday Life

Oisin is one of the most beloved and heroic figures in Irish culture. He appears in several traditional Celtic tales and was the subject of the William Butler Yeats poem *The Wanderings of Oisin* (1889). In 1761, a writer named James MacPherson published what was claimed to be a translation of Oisin's poems. Their authenticity was disproved by Samuel Johnson fourteen years later. In recent times, the name Oisin has been used by geneticist Bryan Sykes to represent a population of people who have a certain group of genetic markers in their DNA. Although members of this population can be found throughout Europe, they are most concentrated in Ireland and Wales.

Read, Write, Think, Discuss

According to legend, Oisin lived for several hundred years in a land of eternal youth. In modern times, people spend billions of dollars each year in an attempt to regain their youthful appearance or energy level. The myth of Oisin seems to suggest that people in centuries past were also concerned with retaining their youth. Do you think people are more concerned now with appearing young than they were in the past? Why or why not?

SEE ALSO Celtic Mythology; Finn

Old Man and Old Woman

Nationality/Culture
American Indian/Blackfoot

Alternate Names
Napi (Old Man), Kipitaki
(Old Woman)

Appears In
Blackfoot creation myths

Lineage
None

Character Overview

Old Man, also known as Napi, is a creator god and trickster figure in the mythology of the Blackfoot Indians of North America. He is said to have created the world and all the creatures in it. His companion was Old Woman, who often argued with Old Man or altered his plans in ways that made life more difficult for people.

Major Myths

To make humans, Old Man fashioned figures out of clay and breathed life into them. Old Man was accompanied by Old Woman as he did this, and their disagreements determined how people were formed and how they lived. For example, Old Man wished to make humans with five fingers on each hand; Old Woman said that five fingers was too many, so they settled on four fingers and one thumb.

Then it came time to decide whether people would live again after they died, or whether they would stay dead forever. To answer the question, Old Man threw a piece of buffalo manure into the river. If the manure floated, he said, humans would die and come back to life after four days. If it sank, they would die and never live again. The manure floated, but Old Woman was not satisfied. She decided to try the test herself. However, instead of a piece of manure, she threw a stone into the water. The stone sank, so Old Man decreed that death for humans would last forever. Old Woman concluded that this would be best, since it meant people would show sympathy for each other.

Another story says that after the world was filled with people, Old Man decided to experience life for himself. He lured a woman to a nest of rattlesnakes, and she mated with one of them. When her husband found out, he cut off her head. But the woman's headless body chased her two children. They saved themselves by throwing a piece of magic moss on the ground. A river formed, and the body drowned. One of the children was Old Man, who continued to live on earth before he died and disappeared behind the mountains.

Old Man and Old Woman in Context

In the myths of Old Man, Old Woman is depicted as always willing to argue and make things difficult. The myths lay the blame on women for making certain tasks—such as tanning buffalo hides—difficult to do, or for denying humans the ability to live forever. It also suggests that decision making is better left to the men, and that the difficult tasks women must perform are deserved, because they would not be difficult if Old Woman did not have her say.

Key Themes and Symbols

The Blackfoot identify Old Man with the **sun**, which also disappears behind the mountains every evening. Like the sun returning in the morning, Old Man is also supposed to come back to earth one day. The theme of deciding humanity's fate is important in the myths of Old Man and Old Woman. Together, they decide all the basics of human life and living, sometimes with very little thought put into the details. The theme of a god longing for the human experience is also present in the stories of Old Man; although he created humans, he still wants to know what it is like to live as one.

Old Man and Old Woman in Art, Literature, and Everyday Life

Old Man and Old Woman are important figures in Blackfoot mythology, but like most American Indian mythical figures, they are not well known in mainstream American society. Stories of Old Man and Old Woman are preserved by the remaining Blackfoot descendants, mostly residing in northern Montana and southern Alberta, Canada. The mythology of the Blackfoot people was also documented by Clark Wissler and D. C. Duvall in their 1908 book *Mythology of the Blackfoot Indians*.

Read, Write, Think, Discuss

In the myth of Old Man and Old Woman, Old Woman states that not allowing people to come back to life after they die will cause them to show more sympathy for each other while they are alive. Why do you think this might be true?

SEE ALSO Native American Mythology; Tricksters

Olorun

Nationality/Culture
West African/Yoruba

Pronunciation
oh-loh-RUN

Alternate Names
Olofin-Orun, Oba-Orun, Olodumare

Appears In
Yoruba creation myths

Lineage
None

Character Overview

In the mythology of the Yoruba people of West Africa, Olorun is the most powerful and wisest god. The all-knowing Olorun takes an active role in the affairs of both **heaven** and earth. Head of the Yoruba pantheon (or collection of recognized gods), Olorun is also known as Olofin-Orun (Lord of Heaven), Oba-Orun (King of the Sky), and Olodumare (Almighty).

Major Myths

According to Yoruba legend, Olorun was one of two original creator gods; the other was the goddess Olokun. In the beginning, the universe consisted only of sky and a formless expanse of marshy water. Olorun ruled the sky, while Olokun ruled the vast marshy waters below. There were thousands of other gods, but none had as much knowledge or power as Olorun.

Although Olokun was content with her watery kingdom, a lesser god named Obatala had ideas about improving her kingdom. He went to Olorun and suggested the creation of solid land, with fields and forests, hills and valleys, and various living things to populate it. Olorun agreed that this would be good and gave Obatala permission to create land.

Obatala went to Orunmila, the eldest son of Olorun, and asked how he should proceed. Orunmila told Obatala to gather gold to make a chain that could be lowered from the sky to the waters below. When the chain was finished, Orunmila gave Obatala a snail's shell filled with sand, a white hen, a black cat, and a palm nut. Obatala lowered himself on the chain and poured the sand on the waters. He then released the hen, which scratched at the sand and scattered it in all directions. Every place the sand fell became dry land. Stepping onto the land—known as Ife—Obatala built a house, grew palm trees from the palm nut, and lived with the black cat as his companion.

Obatala later became lonely and built clay figures. Olorun turned these figures into humans by breathing life into them. Many gods descended from the sky to live on earth, and Olorun told them to listen to the prayers of humans and protect them.

Not pleased by these acts of creation, the water goddess Olokun tried to flood the land to regain the area she had lost. However, Orunmila used his powers to make the waters recede. Angry that the sky god's son had defeated her, Olokun challenged Olorun to a weaving contest to see who was the more powerful. Olokun was a weaver of unequaled skill and knowledge, but every time she made a beautiful cloth, Agemo, the chameleon who carried messages for Olorun, changed the color of its skin to match her weaving. When Olokun saw that even Olorun's messenger could duplicate her finest cloths, she accepted defeat and acknowledged Olorun as the supreme god.

Olorun in Context

For the Yoruba people, the ultimate goal of life is to live in a way that connects one to Olorun and the energy of the world. Becoming one with Olorun leads to a place in the spiritual realm after death. This involves doing things that are helpful for others and the world, and always trying to improve oneself. In this way, Olorun has a profound effect on how all Yoruba people live from day to day.

Key Themes and Symbols

Olorun represents original creation and the father of all the earth. He is closely associated with all things white, including bones, clouds, and—according to Yoruba belief—brains. He is not usually viewed as having a specific physical form.

Olorun in Art, Literature, and Everyday Life

Although he is one of the most important gods in Yoruban mythology, Olorun is not often depicted in human form, and, unlike other figures in the Yoruban pantheon, he is not the focus of an annual celebration. Perhaps because of this, Olorun is not well-known outside the Yoruba culture. However, since many elements of Yoruban culture were brought to the New World during the slave trade, some tales of Olorun have made their way throughout the Caribbean, the southern United States, and South America. Perhaps the most famous mention of Olorun occurs in the 1990 song "Rhythm of the Saints" by Paul Simon, though his variant name Olodumare is used.

Read, Write, Think, Discuss

Many creation myths from around the world include humans originally being crafted from clay, as in the myth of Obatala and Olorun. Why do you think this theme is found in so many different cultures? Do you think the practice of burying the dead supports this notion of humans originally arising from clay? Why or why not?

SEE ALSO African Mythology; Ile-Ife

One Thousand and One Nights

See **Aladdin; Sinbad.**

Nationality/Culture
Greek/Roman

Pronunciation
oh-RYE-uhn

Alternate Names
None

Appears In
Ovid's *Fasti*, Hyginus's *Astronomica*, Homer's *Odyssey*

Lineage
Son of Poseidon

Orion

Character Overview

Orion was a giant in **Greek mythology** who was famed as a hunter and companion of **Artemis** (pronounced AHR-tuh-miss). Some stories say he was the son of **Poseidon** (pronounced poh-SYE-dun), god of the sea, and could therefore walk on water. In other tales, he is born from three fathers—**Zeus** (pronounced ZOOS), Poseidon, and **Hermes** (pronounced HUR-meez)—as an heir for the king of Boeotia (pronounced bee-OH-shuh).

Orion went to the island of Chios (pronounced KY-ohs), where King Oenopion (pronounced ee-NOH-pee-on) asked him to drive all the wild beasts from the land. In return, Oenopion promised Orion his daughter Merope (pronounced MEHR-oh-pee) in marriage. However, the king later refused to honor the agreement. Orion got drunk and raped Merope, and Oenopion blinded him. After recovering his vision, Orion went to Crete to live and hunt with the goddess Artemis.

There are several accounts of his death. One story says that Eos, the goddess of the dawn, fell in love with Orion and that Artemis killed him out of jealousy. According to another version, Orion and Artemis were considering marriage, but she was tricked into killing him by her brother **Apollo** (pronounced uh-POL-oh). In still another myth, Orion pursued seven sisters known as the Pleiades (pronounced PLEE-uh-deez). To save them from Orion's attentions, Zeus, the leader of the gods, turned them into stars. Orion, too, became a constellation, which appears to chase the Pleiades through the heavens.

Orion in Context

Even in ancient times, Orion was best known as a constellation, or group of stars visible in the night sky. The constellation known as Orion earned its name because ancient observers saw the image of a hunter in the arrangement of its stars. Although Orion the mythological character was most likely recognized before Orion the constellation, his link to the constellation undoubtedly led to new tales about him. For example, the myth of Orion and the Pleiades seems likely to have developed after observers noticed the movements of the two groups of stars in the sky. Likewise, in one myth Orion is said to have fought a giant scorpion—a story that may have its origin in the presence of a constellation, near to Orion in the sky, known as Scorpius.

Key Themes and Symbols

Trickery and betrayal runs through the myth of Orion. First, Orion is betrayed by Oenopion, who backs out of his agreement to let Orion marry his daughter Merope. Later, Orion is betrayed by his love, Artemis, who kills him when she is tricked by her brother. The search for love is also a common theme in the tales of Orion, though none of his searches ends happily. Orion is closely associated with hunting, and a club and animal hide are often used to represent him. His dog Sirius (pronounced SEER-ee-uhs) is a constant companion, and represents loyalty.

Orion in Art, Literature, and Everyday Life

Orion's name is easily recognized in modern society, even though existing myths about him are fairly sparse. His appearance in art and literature since the ancient Greek era has also been rather infrequent. He was the subject of a painting by Nicolas Poussin in 1658, and of two operas during the seventeenth and eighteenth centuries. John Keats mentions Orion in his poem *Endymion* (1818), and Richard Henry Horne wrote a successful epic based on Orion in 1843. More recently, science fiction author Ben Bova wrote a series of futuristic novels between 1984 and 1995 centered on Orion. Orion is still probably best known to most people by the constellation that bears his name.

Read, Write, Think, Discuss

Using your library, the Internet, or other available resources, find the constellations of Orion, Scorpius, and the Pleiades on a map of the stars. Where are they in relation to each other? Do they resemble the figures they are meant to represent? Do some further reading about the importance of astrology in ancient Greek and Roman societies. How was astrology regarded by the ancients, compared to what many modern scientists think about it?

Orpheus

Character Overview

In **Greek mythology**, Orpheus is a musician who sang and played so beautifully that even animals, rocks, and trees danced to his tunes. He was the son of Calliope (pronounced kuh-LYE-uh-pee), the Muse of epic poetry, and of the god **Apollo** (pronounced uh-POL-oh). It was Apollo who gave Orpheus his first lyre, the musical instrument that he always played.

Orpheus accompanied **Jason** and the **Argonauts** (pronounced AHR-guh-nawts) on their quest for the **Golden Fleece** and used his music several times to ease their journey. On one occasion, he calmed the sea with his playing; another time, he saved the Argonauts from the deadly **Sirens** by playing so loudly that they could not hear the Sirens' songs. Also, he stopped the Argonauts from quarreling with a song about the origins of the universe.

Orpheus fell in love with the nymph **Eurydice** (pronounced yoo-RID-uh-see). Shortly after their marriage, Eurydice was bitten by a snake and died. The grieving Orpheus refused to play or sing for a long time.

Nationality/Culture
Greek

Pronunciation
OR-fee-uhs

Alternate Names
None

Appears In
Ovid's *Metamorphoses*, Virgil's *Georgics*

Lineage
Son of Calliope and Apollo

Finally he decided to go to the **underworld**, or land of the dead, to find Eurydice. His playing enchanted Charon (pronounced KAIR-uhn), the ferryman who carried the souls of the dead across the river Styx (pronounced STIKS) into the underworld. Charon agreed to take Orpheus across the river, even though he was not dead. Orpheus's music also tamed **Cerberus** (pronounced SUR-ber-uhs), the monstrous three-headed dog who guarded the gates of the underworld. Even **Hades** (pronounced HAY-deez) and **Persephone** (pronounced per-SEF-uh-nee), king and queen of the underworld, could not resist his playing. They agreed to let him take Eurydice back to earth on one condition: he was not to look back at her until they had both reached the surface. Orpheus led his wife from the underworld, and as soon as he reached the surface, he was so overjoyed that he looked back to share the moment with Eurydice. But she had not reached the surface yet, and she immediately disappeared into the underworld.

Orpheus spent the rest of his life grieving for his lost wife. In time his grief infuriated the Maenads (pronounced MEE-nads), a group of women who worshipped the god **Dionysus** (pronounced dye-uh-NYE-suhs). To punish Orpheus for neglecting their attentions, they tore him to pieces. The **Muses** gathered up the pieces of his body and buried them, but the Maenads threw his head and his lyre into the river Hebrus. The head continued to sing and the lyre continued to play, and both eventually floated down to the sea, finally coming to rest on the island of Lesbos. The head became an oracle, or being that communicated messages between the gods and humans. Eventually the head of Orpheus rivaled the famous oracle of Apollo at **Delphi**. The gods placed his lyre in the heavens as a constellation.

Orpheus in Context

Orpheus was much more than a mythological musician to many ancient Greeks. In fact, he was often viewed as a real person who had brought significant religious teachings to his followers. He was said to be the creator of the *Orphic Hymns*, a body of myth that is similar to more traditional Greek beliefs, but emphasizes the importance of certain figures, such as Dionysus and Persephone. Although very little is known about the details of the Orphic religion, its followers appear to have believed in the eternal nature of the human soul, and an **afterlife** that was designed to reward the deserving and punish the

undeserving. This was different from traditional Greek views of the underworld as a rather dismal place where nearly all dead people went, regardless of their virtue.

Key Themes and Symbols

One of the main themes of the myth of Orpheus is the power of true love. After Eurydice dies and passes on to the underworld, Orpheus pursues her out of love. The power of music is also a recurring theme in the stories of Orpheus. The lyre of Orpheus symbolizes this power. Orpheus uses it to drown out the Sirens so the Argonauts do not fall victim to them, and later defuses an argument between the sailors with one of his songs. While pursuing Eurydice, Orpheus uses his lyre to gain entrance to the underworld, and his skill at playing music convinces Hades to let him take Eurydice back to the land of the living. Another important theme in this myth is obedience to the gods. When Orpheus disobeys Hades by looking back at Eurydice before they reach the surface, he breaks his agreement with Hades and Eurydice must return to the underworld.

Orpheus in Art, Literature, and Everyday Life

Over the centuries, the myth of Orpheus has endured as a tragic tale of love lost. Renaissance painters, such as Rubens and Titian, created depictions of Eurydice and Orpheus, and several operas were written about the pair during the seventeenth, eighteenth, and nineteenth centuries. The most famous of these is Jacques Offenbach's 1858 burlesque operetta *Orpheus in the Underworld*, which includes one piece known popularly as the music played during the French dance called the "Can Can."

More recently, the story of Eurydice and Orpheus was adapted for the 1959 film *Black Orpheus* by Marcel Camus. The 1997 Disney animated film *Hercules* used the plot from the myth of Eurydice and Orpheus, but instead had Hercules travel to the underworld in an attempt to save his love, Megara. Eurydice and Orpheus also appear in *The Sandman*, a comic series written by Neil Gaiman.

Read, Write, Think, Discuss

In modern times, many schools are cutting back on music and other arts-based programs in order to focus available funds on core classes, such as science and math. Do you think music programs should be considered necessary for schools? Why or why not? Do you think music is more or less important now than it was in past cultures? Why?

SEE ALSO Argonauts; Eurydice; Muses; Underworld

Osiris

Character Overview

One of the most important deities of ancient Egypt, Osiris was god of the **underworld** and judge of the dead. He also represented the idea of

Nationality/Culture
Egyptian

Pronunciation
oh-SYE-ris

Alternate Names
None

Appears In
The Pyramid Texts

Lineage
Son of Nut and Geb

renewal and rebirth in the **afterlife**. Osiris appears in many Egyptian myths and legends, and his popularity extended beyond Egypt.

Little is known about the origin of Osiris in **Egyptian mythology**. In very ancient times he may have been a local god of the city of Busiris in Lower Egypt. It is possible that he was originally an underworld god or fertility deity or legendary hero. By about 2400 BCE, his worship had become firmly established and began to spread throughout much of Egypt.

Major Myths

In Egyptian mythology, Osiris was the son of the sky goddess **Nut** (pronounced NOOT) and the earth god Geb (pronounced GEB). He was also the brother and husband of **Isis** (pronounced EYE-sis) and the father of **Horus** (pronounced HOHR-uhs). He supposedly served as a ruler of early Egypt, where his followers honored him as both god and man. Credited with civilizing the country, Osiris introduced agriculture and various crafts, established laws, and taught Egyptians how to worship the gods.

Osiris traveled to other parts of the world to civilize people. Upon his return to Egypt, his jealous brother **Set** plotted with others to kill him. They built a beautifully decorated box, tricked Osiris into getting into it, sealed the box, and then threw it into the Nile River. The box floated into the Mediterranean Sea to the land of Byblos (pronounced BIB-luhs) in Phoenicia (pronounced foh-NEE-shuh).

Overcome with grief at the loss of her husband, Isis searched high and low for his body. Eventually she found it. After bringing his body back to Egypt, Isis magically restored Osiris to life long enough to conceive a son, Horus. Isis then hid Osiris's body in a secluded spot. Set discovered it, cut it into pieces, and scattered them throughout Egypt. Isis gathered up the pieces, reassembled them, and restored Osiris to life once again.

Instead of staying on earth, Osiris chose to become lord of the Egyptian underworld. As king of the dead, he sat in judgment of dead souls, measuring the worth of their lives and determining their punishment or reward. The gods **Anubis** (pronounced uh-NOO-bis) and **Thoth** (pronounced TOHT) assisted him. In his role as god of the dead, Osiris became associated with the Egyptian practices of embalming and mummification, methods of preserving the dead so they could safely travel to the afterlife.

Painted wooden figure of the Egyptian god Osiris. HIP/ART RESOURCE, NY.

When Osiris became lord of the underworld, his son Horus became ruler of Egypt. The Egyptians believed that when a pharaoh (king) died he became the god Osiris. The new pharaoh represented Horus, the god of the living.

Osiris in Context

Osiris reflects the ancient Egyptian belief that death and rebirth are intimately connected. To an ancient Egyptian, death represented a chance to become one with Osiris and be given eternal life. This explains why a god of the underworld, usually considered a bringer of death, is also associated with the sprouting of crops and the flooding of the Nile, which leads to an abundance of vegetation. Ancient Egyptians viewed each harvesting of crops as another death for Osiris, with the grain representing his body. Some even planted crop beds in the shape of the god, who would be reborn when the seeds sprouted. In the case of Osiris, lord of the Egyptian realm of the dead, "death-bringer" is a less appropriate description than "eternal life-giver." Although Osiris's main center of worship was at the city of Abydos (pronounced uh-BYE-duhs), the god was worshipped intensely throughout Egypt. The appeal of a god who offered the promise of life after death was so strong that worship of Osiris also spread to other parts of the ancient world, most notably Greece and Rome.

Key Themes and Symbols

Osiris was linked to both death and rebirth for obvious reasons: he was killed twice by his jealous brother Set, and was restored to life twice by his wife and sister Isis. Osiris also represents the provider and teacher in ancient Egyptian myth. He brought knowledge of agriculture to the people and was also thought to be responsible for the growth of plants each year. An important theme in the myth of Osiris is the futility of jealousy and anger. Set kills his brother Osiris because he is jealous, but, in the end, Set still does not get to rule over Egypt—that honor passes to Osiris's son Horus.

In ancient Egyptian art, Osiris is usually portrayed as a bearded king wrapped in cloth like a mummy. He generally wears the crown of Upper Egypt, has an amulet around his neck, and holds a crook and a flail, symbols of his powers as god of fertility and the underworld.

Osiris in Art, Literature, and Everyday Life

In modern times, Osiris is seldom encountered as a character in art or literature. He is, however, sometimes mentioned in works dealing with magic and death. For instance, in the sixth season premiere of the television series *Buffy, the Vampire Slayer* (2001), the title character is brought back to life using an Urn of Osiris.

Read, Write, Think, Discuss

Locate on a map the following places and features mentioned in the myth of Osiris: Busiris, the Nile River, the Mediterranean Sea, Phoenicia, and Abydos. Do you think that the use of real places in the myth helps people to accept it as true? Why or why not?

SEE ALSO Afterlife; Anubis; Egyptian Mythology; Horus; Isis; Nut; Ra; Set; Thoth; Underworld

P

 Character

 Deity

 Myth

 Theme

 Culture

Nationality/Culture
Greek

Pronunciation
PAN

Alternate Names
Faunus (Roman)

Appears In
Ovid's *Metamorphoses*, Nonnus's *Dionysiaca*

Lineage
Son of Hermes and a nymph

Pan

Character Overview

Pan was a Greek fertility god associated with flocks and shepherds. He resembled the mythical creatures known as **satyrs**: from his waist down, he looked like a goat, but above the waist, he had human features, except for goat's ears and horns. The son of the god **Hermes** (pronounced HUR-meez) and a nymph (the name of the nymph differs in various versions of his life), he was abandoned by his mother at birth and raised by other **nymphs**, female nature deities that lived in streams, trees, and other objects. Pan was known for his never-ending love of women.

Major Myths

Pan was an accomplished musician, and the pipe he played is part of a well-known myth. Always in pursuit of a female, Pan was chasing a nymph named Syrinx (pronounced SEER-eenks), who was devoted to the goddess **Artemis** (pronounced AHR-tuh-miss) and not interested in romance, across the countryside. Syrinx reached an impassable stream with sandy banks. To escape from Pan, she called on her sister nymphs within the stream to transform her into a stand of reeds growing along the bank. When Pan reached the stand of reeds, he sighed in despair. The air of his sigh vibrated across the reeds, making a beautiful sound.

Pan cut down the reeds and crafted them into the first flute of its kind, thereafter known as a syrinx.

Pan's musicianship was also the subject of another myth. Pan boasted to his follower **Midas** that his songs were greater than those of anyone else, even greater than those of the god **Apollo** (pronounced uh-POL-oh). Apollo took this as a challenge, and the two played against each other in a contest. Although Pan played well, Apollo's songs were even more masterful. All who heard the contest agreed that Apollo was the winner, except for Pan's follower Midas. When Midas protested Apollo's victory, the god transformed Midas's ears into the ears of a donkey.

Although Pan was a playful figure who enjoyed chasing nymphs, he could be very ill-tempered if his sleep was disturbed. In **Greek mythology**, Pan helped **Zeus** and the other gods of Olympus overthrow the early gods called **Titans**. He did this by blowing into a shell and making a loud roar that frightened the Titans.

Pan in Context

Pan was unique among the Greek gods in ways that reflected the more rural culture of ancient Greece. For one, he was the only Greek god who was said to have died; all other gods were considered immortal, or able to live forever. This created an image of a god who was more like a human, and therefore easier for the average person to relate to. In addition, Pan did not live on Olympus (pronounced oh-LIM-puhs) with the other gods, but instead made his home in the Greek countryside, just like many farmers. Also, there is evidence that Pan—whose name literally means "all"—existed before most of the other Greek gods and was still worshipped after the others had fallen out of fashion. This was perhaps due to his association with nature and farmland, which appealed to small groups that were far removed from the ever-changing cultural centers and tended to retain customs and traditions through many generations.

Key Themes and Symbols

Pan represented the lustful and freewheeling nature of man, as well as the passionate and creative side. He represented animal instincts, as illustrated by his goat-like appearance, as well as fertility. His flute, made from the reeds of Syrinx, symbolized the love he always sought but never seemed to find. To Christians, Pan was a symbol of non-Christian belief that marked the uncivilized.

Pan in Art, Literature, and Everyday Life

Because of his unusual appearance, Pan is a distinctive figure who has appeared in many works of art from ancient to modern times. He was often depicted in pursuit of women and was sometimes shown in the company of the god **Dionysus** (pronounced deye-uh-NEYE-suhs). In modern times, Pan was one of the fantastical characters played by Tony Randall in the 1964 fantasy film *7 Faces of Dr. Lao*. In addition, Pan's ability to cause irrational fear in people lives on in the word "panic."

Read, Write, Think, Discuss

Read *The Great God Pan* by Donna Jo Napoli (2005), the story of Pan from his own viewpoint. In the story, Pan is a youth with an identity crisis who lives under the cloud of a curse: even though he may love, he will never be loved in return. When he falls in love with the human princess Iphigenia, his carefree world is turned upside-down. Author Napoli weaves many different Greek myths into her tale, though the work as a whole is an original work that in some ways differs from the traditional myths.

SEE ALSO Greek Mythology; Satyrs

Pandora

Character Overview

In **Greek mythology**, Pandora was the first woman, infamous for bringing evil into the world and causing humankind's downfall. She was sent to earth by **Zeus** (pronounced ZOOS), king of the gods, who wanted to take revenge on the Titan **Prometheus** (pronounced pruh-MEE-thee-uhs). Prometheus had created mortals and had stolen **fire** from the gods and given it to them. Zeus ordered the divine crafts worker, **Hephaestus** (pronounced hi-FES-tuhs), to form the first

Nationality/Culture
Greek

Pronunciation
pan-DOR-uh

Alternate Names
None

Appears In
Hesiod's *Theogony* and *Works and Days*, Aesop's *Fables*

Lineage
Created by the gods

woman, Pandora, from clay. The goddess **Athena** (pronounced uh-THEE-nuh) gave life to Pandora, **Aphrodite** (pronounced af-ro-DYE-tee) made her beautiful, and **Hermes** (pronounced HUR-meez) taught her to be cunning and deceitful.

Zeus sent Pandora down to earth, but Prometheus—whose name means "forethought"—would have nothing to do with her. However, his brother Epimetheus (pronounced ep-uh-MEE-thee-uhs)—whose name means "afterthought"—married Pandora, who brought with her a sealed box (or often a jar) as a gift from the gods. Some accounts say that Epimetheus opened Pandora's box; others maintain that Pandora herself opened it. Inside the container were disease, old age, poverty, evil, war, and all the other ills that have plagued humans ever since. They flew out into the world when the box was opened, leaving only hope at the bottom of the box to give people a scrap of comfort. A few accounts say that the box contained all the good things that Prometheus planned to give the human race, but when Pandora gave in to curiosity and opened the box, she let all the blessings escape. Pandora and Epimetheus had a daughter, Pyrrha (pronounced PEER-uh), who appears in a Greek myth about a great flood. Pyrrha and her husband, Deucalion (pronounced doo-KAY-lee-uhn), were the flood's sole survivors and became the parents of a new human race.

In one version of the Greek myth, Pandora released evil spirits into the world when she opened the box that held them. PHOTO BY TIME LIFE PICTURES/MANSELL/TIME LIFE PICTURES/GETTY IMAGES.

Pandora in Context

Pandora is viewed much differently today than she was in ancient times. To the ancient Greeks, Pandora was sent to earth as revenge for humans getting fire from Prometheus. The myth, especially as documented by Hesiod, is very clear in its view of women as the bringers of countless troubles to men. However, Hesiod notes that even though women are the source of many problems, a man cannot simply live trouble-free by avoiding marriage—for a man who does not marry will never have heirs and will have no one to care for him when he is old. While no doubt exaggerated for the sake of entertainment, Hesiod's description is likely to be an accurate reflection of how many ancient Greek men viewed women: necessary and vital, but troublesome.

Key Themes and Symbols

For many, Pandora symbolizes curiosity. This comes from her opening the box and releasing bad things into the world (though in some versions she simply brings the box as a gift from the gods). For the ancient Greeks, Pandora was more a symbol of the wiles of womanhood: a potentially dangerous figure who carried out the gods' punishment of men. As the first woman, Pandora also stands as a symbol of femininity, both beautiful and cunning in her way. The box represents the vengeance of the gods, since it contains all the bad things that eventually escape into the world and plague humans for the rest of time.

Pandora in Art, Literature, and Everyday Life

The story of Pandora has endured and transformed itself over the centuries. Most people familiar with the tale today are not aware of the box as punishment by the gods for humans possessing fire, but know instead of a version where Pandora disobeys after she is told not to open the box. Pandora has been the subject of paintings by artists such as John William Waterhouse and Dante Rossetti, and the myth loosely inspired the 1929 G. W. Pabst silent film *Pandora's Box*, starring Louise Brooks. The mythical box of Pandora is often referenced in modern art and culture, and the term "Pandora's box" is commonly used to refer to a thing or situation that can lead to a great deal of unforeseen trouble.

Read, Write, Think, Discuss

Pandora, as the first woman in Greek mythology, can be compared to Eve, the first woman in the Judeo-Christian tradition. Both women are directly responsible for introducing evil into the world, although they had not intended to do so. But while the Greek gods deliberately sent Pandora for that purpose as a punishment to man, Eve had been created by God to be a helper to the first man Adam, and it was only her disobedience that unleashed evil. What does this tell us about the differences between the Greek and Judeo-Christian attitudes towards women, as well as the way the divine relates to mankind?

SEE ALSO Adam and Eve; Greek Mythology; Prometheus

Paris

See **Helen of Troy;** *Iliad, The.*

Parvati

See **Devi.**

Patrick, St.

Nationality/Culture
Christian/Irish

Pronunciation
saynt PAT-trik

Alternate Names
None

Appears In
The *Annals of Ulster*

Lineage
Unknown

Character Overview

In the Christian religion, St. Patrick is the patron saint of Ireland, and was credited with driving evil in the form of snakes out of Ireland. He was born in Britain around 389 CE. He was the son of a Roman official. At the age of sixteen, Patrick was captured by raiders from Ireland and carried back to their homeland. After working as a shepherd for six years, he had a dream in which he was told that a ship was waiting to help him escape his captivity.

The accounts of his journeys at this time differ. He either traveled back to Britain or sailed to Gaul (present-day France). In any event, it seems likely that he visited France, where he joined a monastery and was ordained a priest. According to one of Patrick's personal letters, known in Latin as the *Confessio*, he had another dream, in which the Irish asked him to return to their island. Patrick left his monastery to travel among the non-Christian Irish chieftains, converting them and their people to Christianity.

Several legends have sprung up around St. Patrick, the most famous one claiming that he drove all the snakes out of Ireland and into the sea. A

The Catholic saint known as St. Patrick was famous for supposedly ridding Ireland of all snakes. PHOTO BY TIME LIFE PICTURES/TIME LIFE PICTURES/GETTY IMAGES.

popular myth holds that he used the shamrock, or three-leafed clover, to explain to an Irishman the Holy Trinity, the idea that God consists of three persons: Father, Son, and Holy Spirit. The shamrock is now Ireland's national flower, worn by the Irish on St. Patrick's feast day, March 17.

St. Patrick in Context

St. Patrick's status as a legendary figure reflects the importance of conversion in Christianity. Irish cultures that existed before the spread of Christianity were often described by Christians as "pagan," a term that not only described a belief in more than one god, but also suggested to other Christians an absence of true religious belief. Many Christians such as St. Patrick considered it their duty to convert members of these other belief systems to Christianity, and indeed, many were very successful. The adoption of a specific saint such as Patrick by Ireland allows the converted to retain an individual national character even as their own unique, native belief systems fade from prominence.

Key Themes and Symbols

To most, St. Patrick serves as a symbol of Ireland and its now firmly established Christian tradition. One theme found in the myth of St. Patrick is the personalization of Christianity; Patrick uses a beloved native plant, the shamrock, to explain the Holy Trinity to the Irish people. It has been suggested that the snakes St. Patrick drove from Ireland—a country never known for having many snakes—symbolize the nature-oriented belief systems that existed before the spread of Christianity. In Christian mythology, the serpent also frequently symbolizes evil, as in the myth of the Garden of **Eden**.

St. Patrick in Art, Literature, and Everyday Life

St. Patrick has endured not only in Christian writings and art, but also in Irish works that combine older Celtic legends with more modern beliefs. The twelfth-century work *Tales of the Elders* details a meeting between St. Patrick and members of the Fianna, a band of warriors led by the mythical Irish hero **Finn**. In modern times, St. Patrick's Day is a holiday recognized in many countries, usually celebrated by the wearing of green—a color that reflects Ireland's nickname, the Emerald Isle.

Read, Write, Think, Discuss

Today, many people who are not Irish celebrate St. Patrick's Day, and the religious feast has taken on some secular characteristics. Throughout history, there have been examples of religious holidays transformed into secular celebrations, and secular holidays becoming religious. Using your library, the

Internet, and other available resources, research one major religious holiday. When did it begin? Under what circumstances did it originate? Who were its original practitioners? Then try to trace how it changed over the years and the reasons for those changes.

Pegasus

Character Overview

A winged horse in **Greek mythology**, Pegasus was born from the blood that spurted from the neck of the Gorgon **Medusa** (pronounced meh-DOO-suh) when the hero **Perseus** (pronounced PUR-see-uhs) cut off her head. He is sometimes said to have been fathered by **Poseidon** (pronounced poh-SYE-dun), the god of the sea and tamer of horses. Pegasus served Perseus until his death, and afterward went to the home of the **Muses**. The water that gave the Muses their inspiration had dried up, so Pegasus stamped his hoof and created a spring.

With the help of the goddess **Athena** (pronounced uh-THEE-nuh) and a golden bridle she gave him, the hero **Bellerophon** (pronounced buh-LAIR-uh-fun) tamed Pegasus. He rode the horse when he slew the monster called the Chimaera (pronounced kye-MEER-uh), a fire-breathing creature with the head of a lion, the body of a goat, and the tail of a serpent. Later, Bellerophon tried to ride Pegasus to the top of Mount Olympus (pronounced oh-LIM-puhs) so that he could join the Greek gods. But **Zeus** (pronounced ZOOS), the leader of the gods, was angered by Bellerophon's arrogance. He caused a fly to bite Pegasus, and the horse threw Bellerophon to earth, crippling him for life. Pegasus continued on to Olympus and lived in Zeus's stables, where he became the steed of Eos, the goddess of dawn. At the end of his life, Pegasus was immortalized in the form of a constellation, or a group of stars in the night sky.

Pegasus in Context

For the ancient Greeks, Pegasus must have seemed a natural extension of the human dependence on horses for transportation and labor. Just as horses served their owners dutifully, Pegasus served the various gods and

Nationality/Culture
Greek

Pronunciation
PEG-uh-suhs

Alternate Names
None

Appears In
Ovid's *Metamorphoses*, Hesiod's *Theogony*

Lineage
Born from the blood of Medusa

heroes to whom he was pledged. His ability to fly may have reflected how people felt about travel by horseback, which was considerably faster than any other form of land travel available at the time.

Key Themes and Symbols

One theme found in the myths of Pegasus is faithfulness, or duty. The winged horse is a faithful servant of Perseus throughout his life, perhaps as a duty to the hero who caused Pegasus to be born. Later, he serves Bellerophon fearlessly in a dangerous battle. He does not deliberately betray Bellerophon by throwing him from his back, but merely reacts to Zeus's attempts to distract him. The golden bridle is a symbol of the faithfulness of Pegasus: he approaches Bellerophon as soon as he sees the bridle and allows the hero to ride him.

Pegasus in Art, Literature, and Everyday Life

The image of the winged horse Pegasus can be found throughout ancient and classical art, though not all winged horses are meant to represent

Pegasus. In modern times, Pegasus appeared in the 1981 film *Clash of the Titans* as the steed of Perseus, and played a prominent part in the 1997 Disney animated film *Hercules* as a companion to Hercules. Pegasus is the name of a spaceship in the updated *Battlestar Galactica* television series (2003). Pegasus is also the logo for TriStar Pictures and TriStar television, founded in the 1980s and now owned by Sony Pictures.

Read, Write, Think, Discuss

Airs Beneath the Moon (2006) by Toby Bishop, is a fantasy tale about a teenage farm girl named Larkyn who happens upon an abandoned pregnant mare who dies giving birth to a colt with wings. The colt bonds with Larkyn, and they soon find themselves attending the Academy of the Air, a training center for winged steeds and their riders. As the only person at the Academy not of noble birth, Larkyn struggles to fit in, but she soon discovers that she must foil the evil plans of a newly crowned, power-hungry duke who controls the bloodlines of the steeds.

SEE ALSO Bellerophon; Medusa; Muses; Perseus

Pele

Character Overview

In **Polynesian mythology**, Pele is the **fire** goddess of Hawaii. A powerful and destructive deity, she is said to live in the crater of the volcano of Kilauea (pronounced kee-law-AY-uh) on the big island of Hawaii. Perhaps the best-known deity of Hawaii, Pele appears in many myths and legends.

Major Myths

Like many figures in Polynesian mythology, Pele is a great traveler. She came to Hawaii from the island of Tahiti, but the reasons for her trip vary. Some myths say that she fled Tahiti to escape the anger of her older sister, whose husband she had stolen. In other stories, she was driven from Tahiti by her father, who did not condone her bad temper.

Nationality/Culture
Polynesian

Pronunciation
PAY-lay

Alternate Names
None

Appears In
Polynesian oral myths

Lineage
Daughter of Haumea and Kane Milohai

Pele's arrival in the Hawaiian Islands was accompanied by mighty volcanic eruptions. She visited various islands looking for a place to live, but the sea constantly flooded the sites she chose for a home. She finally found refuge in the volcano of Kilauea.

Once settled in Kilauea, Pele traveled to a neighboring island and fell in love with a young chief named Lohiau. After returning home, Pele sent her younger sister Hi'iaka (pronounced HEE-ee-ah-kah) to fetch the chief. She gave Hi'iaka supernatural powers, which the young woman used to overcome various obstacles during the journey.

When Hi'iaka arrived at the home of Lohiau, she found that the young chief had died of a broken heart caused by his longing for Pele. Hi'iaka caught his spirit and used her magical powers to restore him to life. Meanwhile, Pele became impatient, imagining that her sister had stolen Lohiau's love. The enraged Pele sent a stream of lava that killed Hopoe, Hi'iaka's dearest friend.

When Hi'iaka finally brought the young chief to Kilauea, she learned of the death of Hopoe. Grief stricken, she embraced Lohiau, whom she had come to love. Pele saw this and sent more lava to kill Lohiau. Protected by her magical powers, Hi'iaka later restored Lohiau to life again and went to live with him on his home island.

Many other legends deal with Pele's fiery temper and reveal how unpredictable and dangerous she could be. In some myths, she also appears as a water goddess who caused the seas to encircle the islands of Hawaii. Both Pele and Hi'iaka are considered goddesses of magic and sorcery as well as of the hula, the ancient sacred dance of Hawaii.

Pele in Context

Pele reflects attempts by the Hawaiian people to humanize the volcanoes that both shaped their homeland and have often threatened their very existence. Volcanoes are unpredictable and sometimes deadly. The depiction of this lava deity as a woman indicates a Hawaiian view of females as temperamental and prone to unpredictable moods and behaviors, or as shifting in personality. However, this may also reflect how Hawaiians interpreted some of the physical results of volcano activity. For example, winds around lava flows can create masses of long, thin strands of volcanic glass that resemble a woman's hair. These are commonly called "Pele's hair." Teardrop-shaped beads of volcanic rock are also common, and are known as "Pele's tears"—and would certainly reflect the unpredictable personality of an enraged lava goddess.

According to Polynesian stories, the powerful and destructive fire goddess Pele lives in the volcano of Kilauea on the island of Hawaii. WERNER FORMAN/ ART RESOURCE, NY.

Key Themes and Symbols

Pele symbolized rage, power, and unpredictability. She was the embodiment of the volcanoes that dominated the Hawaiian landscape. The volcano known as Kilauea is often considered to be a symbol of Pele. Rage is a key theme in the myths of Pele, and it plays a role in most of her actions. Her exile from Tahiti and the killing of Hopoe and Lohiau were both the result of rage caused by jealousy.

Pele in Art, Literature, and Everyday Life

Although Pele is one of the best-known deities in Polynesian mythology, she rarely appears in popular culture outside Hawaii. Singer and songwriter Tori Amos titled her 1996 album *Boys for Pele* in honor of the goddess, and the title characters of the 2005 film *The Adventures of Sharkboy and Lavagirl in 3-D* appear to be loosely based on Pele and her brother, who was a shark god.

Pele has also been the subject of a modern legend: in order to keep visitors from stealing rocks as souvenirs from Hawaii's volcano sites, a park ranger invented the myth that Pele would punish anyone who removed volcanic rock from Hawaii. The myth has been quite successful, resulting in many tourists sending stolen rocks back to Hawaii Volcanoes National Park in order to lift the "curse."

Read, Write, Think, Discuss

Many cultures view their gods and natural events in terms of human characteristics and emotions. The term for this is "anthropomorphism." An anthropomorphic view would see the violent and destructive eruption of a volcano as an expression of rage by the gods. Can you find contemporary examples of people viewing a deity or an act of nature in human terms? Do you think this is a helpful way of understanding the world around us? Why or why not?

SEE ALSO Polynesian Mythology

Penates

See **Lares and Penates.**

Penelope

Nationality/Culture
Greek/Roman

Pronunciation
puh-NEL-uh-pee

Alternate Names
None

Appears In
Homer's *Odyssey*

Lineage
Daughter of Icarius and Periboea

Character Overview

The wife of the hero **Odysseus** (pronounced oh-DIS-ee-uhs) in **Greek mythology**, Penelope was celebrated for her faithfulness, patience, and feminine virtue. For the twenty years that her husband was away during and after the Trojan War, Penelope remained true to him and helped prevent his kingdom from falling into other hands.

Penelope's parents were Prince Icarius (pronounced i-KAHR-ee-uhs) of Sparta and Periboea (pronounced pehr-ee-boh-EE-uh), a nymph, or female nature deity. Periboea hid her infant daughter as soon as she was born, knowing that Icarius had wanted a son. As soon as Icarius discovered the baby girl, he threw her into the sea to drown. But a family of ducks rescued her, and seeing this as an omen, or a sign from the gods, Icarius named the child Penelope (after the Greek word for "duck") and raised her as his favorite child.

When Penelope reached womanhood, Odysseus asked for her hand in marriage. Although reluctant to part with his daughter, Icarius agreed, and Penelope went with her new husband to his home on the island of Ithaca (pronounced ITH-uh-kuh). Penelope and Odysseus were deeply in love, so it was with great sorrow that Odysseus later left her and their infant son, Telemachus (pronounced tuh-LEM-uh-kuhs), to fight in the Trojan War.

The Trojan War lasted ten years, and it took Odysseus another ten years to get home to Ithaca. During that time, Penelope received the attentions of many suitors. For a while, she put them off by saying that she would consider marriage only after she finished weaving a shroud for her father-in-law, Laertes (pronounced lay-UR-teez), who was grieving over Odysseus's absence. Each day Penelope would sit weaving the cloth, but at night she would secretly unravel her work. After three years, a servant revealed Penelope's secret, and she had to finish the shroud. When her suitors became insistent again, Penelope announced that she would marry the man who could string a bow that Odysseus had left behind, and shoot an arrow through the loops on a row of twelve axe heads.

Unknown to Penelope, Odysseus had arrived home disguised as a beggar. He wanted to review the situation in his kingdom before revealing his return. The disguised Odysseus won the archery contest and then killed all the suitors with help from his son Telemachus. At first Penelope would not believe that Odysseus was her husband, for the gods had hidden his identity from her. However, Odysseus revealed his true identity by telling Penelope a secret about their marriage that only they knew—that one leg of their bed was made from a still-living olive tree—and the loving couple were finally reunited.

Penelope in Context

Penelope is generally viewed as a reflection of the ancient Greek idea of the perfect wife. She is dutiful, caring for the kingdom while Odysseus is away, and she remains faithful to him despite the many suitors that gather around her. She is also clever, as illustrated by her nightly unraveling of the shroud she weaved, as well as her statement that she would marry the man who could string Odysseus's bow, since she knew no other man could perform the feat. There are passages in the ***Odyssey*** that indicate Penelope was occasionally torn in her devotion to Odysseus, and was even considering choosing one of the suitors. However, as a woman who waited twenty years for her husband's return, fending off over one hundred suitors and enduring the vengeance of gods and goddesses, Penelope undoubtedly served as an example of what ancient Greek husbands hoped for in their wives.

Key Themes and Symbols

Penelope has traditionally been viewed as a symbol of faithfulness and fidelity. The theme of fidelity is an important part of the myth of Penelope, and is shown in her refusal to entertain other suitors in the twenty years her husband is gone. It is also shown in her attempts to keep suitors at bay by unraveling her woven cloth every night, in the hope that Odysseus would return before her trick was discovered. The marriage bed of Penelope and Odysseus also symbolizes their love, with one leg rooted deep into the ground and still alive despite the years.

Penelope in Art, Literature, and Everyday Life

Penelope was the subject of a 1907 opera by the same name composed by Gabriel Fauré. Penelope also appears in the 2004 novel *Waiting for Odysseus* by Clemence McLaren, part of which is written from her point of view. In other media, the myth of Penelope was referenced in the television show *Lost*, in which a character named Penny (short for Penelope) loses her true love as he sails around the world; Penny's faithfulness and dedication in searching for her love leads her to the strange island where he has become trapped.

Read, Write, Think, Discuss

The Penelopiad by Margaret Atwood (2005) offers a darkly humorous retelling of the events of the *Odyssey* from Penelope's point of view. Atwood's version of the tale is quite different from the original myth, with Penelope no longer cast in the role of the eternally faithful wife.

SEE ALSO Greek Mythology; Odysseus; *Odyssey, The*

Persephone

Character Overview

In **Greek mythology**, Persephone was the beautiful daughter of **Zeus** (pronounced ZOOS), king of the gods, and of **Demeter** (pronounced di-MEE-ter), the goddess of agriculture. Persephone became queen of the **underworld**, or land of the dead, when she married **Hades** (pronounced HAY-deez). The Romans knew her as Proserpina (pronounced proh-SUR-puh-nuh).

Major Myths

As a young girl, Persephone traveled around the world with her mother, who ruled over the earth and everything that grew from it. Hades, the god of the underworld, wanted her for his wife. He spoke to his brother Zeus, who agreed to help him. One day Zeus caused a beautiful flower to grow in a place where Persephone was walking. The girl stooped to admire the flower. At that moment, Hades rode out of the underworld on a chariot, seized Persephone, and took her back to his kingdom.

Nationality/Culture
Greek

Pronunciation
per-SEF-uh-nee

Alternate Names
Proserpina (Roman)

Appears In
Ovid's *Metamorphoses*, Hesiod's *Theogony*

Lineage
Daughter of Zeus and Demeter

Unaware of these events, Demeter searched everywhere for her missing daughter. For days she wandered the earth with a flaming torch in each hand and, in her distress, caused all crops to wither and die. Famine threatened. Zeus feared that humankind would perish, leaving no one to perform sacrifices to the gods. He begged Demeter to restore life to the earth, but she refused to do so unless Persephone was returned to her.

Zeus sent Hermes (pronounced HUR-meez), messenger of the gods, to fetch Persephone from the underworld. As she was leaving, Hades gave her a sweet pomegranate, and she ate several of its seeds. Persephone did not realize that eating food from the underworld meant that she could not leave it. As a result, Zeus declared that Persephone would have to spend part of each year in the underworld with Hades and the remainder of the year on earth with her mother.

Persephone in Context

The story of Persephone was used by ancient Greeks and Romans to explain the cycle of the seasons. For most of the year, the earth is alive and covered with growing plants. However, during the barren months when Persephone is with Hades—generally one month for every pomegranate seed she ate, though different versions mention three, four, or even five seeds—Demeter mourns her daughter's absence, and the earth lies bare and lifeless. This use of myth to explain things in the natural world is common to all mythologies around the globe. Myths concerning the origin of the seasons are especially common in cultures centered on agriculture, as ancient Greece was. This reflects an understanding of how the seasons affect crop growth, and the importance of **sun** and rain in the plant growth cycle.

Key Themes and Symbols

Persephone is a symbol of growth and fertility. Although Demeter is generally recognized as the source of growth and fertility, Persephone is often viewed as a younger version of Demeter. The myth of Persephone also contains the theme of innocence lost: after she is abducted by Hades, she is no longer the carefree youth she once was, even during her time away from the underworld. In the myth, the pomegranate offered by Hades represents temptation. Its sweet appearance lures Persephone into tasting some of its seeds, which binds her to the land of the dead forever.

Persephone in Art, Literature, and Everyday Life

Persephone was a very popular subject in ancient art, appearing on many vases and in several surviving sculptures. Persephone was also the subject of a famous sculpture by Giovanni Bernini, as well as paintings by Dante Rossetti and Frederic Leighton, among many others. Although the mythical character of Persephone seldom appears in modern literature or other media, many characters or objects bearing her name have appeared in television series, video games, films, and songs. She has also lent her name to an asteroid, a publishing company, and even a musical instrument.

Read, Write, Think, Discuss

The pomegranate originally came from the Indian subcontinent, but has been cultivated throughout the Mediterranean region since ancient time. It has deep cultural significance in many Near Eastern civilizations. Today, it is a popular ingredient in everything from health drinks to beauty creams. Using your library, the Internet, and other available sources, find out more about the cultural history of the pomegranate—that is, how it is viewed and used by different cultures—and write a paper tracing the pomegranate's history from ancient to modern times.

SEE ALSO Demeter; Hades; Underworld

Perseus

Nationality/Culture
Greek/Roman

Pronunciation
PUR-see-uhs

Alternate Names
None

Appears In
Ovid's *Metamorphoses*, Hesiod's *Theogony*

Lineage
Son of Zeus and Danaë

Character Overview

In **Greek mythology**, Perseus was the heroic slayer of the Gorgon **Medusa** (pronounced meh-DOO-suh). His mother was **Danaë** (pronounced DAN-uh-ee), daughter of King Acrisius (pronounced uh-KRIZ-ee-uhs) of Argos. Before Perseus's birth, an oracle—or person who could communicate with the gods—predicted that Danaë would bear a child who would one day kill his grandfather. Terrified by this prediction, Acrisius imprisoned his daughter in a tower. However, Danaë received a visit in the tower from **Zeus** (pronounced ZOOS), the king of the gods, who had taken the form of a shower of gold, and she became pregnant with Zeus's child.

After Danaë gave birth to Perseus, Acrisius had his daughter and her child locked in a box, which he threw into the sea. The box came ashore on the island of Seriphos (pronounced SEHR-uh-fohs) and was found by Dictys (pronounced DIK-tis), a fisherman. Dictys sheltered Danaë and Perseus in his home, and they remained with him for many years.

When Perseus had grown into a young man, King Polydectes (pronounced pol-ee-DEK-teez) of Seriphos fell in love with Danaë and tried to persuade her to marry him. Danaë refused, and Perseus protected his mother from the king's unwanted advances. Hoping to rid himself of Perseus, Polydectes set him a seemingly impossible task: to obtain the head of Medusa, a monster so hideous that anyone who even glanced at her face turned to stone.

Perseus received gifts from the gods **Hermes** (pronounced HUR-meez) and **Athena** (pronounced uh-THEE-nuh) to help him in his task: a pair of winged sandals, an adamantine sword, a helmet that made the wearer invisible, and a bronze shield that was polished to shine like a mirror. Perseus then visited the Graeae (pronounced GREE-ee), three old hags who were sisters of the **Gorgons** and who shared a single eye. Seizing their eye, he demanded to know where he could find the Gorgons. When they told him, Perseus threw the eye into a lake so that the Graeae could not warn their sisters.

With the winged sandals, Perseus flew to the home of the Gorgons. When he reached their cave, he advanced toward Medusa using Athena's shield as a mirror to avoid looking directly at the monster. Then he took the sword and cut off Medusa's head, which he placed in a bag. Several drops of Medusa's blood touched the ground and changed into the winged horse **Pegasus** (pronounced PEG-uh-suhs). Wearing the helmet that made him invisible, Perseus flew off on Pegasus.

On his way home, Perseus came upon the giant, **Atlas** (pronounced AT-luhs), who held up the sky. Atlas tried to stop Perseus, but the hero took out the head of Medusa and turned the giant to stone. Next, Perseus saw a beautiful woman chained to a rock. This was **Andromeda** (pronounced an-DROM-i-duh), left as a **sacrifice** to a sea monster after her mother, Cassiopea (pronounced kas-ee-oh-PEE-uh), had boasted of her beauty and offended the sea god **Poseidon** (pronounced poh-SYE-dun). Perseus killed the sea monster, rescued Andromeda, and asked her to marry him.

Arriving back on the island of Seriphos, Perseus found that his mother had taken refuge in the temple of Athena to avoid the advances of Polydectes. Furious, Perseus used Medusa's head to turn Polydectes and his soldiers to stone. Perseus returned the winged sandals, helmet, and shield to the gods and gave the head of Medusa to Athena, who placed it on her shield. He then took Andromeda to Argos, the kingdom of his grandfather Acrisius.

Hearing that Perseus had arrived, Acrisius fled to a region of Greece known as Thessaly (pronounced THESS-uh-lee), mindful of the prophecy made years before. Later, however, Perseus took part in an athletic contest there and threw a discus—a heavy disc thrown for sport—that accidentally killed Acrisius. The prophecy was fulfilled.

Perseus in Context

The myth of Perseus is largely meant to warn ancient Greeks against trying to escape fate or the will of the gods. Perseus serves as an instrument of fate and the gods to carry out events in the human realm.

This reflects the ancient view that the gods were often not direct players in the affairs of humans, but acted indirectly to sway events. This helped to explain why gods were not seen interacting directly on a daily basis with humans.

Key Themes and Symbols

The intervention of the gods in the world of humans is an important theme in the story of Perseus. Zeus first intervenes by visiting Danaë in the form of a shower of gold and conceiving Perseus. Later, when Perseus is sent on an almost impossible mission to bring back the head of Medusa, Athena and Hermes intervene by providing him with weapons and armor. The inescapable nature of fate is also an important theme in the tale of Perseus. Acrisius tries to escape his fate on many occasions: he locks his daughter in a tower so she cannot have a child; after she has a son, Acrisius seals both mother and son in a box and sends them out to sea; and much later, when Acrisius discovers that Perseus is still alive, he flees to another region of Greece. In the end, Acrisius cannot escape his fate and is accidentally killed by his grandson during an athletic event.

Perseus in Art, Literature, and Everyday Life

Perseus was a popular hero in ancient Greek and Roman art, appearing frequently on pottery and in murals. He has been the subject of famous sculptures by Benvenuto Cellini, Antonio Canova, and Salvador Dali, and paintings by artists such as Piero di Cosimo and Edward Burne-Jones. In modern times, the myth of Perseus was used as the main storyline for the 1981 fantasy film *Clash of the Titans*, although some elements of the myth were changed. The actor who played Perseus in the movie, Harry Hamlin, also provided the voice of Perseus—this time portrayed as a villain—in the PlayStation 2 video game *God of War II*.

Read, Write, Think, Discuss

Legends about **heroes** often include tales about the slaying of great monsters or beasts, such as the sea monster Perseus defeats in order to save Andromeda. Although this theme is also found in stories today, modern heroes are often depicted fighting against human enemies, such as criminals. Why do you think older mythologies placed a strong emphasis on defeating beasts? Why do you think modern legends focus instead on human foes?

SEE ALSO Andromeda; Athena; Atlas; Danaë; Gorgons; Heroes; Medusa; Pegasus

Persian Mythology

Persian Mythology in Context

Persian mythology developed in what is now Iran around 1500 BCE. About a thousand years later, a religion known as Zoroastrianism (pronounced zor-oh-AS-tree-uhn-iz-m) emerged in the region. It held on to many of the earlier beliefs but added new themes, gods, and myths. The result was a mythology based on a vision of grand-scale conflict between good and evil.

The roots of Persian mythology lie in the steppes—grass-covered plains—of southern Russia and Central Asia. Between 1500 and 1000 BCE, Indo-European peoples migrated south from the steppes into the regions now known as Turkey, Iran, and northern India. Those who settled in Iran became the Persians. Their mythology had much in common with that of the early Hindus and probably developed from a common source. In time, the Persians also absorbed influences from an area called Mesopotamia (pronounced mess-uh-puh-TAY-mee-uh) on their western border.

A religious leader named Zoroaster (pronounced ZOR-oh-as-tur; probably born around 628 BCE), founded the faith that was most popular in Persia until the arrival of Islam in the 600s CE. The best information about Persian mythology comes from Zoroastrianism's sacred book, the *Zend-Avesta* or *Avesta*. Much of the original *Zend-Avesta* was lost after Alexander the Great conquered Persia in 334 BCE. What survives is a set of writings gathered and arranged between 200 and 600 CE. One section, the *Gathas*, consists of songs believed to have been composed by Zoroaster. Much mythological material can be found in another section containing *Yashts*, hymns addressed to **angels** and **heroes**.

Core Deities and Characters

The driving forces of Persian mythology were two powerful gods, sometimes presented as twin brothers: **Ahura Mazda** (pronounced ah-HOO-ruh MAHZ-duh), the creator god of light, truth, and goodness; and his enemy **Ahriman** (pronounced AH-ri-muhn), the spirit of darkness, lies, and evil who created only destructive things, such as vermin, disease, and demons. The world was their battlefield, and, although they were equally matched during this period of history, Ahura Mazda was fated to win the fight. For this reason, Ahura Mazda, the Wise Lord, was the most important deity or god of Persian mythology. The Zoroastrians identified him with **fire**, and tended fires on towers as part of their worship.

The ancient Persian pantheon—collection of recognized gods—also included **Mithras** (pronounced MITH-rahs), a god associated with war, the **sun**, and law and order. Anahita (pronounced ah-nuh-HEE-tuh) was a goddess of water and fertility. Bahram, a god of war and victory, appeared on earth in ten forms: as wind, a bull, a horse, a camel, a boar, a youth, a raven, a ram, a buck, and a man. Zoroaster reduced the role of these and other traditional deities and emphasized Ahura Mazda as the supreme god. Religious scholars see this move as an early step toward monotheism, or the belief in a single, powerful god. However, Ahura Mazda was said to have created seven archangels, called the Amesha Spentas, who represented truth, power, immortality (ability to live forever), and other aspects of his being. These archangels may have taken over some features of the pre-Zoroastrian gods.

Perhaps influenced by stargazing Babylonian (pronounced bab-uh-LOH-nee-uhn) astronomers, the ancient Persians associated some of their deities with the stars. The star Sirius (pronounced SEER-ee-uhs) represented the rain god Tishtrya, whose main role was to battle Apausha, an evil star of drought. Tishtrya, in the form of a white stallion, and Apausha, in the form of a hideous black horse, fought for three days. Then with Ahura Mazda's help, Tishtrya defeated Apausha. Tishtrya and other star gods who protected agriculture also took charge of battling meteors, or shooting stars, which the Persians believed to be witches.

Heroes and kings also figured in Persian myth and legend. The hero Threataona battled Azhi Dahaka, a three-headed demon controlled by Ahriman. When Threataona stabbed the demon in the chest, snakes and lizards poured from the wound. To prevent the demon from poisoning the world, Thraetaona locked him inside a mountain where he will remain until the world comes to an end. At that time Azhi Dahaka will break free, but another hero, Keresaspa, will kill him.

The legendary King Bahram Gur appeared often in poems and tales as the inventor of poetry and as a mighty hunter. The greatest hero was the warrior Rustum, whose adventures appear in the epic *Shah Namah* (*Book of Kings*), written by the poet Firdawsi around 1010 CE.

Major Myths

Ahura Mazda made the world. Creation began when he cast a beam of his pure light into the empty void between him and Ahriman, who had attacked him. Ahura Mazda uttered a prayer that silenced Ahriman for three thousand years. Ahura Mazda created the Amesha Spentas, or archangels, and the Yazatas (pronounced yah-ZAH-tuhz), divine beings. His final creation was Gayomart, the first man. Ahriman then awoke and began his evil work, sending a female demon to make Gayomart sicken and die.

Gayomart's body became the silver and gold in the earth, and in death he fertilized the ground so that a plant grew and became a man and a woman. These two people, Masha and Mashyoi, were the parents of the human race. Ahriman deceived them into thinking that he was their creator, and when they repeated this lie, evil and suffering entered the world. Zoroastrians believed that after three thousand years, Zoroaster came into the world to break Ahriman's hold, leaving the two powers to fight into the future.

The legend of Rustum shows the part human heroes play in the great drama of good and evil. Rustum was so strong and brave that the king made him head of the army. Then the White Demon seized the king, and Rustum set out to rescue him. In the course of his travels, Rustum encountered a lion, a desert, a dragon, a demoness, and a demon army. He overcame all these obstacles with the help of his faithful horse Ruksh and a warrior named Aulad, whom he defeated in combat and who then became an ally. Rustum's adventure ended in a cave, the lair of the White Demon, where Rustum tore out the demon's heart.

Death in Persian mythology involved a journey into the **afterlife**. The soul of the dead person had to cross a bridge called Chinvat. Good souls found the bridge to be a wide and comfortable beam leading to **heaven**. For the wicked, it was a razor-sharp blade from which they fell headlong into **hell**.

Zoroastrianism was one of the first belief systems to include a vision of the end of the world. It would be signaled by the appearance of three saviors, sons of Zoroaster. Upon the arrival of Hushedar, the first savior, the sun would stand still for ten days, and people would stop eating meat. When Hushedar-mar, the second savior, appeared, the sun would halt for twenty days, and people would stop drinking milk. Just as the world neared a state of purity, however, the evil demon Azhi Dahaka would break free from his mountain prison. Only after he had been killed would Soshyant, the third savior, arrive. People would stop eating plants and live only on water, and each soldier of good would fight and defeat a particular evil enemy. Then the world would be enveloped in fire and molten metal for three days. Everyone who has ever lived would return to life to cross the fire, but only the wicked would suffer from the heat. This final judgment would purge sin and evil from the world, leaving an innocent human race in a cleansed world to worship Ahura Mazda.

Key Themes and Symbols

The main theme of Persian mythology was the battle between good and evil. Ahura Mazda and Ahriman were not the only ones involved. Hosts of Yazatas and good spirits (*ashavans*) fought on Ahura Mazda's side. Ahriman headed an army of evil spirits known as *dregvants*, and demons called *devas* (pronounced DAY-vuhz). Humans took part in the conflict as well. Each person had to choose whether to follow the truth or the lie. Plants, animals, and other things could be good or evil, depending on whether Ahura Mazda or Ahriman created and controlled them. This theme is also shown in the story of the hero Rustum, and in the final battle between Azhi Dahaka and the sons of Zoroaster.

Another theme found in Persian mythology is judgment in the afterlife. This is shown in the idea of the Chinvat bridge, where people are judged according to their deeds while living, and are either rewarded or punished based on those deeds. This theme also plays a critical role in the final judgment that takes place after Azhi Dahaka is defeated: only those with pure spirits would be reborn into the world, while impure souls would burn in fire.

Persian Mythology in Art, Literature, and Everyday Life

Persian religion and mythology had a far-reaching influence. Historians of mythology think that certain beliefs in the Jewish, Christian, and Islamic faiths probably grew out of Persian traditions. The tendency of Zoroastrianism toward monotheism—the belief in one god—may also have helped shape those faiths.

Unlike some ancient belief systems, Persian mythology remains alive outside the covers of old books. It has survived continuously for thousands of years, and isolated groups of Iranians still worship Ahura Mazda. Other Zoroastrian communities exist in India, where the descendants of immigrants from Iran are known as Parsis or Parsees, a reference to their Persian origin.

As the most important god in Persian mythology, Ahura Mazda was well-represented in ancient art, and many stone reliefs and statues of the god have been found at ancient Persian sites. But as the religion became less popular over the centuries, depictions of Ahura Mazda also became less abundant. Recently, however, Ahura Mazda has seen new life as a character in comic books. Notable appearances include the long-running DC Comics series *Wonder Woman*, and the miniseries *Dawn: Lucifer's Halo* by Joseph Michael Linsner (1999). Similarly, Ahriman has appeared several times in the *Final Fantasy* video game series as an enemy to be fought by the player. In the series, he takes the names Ahriman and Angra Mainyu, and is usually depicted as a winged monster with a single eye. Ahriman has also appeared as a demon in the DC Comics series *Wonder Woman*.

Read, Write, Think, Discuss

Much of Persian mythology is based on the idea of a good or positive force battling an evil force for control of humankind. This theme is one of the most enduring in all of modern storytelling. List three different examples of this theme that you have encountered in books you have read or movies you have seen. They can be based on true stories or they can be fictional. Are there similarities between the way the various "good sides" are depicted? How about the "evil sides" and their depictions? Are there any important differences?

SEE ALSO Ahriman; Ahura Mazda; Angels

Phoenix

Character Overview

The phoenix is a legendary bird mentioned in Greek, Roman, and **Egyptian mythology**. According to ancient writers, the phoenix lived for five hundred years, then died and was reborn. It had brilliant golden and scarlet feathers and grew to the size of an eagle.

Just before dying, the phoenix built a nest of fragrant herbs and spices, including cinnamon and myrrh. Then it set the nest on **fire** and died in the flames. A new phoenix then arose from the ashes. According to Egyptian myth, when the young bird was strong enough, it placed the ashes of the dead phoenix in an egg made of myrrh. Then the young

Nationality/Culture
Greek, Roman, Egyptian

Pronunciation
FEE-niks

Alternate Names
Bennu (Egyptian)

Appears In
Ovid's *Metamorphoses*, Herodotus's *Histories*

Lineage
Unknown

The phoenix is a legendary bird that died in flames and then rose from the ashes to live again. THE ART ARCHIVE/BODLEIAN LIBRARY OXFORD/THE PICTURE DESK, INC.

phoenix carried the egg to Heliopolis (pronounced hee-lee-OP-uh-luhs), the Egyptian city of the **sun**, and placed it on the altar of the sun god **Ra**.

The Phoenix in Context

The myth of the phoenix may reflect ancient observations of nature, particularly in areas of fire. When many types of hardwood trees are burned to ash in a fire, they return important minerals such as potassium to the soil. This fertilizes the soil to help more trees and vegetation grow. In this way, fire destroys the existing trees, and their ashes provide a way for new trees to appear—much like the myth of the phoenix. Indeed, the creation of the fertilizing compound potash from the ashes of trees was a lucrative business in Europe for centuries, and continues even today.

Key Themes and Symbols

The phoenix was associated with immortality—the ability to live forever—and rebirth. Early Christians saw the phoenix as a symbol of resurrection, or the act of rising from the dead. The main theme of the myth of the phoenix is the eternal or everlasting nature of the spirit, with the phoenix symbolizing that spirit. In the myth, fire represents death as the bird is consumed in flames.

The Phoenix in Art, Literature, and Everyday Life

The phoenix was a popular figure in many cultures beyond Egypt. Romans used it on coins to symbolize Rome, the Eternal City. The bird also appears as a sacred figure in both Chinese and **Japanese mythology**, and was the subject of Japanese comic creator Osamu Tezuka's masterwork, a twelve-book series titled simply *Phoenix*. More than one American comic book character has gone by the identity of Phoenix, most notably several characters in the Marvel Comic Universe. Albus Dumbledore, the headmaster of Hogwarts School in J. K. Rowling's Harry Potter series, has a phoenix named Fawkes. The name has also been used by a number of cities and places around the world that have been "reborn" from previous settlements, most notably Phoenix, Arizona.

Read, Write, Think, Discuss

The idea of something new rising from the ashes of something older is taken from the myth of the phoenix. In modern times, this idea is often used when referring to rebuilding in the wake of tragedies or disasters, such as the destruction of the World Trade Center or the flooding of New Orleans during Hurricane Katrina. In what ways do these events function as modern versions of the myth of the phoenix? Can you think of other examples?

Pluto

See **Hades.**

Polynesian Mythology

Polynesian Mythology in Context

Polynesia is a vast region of the Pacific Ocean consisting of many hundreds of widely separated, culturally and politically diverse island groups. Ranging from Midway and Hawaii in the north to New Zealand in the south, the triangular area called Polynesia also includes Tahiti, Samoa, Tonga, Tuamotu (pronounced too-ah-MOH-too), the Cook Islands, and the Pitcairn Islands. Although the mythology of Polynesia varies from one island to the next, many of the basic stories, themes, and gods are surprisingly similar throughout the region.

Scholars believe that humans first migrated to Polynesia from Southeast Asia about two thousand years ago. These people carried with them their mythological traditions about events, deities, and **heroes**. As time passed and people moved to different island groups, they adapted their mythology and religious beliefs to suit their new environments. In the process, they added new characters and events to the traditional myths and legends. Nevertheless, the basic elements of religion and myth remained relatively unchanged throughout the island groups, and a fairly distinct pantheon—group of recognized gods and goddesses—emerged.

Polynesian religion and mythology placed great emphasis on nature, particularly the ocean environment. The Polynesians became masters of navigation and other seafaring skills, and their religion and myths strongly reflected the importance of nature and the sea. Polynesians believed that all things in nature, including humans, contained a sacred and supernatural power called mana. Mana could be good or evil, and individuals, animals, and objects contained varying amounts of mana.

Because mana was sacred, Polynesians invented complicated rules—known as *tapus*, the source of the word "taboo"—to protect it. For example, ordinary people were not allowed to touch even the shadow of a great chief, nor could they step inside sacred groves or temples. The punishment for breaking important rules was often death, while illness and misfortune were believed to be the penalties for breaking minor tapus.

The Polynesian religion included many gods, local deities as well as the great gods of their pantheon. The people felt a close personal connection to their deities and to the various heroes, demigods (half human and half god), and **tricksters** of their mythology. The most popular character was **Maui** (pronounced MOU-ee), a hero-trickster well known throughout Polynesia.

Worship of the gods involved chants and prayers, elaborate rituals or ceremonies, and sacrifices (including human sacrifice). Magic was also important among the Polynesians, who used chants, charms, and spells to summon the gods or ask for their guidance or assistance. Priests usually organized and led religious festivals and celebrations. In some places, special groups consisting of storytellers, musicians, dancers, and other performers took charge of staging ceremonial activities. Sacred ceremonies often included singing, dancing, storytelling, and dramatic performances. The Hawaiian hula dance originated as a sacred ceremonial dance.

Core Deities and Characters

The most important gods of the Polynesian pantheon were those associated with creation myths and legends. Best known were Rangi (pronounced RANG-gee, meaning Father Sky) and Papa (Mother Earth), the two supreme creator gods of the Maori people of New Zealand. According to Maori legend, **Rangi and Papa** served as the source from which all things came.

The counterparts of Rangi and Papa in Hawaiian mythology were Ao and Po. Ao represented the male force in the universe and was associated with the sky, the day, and light. Po, the feminine force, was linked with the earth, darkness, and night. According to Hawaiian myth,

Polynesian Deities

Haumia: god of wild plants and vegetables.

Kamapua'a: pig god.

Kane: god of creation and growth.

Ku: creator god.

Lono: god of the heavens.

Maui: trickster god and hero.

Oro: war god.

Papa, Po: supreme creator goddess, mother earth.

Pele: fire goddess.

Rangi, Ao: supreme creator god, father sky.

Rongo: god of cultivated plants.

Ta'aroa, Rua-i-tupra: supreme creator god.

Tane: god of the forest.

Tangaroa, Kanaloa, Tangaloa: god of the seas.

Tawhiri: god of the wind and storms.

Tu: god of war.

a creator god named Ku separated Ao from Po. Ku then worked with Lono, god of the heavens, and Kane, the chief god of generation and growth, to create the earth and all living things. After Kane made the first man and woman, he became angry at their bad behavior and decided that humans would be subject to death. He then left the earth and went to live in **heaven**.

In Tahitian mythology, the supreme creator deity was Ta'aroa (pronounced tah-uh-ROH-uh), also called Rua-i-tupra (source of growth). Ta'aroa emerged from an ancient egg and started the process of creation. To fill the emptiness around him, he used part of the egg to make the sky and the other part to create the earth. Satisfied with his accomplishment, he filled the world with all the creatures and things that are now found in it. The Tahitians believed that Ta'aroa sent both blessings and curses, and they tried to appease him with human sacrifices.

The Maori version of Ta'aroa was Tangaroa, a god of the sea and child of Rangi and Papa. According to legend, Tangaroa fled to the sea to escape the wrath of his brother Tawhiri (pronounced tah-FEE-ree), the storm god. Tangaroa later quarreled with another brother, the forest god Tane (pronounced TAH-nee), and forever after he enjoyed sinking

The carving on this **hei tiki** *jade pendant is a fertility symbol in the mythology of the Maori people of New Zealand. The figure represents the first man, Tiki, in the stories of other Polynesians.* WERNER FORMAN/ART RESOURCE, NY.

canoes made from wood from Tane's forests. In Hawaiian mythology, Tangaroa was called Kanaloa, and the Hawaiian counterpart of Tane was Kane. The Samoans and Tongans knew Tangaroa as Tangaloa.

Perhaps the best-known and most feared deity in Hawaii was the **fire** goddess **Pele** (pronounced PAY-lay), a violent figure associated with volcanoes. Renowned for her beauty but also for her ability to destroy, Pele symbolized the power of natural forces. Many Hawaiian legends deal with her unpredictable temper and dangerous nature.

Another prominent deity in Hawaiian mythology was Kamapua'a (pronounced kah-mah-poo-AH-uh), the pig god. Known both for his warlike nature and for his romantic exploits, this energetic god appeared in many tales. The Hawaiians often sought Kamapua'a as an ally during war and used his adventures to explain various natural phenomena.

By far the most popular figure in Polynesian mythology was Maui, the trickster god and hero. Though small in stature, he displayed amazing strength and had various magical powers. The many tales about his adventures reveal a cunning and determined hero who performed many great and wondrous deeds, including creating the Pacific islands with a magical hook and providing humans with more hours of daylight by slowing the **sun**'s passage across the sky. Maui also tried, but failed, to become immortal (able to live forever).

Major Myths

The best-known myths in Polynesia deal with creation and with the origin of gods, humans, and other living things. The adventures of characters such as Pele and Maui also figure prominently. Some Polynesian myths describe creation as a process of growth or evolution from a state of disorder, nothingness, or darkness. The Hawaiian myths of Ao and Po, the male and female forces of the universe, reflect this idea. From a great watery chaos at the beginning of time, the creator god Ku separated Ao and Po, thus producing day and night and making the world possible.

Other Polynesian creation myths focus on a pre-existing creator who lives alone and forms all things from nothingness. This idea is expressed in stories from Samoa and Tonga about Tangaloa. According to legend, while Tangaloa ruled over a vast expanse of ocean, his messenger, the bird Tuli, searched endlessly for somewhere to rest. Tangaloa eventually threw some rocks into the water, and these became the islands of Samoa and Tonga.

In the Maori creation myth, two primal beings—Te Po (Night) and Te Kore (Darkness)—existed in a realm of nothingness at the beginning of time. From them sprang Rangi and Papa, the first gods of the universe. For many ages, Rangi and Papa were locked in an embrace, and their offspring, including numerous gods, were caught between them. The gods grew weary of their confinement and finally separated Rangi from Papa, thus providing room for themselves and for all things to grow and multiply.

The origin of humans and other living things is explained in various ways. According to myths about Tangaloa, after he created the islands of

Captain Cook and the Gods

In 1778 English explorer Captain James Cook became the first European to visit the Hawaiian Islands. He arrived during a period of political turmoil, and some scholars believe that a misunderstanding about the native religion cost him his life. When Cook came ashore, the people thought that he was the god Lono. They escorted him to their temple, where he took part in their rituals, unaware that doing so confirmed their beliefs that he was Lono. The Hawaiians believed that Lono would ritually "die" and then leave them. Cook left, but soon returned, which confused the islanders. Anxious to make sure that Lono died as he was supposed to, the Hawaiians killed Cook.

the Pacific, he used a vine to cover the bare land and provide shade. The vine spread, and parts of it decayed and became full of maggots. Tangaloa took the maggots and shaped them into humans. When he gave them a heart and soul, they came to life. In Maori myth, several of the gods—especially Tane-mahuta, Tangaroa, and Rongo-ma-tane (the god of cultivated crops)—played an active role in creating lands, plants, and humans. According to some legends, all living creatures, including humans, emerged from Tangaroa's vast body.

In another myth, the god Tane went searching for a wife. He united with several different beings and produced mountains, rivers, and other living and nonliving things. Tane longed for a partner with a human shape, however, so he formed a woman out of sand and breathed life into her. This woman's name was Hine-hauone (Earth-formed Maiden), and she had a daughter named Hine-titama (Dawn Maiden). Tane later took the girl—who did not know he was her father—as his wife, and they had many children. When Hine-titama discovered Tane's identity, she fled to the **underworld**, or land of the dead, dragging her children after her. The relationship between Tane and his daughter resulted in the arrival of death for humans.

A Hawaiian myth tells how Kane longed for a companion in his own image. His mother, Papatuanuku (pronounced pah-pah-too-ah-NOO-koo), told him to make a likeness of himself from clay and to embrace it. When he did as she suggested, the clay figure came to life and became the first woman.

Numerous myths explain the origin of various plant foods and other items of value. According to some stories, humans had to steal food from the gods or trick them into giving up certain foods. In other stories, the gods felt sorry for humans and generously gave food to them. A number of myths also explain that foods were the offspring of a particular god or grew from part of the body of a god.

The yam, or sweet potato, is one of the basic food crops of Polynesia. A number of myths explain the origin of this important food. One Maori (pronounced MAH-aw-ree) myth tells how the god Rongo-maui went to heaven to see his brother Wahnui (pronounced wah-NOO-ee), the guardian of the yam. Rongo-maui stole the yam, hid it in his clothing, and returned to earth. Soon after, his wife Pani became pregnant, and she later gave birth to a yam, the first on earth. Rongo-maui gave this food to humans.

Some Polynesian myths tell about characters who possessed extraordinary or supernatural powers and acted as miracle workers, mischief makers, or tricksters. The Hawaiians called these figures *kapua* (pronounced kah-POO-ah) and loved to hear about their many adventures. The kapua were often raised by grandparents who used magic to help them in their adventures. They generally grew up to be monstrous creatures who could change shape and perform great feats of strength. Among the more popular tales were those in which the kapua slayed monsters, rescued maidens, defeated rivals, and competed with the gods.

Key Themes and Symbols

As in many cultures around the world, one of the main themes in Polynesian mythology is creation as an act of the gods. This theme occurs in origin myths about men and women, as well as plants and animals important to the region. Central to the theme of creation is the idea of overcoming nothingness or darkness in order to bring the world into being—another element common to many of the world's mythologies.

Another theme in Polynesian mythology is that of humans having to deal with uncooperative or unfriendly gods in some way. This is shown in myths about humans acquiring different types of foods by stealing them from the gods or tricking the gods into providing them. This is seen in the myth of Maui, often identified more as a hero to humans

Captain James Cook visited the Hawaiian islands in 1778. When he came ashore, the people mistook him for one of their gods. This illustration shows the Hawaiians offering gifts to the English captain. © PRIVATE COLLECTION/THE STAPLETON COLLECTION/THE BRIDGEMAN ART LIBRARY.

than as a god, who tries to trick the goddess Hina into making him immortal.

Polynesian Mythology in Art, Literature, and Everyday Life

Maui is perhaps best known for lending his name to one of the Hawaiian Islands, and sometimes appears in art carvings of the Pacific Islanders. His hook, which was used to pull the islands to the surface of the ocean, is also a popular object represented in Polynesian art. With the introduction of Christianity to Polynesia in the 1700s, traditional religious beliefs began to fade. Although the Polynesian gods no longer play a major religious role in most parts of the region, the rich heritage of myths and legends remains part of the literature, folklore, and imagination of native cultures.

Read, Write, Think, Discuss

The idea that people must struggle against uncooperative gods is not unique to Polynesian mythology. Using your library, the Internet, or other available resources, research one culture whose principal deity is friendly and protective, and one whose principal deity is stern and more likely to punish. Why do you think some cultures primarily view gods as unfriendly, while others view them mostly as protectors and providers? Does this reflect a different cultural view of the world, or the different environments in which these cultures exist?

SEE ALSO Creation Stories; Maui; Melanesian Mythology; Micronesian Mythology; Pele; Rangi and Papa; Tricksters

Popol Vuh

Myth Overview

The *Popol Vuh*, a book of myths belonging to the Quiché (pronounced kee-CHAY) Mayans of highland Guatemala, is divided into five parts. The first contains an account of the creation of the world and of the failed attempts to produce proper human beings. The second and third parts tell of the adventures of the Hero Twins, Hunahpú (pronounced WAH-nuh-pwuh) and Xbalanqúe (pronounced shi-BAY-lan-kay). The last two parts deal with the issue of creating humans from **corn**, and then tell the story of the Quiché people from the days before their history began to accounts of tribal wars and records of rulers up until 1550.

Creation of the World At the beginning of time, the gods Huracan (pronounced wah-ruh-KAHN) and Gukumatz (pronounced gwah-kwuh-MAHTS) shaped the earth and its features and raised the sky above it. The gods then placed animals on the earth, hoping that they would sing the praises of the gods.

When the gods discovered that the animals could not speak, they tried again to make a creature that could praise its creator. Huracan and Gukumatz called on the ancestral beings Xpiyacoc (pronounced shpee-YAH-kok) and Xmucane (pronounced SHMOH-kah-nay) to help, and

Nationality/Culture
Mayan

Pronunciation
poh-POHL VOO

Alternate Names
None

Appears In
Ancient Mayan culture

together they created men of mud. But these creatures talked endlessly and dwindled away. Next the gods fashioned humans out of wood. These beings populated the earth but soon forgot about their creators. The angry gods sent **floods** and various objects to destroy them.

The Hero Twins In Part Two of the *Popol Vuh*, **Hunahpú and Xbalanqúe** appear and take on the self-important Vucub-Caquix (pronounced voh-KOHB kah-kwish), as well as his sons, Zipacna (pronounced sip-AK-nah) and Earthquake. Using blowpipes, the **twins** knocked out Vucub-Caquix's jeweled teeth, which gave him his radiance. Vucub-Caquix accepted corn as a replacement for his teeth. But because he could not eat with his corn teeth and because they did not shine, he was defeated.

In Part Three of the *Popol Vuh*, the story goes back to an earlier time, to Hun-Hunahpú (pronounced wahn-WAHN-uh-pwah) and Vucub Hunahpú (pronounced voh-kohb WAHN-uh-pwah), the father and uncle of the Hero Twins. These two disturbed the lords of Xibalba (pronounced shi-BAHL-buh)—the **underworld**, or land of the dead—with their constant ball playing. The lords commanded the brothers to come to the underworld for a contest. Tricked by the lords, the brothers lost the contest and, as a result, were sacrificed and buried in the ball court. However, the head of Hun-Hunahpú remained unburied and was placed in a tree.

A young goddess heard of a strange fruit in a tree and went to see it. The fruit was actually the head of Hun-Hunahpú, which spat in her hand and made her pregnant. She later gave birth to the Hero Twins. Hun-Hunahpú already had another set of twins, Hun Batz and Hun Chuen, who resented their baby brothers. When the Hero Twins grew old enough, they outsmarted the older twins and turned them into monkeys.

The Hero Twins became great ball players, as their father and uncle had been, and one day the lords of Xibalba summoned them to the underworld for a contest. The twins saw this as an opportunity to avenge their father's death. Challenged to a series of trials, they passed every one they were given. They survived a night in the House of Cold, escaped death in the House of Jaguars, and passed unharmed through the House of Fire. They almost met defeat in the House of Bats, when a bat cut off Hunahpú's head. The lords of Xibalba took the head to the ball court as a trophy, but Xbalanqúe managed to return the head to his brother and restore him.

Knowing they were immortal, or able to live forever, the Hero Twins now allowed the lords of Xibalba to defeat and "kill" them. Five days later, the twins reappeared, disguised as wandering performers, and entertained the lords with amazing feats. In one of these feats, Xbalanqúe sacrificed Hunahpú and then brought him back to life. Astounded, the lords of Xibalba begged to be sacrificed themselves. The Hero Twins agreed to the request but did not restore the lords of Xibalba to life. The twins then dug up the bodies of their father and uncle and brought them back to life.

Creation of the Maya The final two parts of the *Popol Vuh* tell how the gods once again tried to make humans who would praise the gods. The four men they created from maize—their skin a mix of white and yellow corn, and their limbs shaped from corn meal—became the founders of the Quiché Maya. These people praised their creators and flourished. The generations that followed them are listed in the closing section of the *Popol Vuh*.

The *Popol Vuh* in Context

The *Popol Vuh* is the most important source of information on the mythology of the ancient Maya. A sacred book of the Quiché Maya of Guatemala, it was written down in the mid-1500s. A Spanish priest discovered the *Popol Vuh* manuscript in the early 1700s. After copying the text, he translated it into Spanish.

Key Themes and Symbols

One important theme in the *Popol Vuh* is the creation of life from natural materials. The gods try to create humans from mud, and later from wood. These are failures, and the gods destroy them. Finally, the first successful humans are created from corn—a crucial food in the Mayan diet. In this way, corn symbolizes life to the Mayan people. Corn is also used as the substitute for Vucub-Caquix's teeth after Hunahpú and Xbalanqúe knock out his real teeth.

Another important theme found in the *Popol Vuh* is the interaction of the living with the dead. This is seen throughout the myth of Hunahpú and Xbalanqúe, beginning with the head of their father talking to (and impregnating) a goddess while hanging from a tree. It is also seen when the twins journey to the underworld for a ball-playing contest;

Hunahpú loses his head in the House of Bats, but is brought back to life, and both brothers later allow themselves to be killed and brought back to life. Then, after killing the lords of the underworld, the brothers bring their father and uncle back from the dead and return with them to the land of the living.

The *Popol Vuh* in Art, Literature, and Everyday Life

Although the Mayan civilization has dwindled greatly in the centuries following Spanish occupation, the myths recorded in the *Popol Vuh* still play an important part in the culture of the region. Stories in Charles Finger's *Tales from the Silver Lands* and Miguel Angel Asturias's *Men of Maize* are based on the *Popol Vuh*. The myths of the *Popol Vuh* also served as inspiration for Louis L'Amour's supernatural Western novel *The Haunted Mesa* (1987). The underworld of Xibalba appears in the 2006 Darren Aronofsky film *The Fountain*.

Read, Write, Think, Discuss

Mayan civilization had largely disappeared by the time Spanish explorers arrived in the New World. Some modern historians view the fall of the Maya as an example for modern society to learn from and avoid. Using your library, the Internet, or other available resources, research the collapse of the Mayan civilization. Can you find any similarities between the fall of Mayan civilization and the current state of modern societies like the United States? How are they different? Do you think there are lessons to be learned from the Maya? If so, what are they?

SEE ALSO Hunahpú and Xbalanqúe; Mayan Mythology; Quetzalcoatl; Twins; Underworld

Poseidon

Character Overview

One of the major deities (gods) in **Greek mythology**, Poseidon was the supreme ruler of the seas. The Romans called him Neptune (pronounced

Nationality/Culture
Greek

Pronunciation
poh-SYE-dun

Alternate Names
Neptune (Roman)

Appears In
Homer's *Iliad*, Hesiod's *Theogony*

Lineage
Son of Cronus and Rhea

NEP-toon). An awesome, unruly, and powerful god, Poseidon was associated with storms, earthquakes, and some other violent forces of nature. When angry, he could stir the sea to a fury, but he could also calm the raging waters with just a glance. One of his titles, translated as "Earth-shaker," reflected his ability to cause earthquakes by striking the earth and mountains with his three-pronged spear known as a trident. Another name for Poseidon was Hippios (pronounced HIP-ee-ohs), meaning lord of horses, a reference to the fact that he was believed to be the creator of the first horse.

Poseidon rode the waves in a swift chariot drawn by golden sea horses. He used his mighty trident not only to create earthquakes and stir ocean waves, but also to raise new land from beneath the sea or cause existing land to sink below the waters. Although often helpful to humans—protecting sailors at sea, guiding ships to safety, and filling nets with fish—Neptune could be a terrifying figure as well. Quick to anger, he directed his fury at anyone who acted against him or failed to show proper respect.

Major Myths

The son of the **Titans Cronus** (pronounced KROH-nuhs) and Rhea (pronounced REE-uh), Poseidon was swallowed at birth by his father. He was saved by his brother **Zeus** (pronounced ZOOS), who tricked Cronus into taking a potion that caused him to vomit up Poseidon and the other siblings—**Hades** (pronounced HAY-deez), **Demeter** (pronounced di-MEE-ter), **Hera** (pronounced HAIR-uh), and Hestia (pronounced HESS-tee-uh). Poseidon later joined Zeus and Hades in overthrowing Cronus, and the three brothers then divided the universe among themselves. Zeus received the sky, Hades ruled the **underworld** or land of the dead, and Poseidon became god of the seas.

Although Zeus was king of the gods, Poseidon often asserted his independence. Once he even plotted with the goddesses Hera and **Athena** (pronounced uh-THEE-nuh) to overthrow Zeus. Together they managed to put Zeus in chains. However, the sea goddess Thetis (pronounced THEE-tis) saved Zeus by bringing a giant from Tartarus (pronounced TAR-tur-uhs)—a realm beneath the underworld—to release the king of the gods from his chains. As punishment for this rebellion, Zeus made Poseidon serve as a slave to King Laomedon (pronounced lay-OM-uh-don) of Troy for a year. During this time,

Poseidon helped build great walls around the city. When the king refused to pay for this work, Poseidon took revenge by siding with the Greeks against Troy in the Trojan War.

Love, Life, and Children Poseidon had a turbulent love life and fathered many children, including a number of monsters and sea creatures. With his wife, the sea nymph Amphitrite (pronounced am-fi-TRY-tee), he had three offspring. One of the children, Triton (pronounced TRY-tun), was a sea god and a merman (male version of a **mermaid**) who resembled a human above the waist and a fish from the waist down.

Poseidon had children with other partners as well. After seducing his sister Demeter while disguised as a horse, he had two children: the divine horse Arion (pronounced uh-RYE-uhn) and a daughter Despina (pronounced des-PEE-nuh). **Medusa** (pronounced meh-DOO-suh) is also sometimes mentioned as a lover of Poseidon. According to myth, Medusa was once a beautiful woman, and Poseidon seduced her inside one of the goddess Athena's temples. Athena, angered by this sign of disrespect, transformed Medusa into a hideous Gorgon. The two children of Poseidon and Medusa were born from the blood spilled when the hero **Perseus** (pronounced PUR-see-uhs) cut off Medusa's head. These two children were the winged horse **Pegasus** (pronounced PEG-uh-suhs), and a son named Chrysaor (pronounced kree-SAY-ohr). Through his son Chrysaor, Poseidon became ancestor to some of the most fearsome monsters in Greek mythology, including the three-headed hound **Cerberus** (pronounced SUR-ber-uhs), the Hydra (pronounced HYE-druh), the Nemean (pronounced ni-MEE-uhn) Lion, and the **Sphinx**.

Gaia (pronounced GAY-uh), the earth, bore Poseidon two children: Antaeus (pronounced an-TEE-uhs), a giant, and Charybdis (pronounced kuh-RIB-dis), a sea monster that almost destroyed **Odysseus** (pronounced oh-DIS-ee-uhs) during his journey home after the Trojan War. Another giant offspring of Poseidon—the one-eyed Cyclops Polyphemus (pronounced pol-uh-FEE-muhs)—also threatened Odysseus on his voyage home. When Odysseus blinded the giant, he became a target of Poseidon's hatred.

When Poseidon tried to seduce the beautiful sea nymph Scylla (pronounced SIL-uh), his wife Amphitrite became jealous and transformed her into a horrible sea monster with six dog-heads. Like Charybdis, Scylla terrorized sailors, and she devoured several of Odysseus's companions.

Poseidon was the god of the seas in Greek mythology. The Romans called him Neptune.
PURESTOCK/GETTY IMAGES.

Among Poseidon's other children were the evil Cercyon (pronounced SUR-see-on) and Sciron (pronounced SKEE-ron), normal-sized offspring who threatened and killed travelers in Greece, and the giant Amycus (pronounced AM-i-kuhs), who forced people to fight with him and then killed them. Various ordinary mortals also claimed Poseidon as their father, including the famous Greek hero **Theseus** (pronounced THEE-see-uhs).

Poseidon's Quarrels Poseidon had numerous quarrels with other gods. One of his most famous disputes involved the goddess Athena. Both Poseidon and Athena claimed the region of Attica (pronounced AT-i-kuh) and its capital city as their own. A contest was held to see which god could give Athens the best gift; whoever won would have the capital city named after them. Athena created an olive tree; Poseidon produced a saltwater spring (or, in some versions, the first horse). When the citizens judged Athena's gift to be superior, the angry Poseidon flooded the surrounding plain.

Poseidon also quarreled with the **sun** god Helios (pronounced HEE-lee-ohs) over control of the Greek city of Corinth. The giant Briareus (pronounced bry-AHR-ee-uhs) settled the argument by giving the hill overlooking the city to Helios and the surrounding land to Poseidon. Satisfied with this decision, Poseidon caused no problems for the people of Corinth.

Another of Poseidon's famous quarrels was with Minos (pronounced MYE-nuhs), the king of Crete (pronounced KREET). Minos asked Poseidon to send him a bull that he could **sacrifice** to the god. Poseidon sent such a magnificent bull that the king decided to keep it for himself instead of sacrificing it. Furious, Poseidon caused Minos's wife, Pasiphaë (pronounced pa-SIF-ah-ee), to fall in love with the bull and to give birth to the **Minotaur** (pronounced MIN-uh-tawr), a monstrous beast that had the body of a man and the head of a bull.

Poseidon in Context

As the god of the sea, Poseidon reflects the way ancient Greeks and Romans viewed the seas and oceans upon which they relied for trade and commerce. Poseidon is depicted as a god prone to violent outbursts that occur almost without warning. This is similar to how a calm sea can quickly give way to stormy, dangerous swells. In addition, his frequent outbursts at not receiving proper respect may have been viewed as cautionary tales: looking at the available historical evidence, some experts believe that Poseidon was among the most worshiped of all the Greek and Roman deities. This may also reflect the importance these people placed upon the sea as both a provider and a pathway to trade. But though the Greeks worshipped and respected Poseidon, it is important to note that places of worship to Poseidon were always located outside city walls, indicating that he was too violent and unpredictable for civilized, orderly city life.

Key Themes and Symbols

Poseidon represents the untamed and wild power of nature. While he ruled the sea and could cause the waters to become violent, he also had a strong connection to the earth, as shown in his association with earthquakes that the Greeks believed he started with his mighty trident. The trident—itself an important symbol of Poseidon—indicates his stronger association with fishermen than sailors, since the trident is an important tool in the fishing trade.

Poseidon also had a strong connection to horses, particularly the wild and powerful aspects of horses. The Greeks would pray to him before and after a horse race, although they prayed to his sister Athena during the race, as she was responsible for the actual technique of horse-racing. Another animal associated with Poseidon is the dolphin; a sighting of a dolphin by Greek sailors was considered a good sign of a smooth trip.

Poseidon in Art, Literature, and Everyday Life

In ancient art, Poseidon was often portrayed riding in a chariot pulled by horses or hippocamps—creatures with front halves similar to horses and back halves like fish. He was usually seen holding his trident. In modern times, he is perhaps best known by his Roman name, Neptune. Sculptures of Neptune are popular in city fountains and can be found in cities such as Copenhagen, Florence, Mexico City, and Virginia Beach. Neptune also makes an appearance in the animated film *The SpongeBob SquarePants Movie* (2004), with actor Jeffrey Tambor providing the voice of King Neptune. Poseidon plays a key part in the 2005 novel *The Lightning Thief*, by Rick Riordan, which follows the adventures of a demigod (half god, half human) named Percy Jackson.

Read, Write, Think, Discuss

Poseidon made his home at the bottom of the sea, in a palace made of coral. Over two-thirds of our planet's surface is covered by water. As the human population continues to grow, the amount of land available for people to live on will become ever smaller. Do you think that humans will someday live in communities on or under the oceans of the world? What unique problems would humans face living in the realm of Poseidon?

SEE ALSO Athena; Cerberus; Cyclopes; Demeter; Gaia; Hades; Hera; Medusa; Odysseus; Pegasus; Sphinx; Theseus; Zeus

Prometheus

Character Overview

Prometheus, one of the **Titans** in **Greek mythology**, was a master craftsman and was considered the wisest of his race. He was credited with the creation of humans and with giving them **fire** and various types of skills and knowledge. His name means "forethought."

Prometheus was the son of the Titan Iapetus (pronounced eye-AP-uh-tus) and the sea nymph Clymene (pronounced KLEM-eh-nee). **Atlas** (pronounced AT-luhs) and Epimetheus (pronounced ep-uh-MEE-thee-uhs, meaning "afterthought") were his brothers and Hesione (pronounced hee-SYE-oh-nee), daughter of the Titan Oceanus (pronounced oh-SEE-uh-nuhs), was his wife.

When **Zeus** (pronounced ZOOS), the king of the gods, and the other Olympian gods rebelled against the Titans, Prometheus sided with the gods and thus won their favor. He held Zeus's aching head so that **Hephaestus** (pronounced hi-FES-tuhs), the god of fire and metalworking, could split it open and release the goddess **Athena** (pronounced uh-THEE-nuh). To show her gratitude, Athena taught Prometheus astronomy, mathematics, architecture, navigation, metalworking, writing, and other useful skills. He later passed this knowledge on to humans.

Friend to Humans Prometheus created humans by shaping lumps of clay into small figures resembling the gods. Athena admired these figures and breathed on them, giving them life. Zeus disliked the creatures, but he could not uncreate them. He did, however, confine them to the earth

Nationality/Culture
Greek

Pronunciation
pruh-MEE-thee-uhs

Alternate Names
None

Appears In
Ovid's *Metamorphoses*, Hesiod's *Theogony*

Lineage
Son of Iapetus and Clymene

and denied them immortality, or the ability to live forever. Prometheus felt sorry for humans, so he gave them fire and taught them various arts and skills.

Prometheus was given the task of determining how sacrifices were to be made to the gods. He cut up a bull and divided it into two portions. One portion contained the animal's flesh and skin, but they were concealed beneath the bull's stomach, the least appetizing part of the animal. The other portion consisted of the bones, wrapped in a rich layer of fat. Prometheus then asked Zeus to choose a portion for himself, leaving the other for humans. Fooled by the outward appearance of the portions, Zeus chose the one containing the bones and fat. Prometheus thus ensured that humans got the best meat.

Angered by this trick, Zeus punished humans by withholding fire from them so they would have to live in cold and darkness and eat meat raw. Prometheus promptly went to Olympus (pronounced oh-LIM-puhs), stole a spark of fire from Hephaestus, and carried it back to humans. When Zeus discovered what Prometheus had done, he swore revenge. He ordered Hephaestus to create a woman from clay, and he had the winds breathe life into her. Athena and other goddesses clothed the woman, whose name was **Pandora** (pronounced pan-DOR-uh).

Zeus sent Pandora as a gift to Prometheus's brother Epimetheus, who married her despite warnings from Prometheus not to accept any gift from Zeus. Pandora brought with her a box containing evil, disease, poverty, war, and other troubles. When Pandora opened the box, she released these sorrows into the world, and Zeus thus gained his revenge on humankind.

Prometheus's Punishment To punish Prometheus, Zeus chained the god to a rock on a mountain peak. Every day an eagle tore at Prometheus's body and ate his liver, and every night the liver grew back. Because Prometheus was immortal, he could not die. Instead he suffered endlessly.

Prometheus remained chained and in agony for thousands of years. The other gods begged Zeus to show mercy, but he refused. Finally, Zeus offered Prometheus freedom if he would reveal a secret that only he knew. Prometheus told Zeus that the sea nymph Thetis (pronounced THEE-tis) would bear a son who would become greater than his father. This was important information. Both Zeus and his brother **Poseidon** (pronounced poh-SYE-dun) desired Thetis, but they arranged for her to marry a mortal so that her son would not pose a challenge to their power.

Zeus sent **Heracles** (pronounced HAIR-uh-kleez) to shoot the eagle that tormented Prometheus and to break the chains that bound him. After his years of suffering, Prometheus was free. To reward Heracles for his help, Prometheus advised him how to obtain the golden apples of the Hesperides (pronounced hee-SPER-uh-deez), one of the twelve labors the famous hero had to accomplish.

Prometheus in Context

The myth of Prometheus reflects an interesting change over the centuries regarding the ancient Greek gods and how followers viewed them. In the earliest versions of the myth, recorded by Hesiod in the seventh or eighth century BCE, Prometheus was portrayed as a betrayer of the gods who was rightfully punished for his wickedness. Prometheus and his trickery, it is suggested, was the reason that humans suffered in their labors instead of being able to perform their work quickly and easily. In later versions of the myth, recorded two hundred years or more after Hesiod's text, Prometheus was depicted as a hero who defied the gods in order to help humanity. This reflected a growing view among the ancient Greeks that the gods were not infallible and all-powerful, but instead displayed many of the same faults as humans.

Key Themes and Symbols

An important theme in the myth of Prometheus is the idea of humans and gods as adversaries, or opposing groups. In the myth, Prometheus creates humans in the image of the gods. Zeus, however, does not think that people deserve to keep the best meats for themselves and becomes angry when he discovers that Prometheus has tricked him. He punishes people by keeping fire away from them so they cannot cook their meat. Ultimately, even though humans receive the power of fire, disease and other awful things are released into the world by the gods as revenge. In the myth, fire symbolizes knowledge; Prometheus represents the teacher of humankind and provider of useful information and skills.

Prometheus in Art, Literature, and Everyday Life

The story of Prometheus's suffering and ultimate release from his torment has inspired artists and writers for centuries. Among the most important early works dealing with the myth was a series of plays written by the Greek

playwright Aeschylus (pronounced ES-kuh-luhs). Only one of these works, *Prometheus Bound*, survives. The Roman poet Ovid incorporated parts of the story in his work the *Metamorphoses*. Prometheus has also been the subject of more modern works of art, music, and literature by such individuals as the composer Ludwig van Beethoven and the poets Lord Byron, Percy Shelley, Johann Wolfgang von Goethe, and Henry Wadsworth Longfellow. The myth also loosely inspired Mary Shelley to write the novel *Frankenstein*, the subtitle of which was *The Modern Prometheus*.

Read, Write, Think, Discuss

A popular modern interpretation of the myth of Prometheus is that there are some things humans are not meant to know about. This dangerous knowledge is symbolized by fire, but could represent anything—nuclear fission, cloning, tissue regeneration, or artificial intelligence, to name a few. Using your library, the Internet, or other available resources, research a current debate about one of these issues and make a list of the pros and cons involved in the quest for new knowledge. Then write a brief essay on what you think about the issue.

SEE ALSO Atlas; Greek Mythology; Hephaestus; Heracles; Pandora; Titans; Zeus

Proserpina
See **Persephone.**

Proteus

Nationality/Culture
Greek

Pronunciation
PRO-tee-uhs

Alternate Names
None

Appears In
Ovid's *Metamorphoses*, Homer's *Odyssey*, Virgil's *Georgics*

Character Overview

Proteus was an ancient Greek god also known as the old man of the sea. He served as a shepherd for the sea god **Poseidon** (pronounced poh-SYE-dun), who is sometimes named as his father. Proteus watched over Poseidon's flocks of seals, and in return, Poseidon gave Proteus the gift of prophecy, or the ability to see the future.

Major Myths

Proteus possessed knowledge of all things—past, present, and future—but was reluctant to reveal his knowledge. He would answer questions

Greek mosaic of Proteus, the Old Man of the Sea. © NATIONAL ARCHAEOLOGICAL MUSEUM, ATHENS, GREECE/ANCIENT ART AND ARCHITECTURE COLLECTION LTD./THE BRIDGEMAN ART LIBRARY.

only if caught. The only way to catch him was to sneak up on him at noontime when he took his daily nap. However, Proteus also had the ability to change shape at will. Once he was seized, it was necessary to hold him tightly until he returned to his natural form. Then he would answer any question put to him.

According to one myth, Aristaeus (pronounced a-ris-TEE-uhs), a son of the god **Apollo** (pronounced uh-POL-oh) and a beekeeper, discovered one day that all of his bees had died from an unknown sickness. His mother suggested that he locate Proteus, who would know how to solve his bee problem. Aristaeus found Proteus and held on tight to him, despite his attempts to change shape and escape. Eventually Proteus gave up and agreed to answer whatever question Aristaeus might ask. Aristaeus asked how to get back his bees; Proteus told him to **sacrifice** twelve animals at an altar, and return to the altar after three days. When Aristaeus returned to the altar, the corpse of one of the animals was filled with bees. Aristaeus kept these bees, and they never again fell ill.

Proteus in Context

The idea of Proteus, a sea god, may reflect ancient Greek observations about the nature of the sea. Many observers throughout the centuries have noted the constantly changing nature of the sea, with its ever-shifting surface and ability to turn from calm to violent very quickly. Proteus may also reflect an ancient view of the gods as often being unwilling to help others, especially humans.

Key Themes and Symbols

One of the main themes found in the myth of Proteus is the reluctant seer—a being who possesses great knowledge, but is unwilling to share it except when forced. Proteus never offers his wisdom willingly, as shown in the myth of Aristaeus and the bees. Another theme is ancient wisdom: although Proteus was often referred to as the son of Poseidon, he was always pictured as an old man, and it was rumored he existed in myth long before many of the Olympian gods.

Proteus in Art, Literature, and Everyday Life

The legend of Proteus gave rise to the term *protean*, which means able to assume different forms. Although Proteus seldom appears as a character in art or literature after ancient times, he has been mentioned in the works of John Milton, William Shakespeare, and William Wordsworth, and the concept of Proteus as a shape-shifter has endured both literally and figuratively. Kurt Vonnegut gave the main character of his novel *Player Piano* (1952) the last name of Proteus, a reference to his shifting identity. Proteus, and shape-shifting creatures known as Proteans, appear often in role-playing games such as *Vampire: The Masquerade*. Proteus is also the name given to a satellite of the planet Neptune.

Read, Write, Think, Discuss

The term "protean" is used to refer not only to beings that can change shape, but also to people who can exhibit different moods or personalities in different situations. In modern times, such people might be classified as having a mood or personality disorder. Looking at the actions and behaviors of the other Greek gods, how do you think they would be viewed by modern people? Why? Provide examples to illustrate your point.

SEE ALSO Greek Mythology; Poseidon

Psyche

Character Overview

In Greek and **Roman mythology**, Psyche was a princess of such stunning beauty that people came from near and far to admire her. In turning their adoration toward Psyche, however, they neglected to worship the goddess **Aphrodite** (pronounced af-ro-DYE-tee). Jealous that so much praise was flowing to a mortal girl, Aphrodite decided to punish Psyche.

In Psyche's myth, the goddess Aphrodite summoned her son **Eros** (pronounced AIR-ohs and also known as Cupid), the god of love, and told him to make Psyche fall in love with some ugly, mean, and unworthy creature. Eros prepared to obey his mother's wishes, but when he laid eyes on the beautiful Psyche, he fell in love with her.

Eros asked the god **Apollo** (pronounced uh-POL-oh) to send an oracle—or messenger of the gods—to Psyche's father, telling him to prepare his daughter for marriage. He was to send her to a lonely mountain, where an ugly monster would meet her and take her for his wife. Full of sorrow for his daughter but afraid of making the gods angry, Psyche's father obeyed.

While Psyche stood on the mountain, Zephyrus (pronounced ZEF-er-uhs), the god of the west wind, sent a breeze to pick her up and carry her to a beautiful palace in a valley. When Psyche entered the palace, a friendly voice guided her around, and invisible attendants waited upon her and fulfilled her every need.

That night and on the nights that followed, Eros came to Psyche in the darkness of her bedroom. Psyche could not see Eros in the darkness, but he told her that he was her husband. He also warned Psyche not to

Nationality/Culture
Greek/Roman

Pronunciation
SYE-kee

Alternate Names
None

Appears In
Lucius Apuleius's *The Golden Ass*

Lineage
Unknown

ask his identity and never to look at him. Psyche grew to love her unseen husband, but she felt very lonely.

When she asked if her sisters might visit, Eros reluctantly agreed. Her sisters admired her palace and life of luxury, but when they discovered that Psyche had never seen her husband, they told her that he must be a monster and might kill her. They convinced her to take a knife and lamp to bed with her.

When Eros fell asleep that night, Psyche lit the lamp and prepared to stab her husband. But instead of a monster, she saw the handsome god of love. Startled, she let a drop of hot oil from the lamp fall on Eros. He awoke, realized that Psyche knew his identity, and flew away. Psyche fainted. When she awoke, the palace had vanished, and she found herself alone in a strange country.

Psyche wandered the countryside searching for Eros. Finally she asked Aphrodite for help, and the goddess gave her a set of seemingly impossible tasks. With the help of other gods, however, Psyche managed to sort a roomful of grain in one night and gather golden fleeces from a flock of sheep. For the final task, Aphrodite told Psyche to go to the **underworld**, or land of the dead, and bring back a sealed box from the goddess **Persephone** (pronounced per-SEF-uh-nee). Psyche retrieved the box and on her way back, overcome by curiosity, peeked inside it. The box released a deep sleep that overpowered her.

By this time Eros could no longer bear to be without Psyche. He flew to where she lay sleeping, woke her, and took her to the home of the gods on Mount Olympus (pronounced oh-LIM-puhs). **Zeus** commanded that the punishment of Psyche cease and gave permission for the lovers to marry. Zeus then gave Psyche a cup of ambrosia (pronounced am-BROH-zhuh), the food of the gods, which made her immortal—or able to live forever.

Psyche in Context

The myth of Psyche can be seen as a reinforcement of male authority in marriages in ancient Greece and Rome. First, Psyche is offered up in marriage by her father without her consent and without ever meeting her husband. This was not out of the ordinary for weddings in ancient times, though in this case Psyche's father gives up control over his daughter to the gods. Psyche is treated to a beautiful palace and an army of servants to care for her, and she enjoys the company of her husband each night in

darkness. However, her husband never lets her see him. It is only when Psyche, driven to fear by her jealous sisters, questions his authority that the otherwise perfect marriage is ruined. Psyche then spends the rest of the story trying to win back her husband.

Key Themes and Symbols

One of the main themes found in the myth of Psyche is disobeying the will of the gods. Psyche does this twice: first, by looking at her husband while he sleeps (though she does not know that he is a god); and second, by opening the box she retrieves from Persephone. In both cases, disobeying the will of the gods leads to tragic circumstances. Another theme is the association of beauty and love. Eros falls in love with Psyche when he gazes upon her beauty; Psyche does not truly feel love for Eros until she is finally able to see him as he sleeps.

Psyche in Art, Literature, and Everyday Life

Although the tale of Psyche and Eros is only marginally accepted as a genuine myth, its impact throughout the centuries has been profound. Poets such as Mary Tighe, Robert Bridges, and John Keats have all written their own versions of the tale, and artists such as William Adophe Bouguereau, Jacques-Louis David, and Edward Burne-Jones have captured the characters on canvas. The tale of Psyche and Eros is similar in many ways to the eighteenth-century French fairy tale "Beauty and the Beast," and may have served as inspiration for it.

Read, Write, Think, Discuss

The 1956 fantasy novel *Till We Have Faces: A Myth Retold* by C. S. Lewis is a new version of the myth of Eros and Psyche told from the point of view of Orual, Psyche's sister. The book is considered a parallel novel, meaning it covers the same events as the original myth, but from a different perspective.

SEE ALSO Aphrodite; Eros; Greek Mythology

Pygmalion and Galatea

Nationality/Culture
Greek/Roman

Pronunciation
pig-MAY-lee-uhn and gal-uh-TEE-uh

Alternate Names
None

Appears In
Ovid's *Metamorphoses*

Myth Overview

In **Greek mythology**, Pygmalion was a king of the island of Cyprus and a sculptor who may have been a human son of the sea god **Poseidon** (pronounced poh-SYE-dun). He spent many years carving an ivory statue of a woman more beautiful than any living female. According to myth, Pygmalion became fascinated by his sculpture and fell in love with it. He pretended it was an actual woman. He brought it presents and treated it as if it were alive. However, the statue could not respond to his attentions, and Pygmalion became miserable. Finally, he prayed to **Aphrodite** (pronounced af-ro-DYE-tee), the goddess of love, to bring him a woman like his statue. Aphrodite did even better. She brought the statue to life. Pygmalion married this woman, often called Galatea (pronounced gal-uh-TEE-uh), who gave birth to a daughter (or, in some versions, a son).

Pygmalion and Galatea in Context

The myth of Pygmalion and Galatea reflects the ancient Greek view of the ideal wife. Pygmalion's statue is beautiful and without voice or opinion. Even after the statue comes to life, she is only described as blushing at Pygmalion's kiss and giving birth to his child. She does not perform any other actions beyond these simple duties—a reflection of the ancient Greek ideal in a society dominated by men. The myth of Pygmalion also reflects ancient Greek and Roman achievements in sculpture: at the time they were created, the works of Greek and Roman sculptors were arguably the most lifelike representations of the human form ever crafted. Without this crucial quality, it is unlikely that the myth of Pygmalion would have been as popular as it was. In fact, the myth itself can be viewed as a celebration of such artistic achievement.

Key Themes and Symbols

The main theme of Pygmalion's myth is the artist's love of his own creation. Pygmalion becomes so infatuated with his work that he begins to treat it as if it were a real person. Another important theme, common in Greek mythology, is the equation of physical beauty with perfection. The statue's flawless physical appearance, suggests that it is the perfect woman—though there is never any evidence of Galatea's personality or character.

Pygmalion and Galatea in Art, Literature, and Everyday Life

The myth of Pygmalion and his sculpture has appealed to many artists over the centuries, perhaps because the myth speaks directly to the act of artistic creation. Artist Jean-Léon Gérome created an astounding pair of paintings, both titled *Pygmalion and Galatea*, depicting similar scenes of sculptor and sculpture from two different angles. Images of Pygmalion and his creation have also been captured by modern artists, such as Boris Vallejo.

The myth was the subject of two operas in the seventeenth and eighteenth centuries, as well as a humorous play by W. S. Gilbert (later of Gilbert and Sullivan fame) in 1871 titled *Pygmalion and Galatea*. The writer George Bernard Shaw took the name *Pygmalion* as the title of his play about an English professor who turns a poor girl from the streets

into a fashionable society woman, which touches upon some of the same themes as the original myth. In the play, the professor "creates" a beautiful woman out of a poor wretch, just as Pygmalion creates a flawless beauty out of a chunk of ivory. Shaw's story was the basis of the later Broadway musical and movie *My Fair Lady*. Another updated version of the myth of Pygmalion can be found in the 1987 comedy film *Mannequin*, where the object of the artist's affection is a department store mannequin rather than a statue.

The Fat Girl by Marilyn Sachs (1984) is a novel that updates the myth of Galatea and Pygmalion to include modern issues that many adolescents face. The narrator, Jeff, is a popular boy with a beautiful girlfriend. When he makes a remark about an overweight girl named Ellen in his ceramics class and she overhears, he feels bad and becomes friendly with her to make up for his cruel act. He helps her gain self-confidence and blossom into a successful young woman, though his motives may not be entirely charitable, and the result may not be what he expects.

Read, Write, Think, Discuss

The idea of creating the perfect companion—whether it is a friend or romantic partner—is one of most enduring elements of the myth of Pygmalion. It appears frequently in modern forms of storytelling. Think of an example of this that you have encountered in books, songs, on television, or in movies. (One example would be *Pinocchio*.) How does your example use the theme of creating the perfect companion? Are there other similarities to the tale of Pygmalion?

Where to Learn More

African

Altman, Linda Jacobs. *African Mythology.* Berkeley Heights, NJ: Enslow Publishers, 2003.

Ardagh, Philip, and Georgia Peters. *African Myths & Legends.* Chicago: World Book, 2002.

Giles, Bridget. *Myths of West Africa.* Austin, TX: Raintree Steck-Vaughn, 2002.

Husain, Shahrukh, and Bee Willey. *African Myths.* 1st ed. North Mankato, MN: Cherrytree Books, 2007.

Lilly, Melinda. *Spider and His Son Find Wisdom: An Akan Tale.* Vero Beach, FL: Rourke Press, 1998.

Lilly, Melinda. *Warrior Son of a Warrior Son: A Masai Tale.* Vero Beach, FL: Rourke Press, 1998.

Lilly, Melinda. *Zimani's Drum: A Malawian Tale.* Vero Beach, FL: Rourke Press, 1998.

Schomp, Virginia. *The Ancient Africans.* New York: Marshall Cavendish Benchmark, 2008.

Seed, Jenny. *The Bushman's Dream: African Tales of the Creation.* 1st American ed. Scarsdale, NY: Bradbury Press, 1975.

Anglo-Saxon/Celtic

Ardagh, Philip, and G. Barton Chapple. *Celtic Myths & Legends.* Chicago: World Book, 2002.

Crossley-Holland, Kevin, and Peter Malone. *The World of King Arthur and His Court: People, Places, Legend, and Lore.* New York: Dutton Children's Books, 2004.

Hicks, Penelope, and James McLean. *Beowulf.* New York: Kingfisher, 2007.

Lister, Robin, Alan Baker, and Sir Thomas Malory. *The Story of King Arthur.* Boston: Kingfisher, 2005.

Martell, Hazel Mary. *The Celts.* 1st American ed. New York: Peter Bedrick, 2001.

Morris, Gerald. *The Lioness & Her Knight.* Boston: Houghton Mifflin, 2005.

Whittock, Martyn J. *Beliefs and Myths of Viking Britain.* Oxford: Heinemann, 1996.

Williams, Marcia, ed. *Chaucer's Canterbury Tales.* London: Walker, 2008.

Asian/Pacific

Behnke, Alison. *Angkor Wat.* Minneapolis: Twenty-First Century Books, 2008.

Carpenter, Frances. *Tales of a Korean Grandmother.* Boston: Tuttle Pub., 1973.

Coburn, Jewell Reinhart. *Encircled Kingdom: Legends and Folktales of Laos.* Rev. ed. Thousand Oaks, CA: Burn, Hart, 1994.

Coulson, Kathy Morrissey, Paula Cookson Melhorn, and Hmong Women's Project (Fitchburg, MA). *Living in Two Worlds: The Hmong Women's Project.* Ashburnham, MA: K. M. Coulson and P. C. Melhorn, 2000.

Dalal, Anita. *Myths of Oceania.* Austin, TX: Raintree Steck-Vaughn, 2002.

Green, Jen. *Myths of China and Japan.* Austin, TX: New York: Raintree Steck-Vaughn Publishers, 2002.

Htin Aung, U., G. Trager, and Pau Oo Thet. *A Kingdom Lost for a Drop of Honey, and Other Burmese Folktales.* New York: Parents' Magazine Press, 1968.

Kanawa, Kiri Te. *Land of the Long White Cloud: Maori Myths, Tales, and Legends.* 1st U.S. ed. New York: Arcade Pub., 1989.

Sakairi, Masao, Shooko Kojima, and Matthew Galgani. *Vietnamese Fables of Frogs and Toads.* Berkeley, CA: Heian International, 2006.

Sakairi, Masao, Shooko Kojima, and Matthew Galgani. *Vietnamese Tales of Rabbits and Watermelons.* Berkeley, CA: Heian International, 2006.

Egyptian

Ardagh, Philip, and Danuta Mayer. *Ancient Egyptian Myths & Legends.* Chicago: World Book, 2002.

Broyles, Janell. *Egyptian Mythology.* 1st ed. New York: Rosen Pub. Group, 2006.

Cline, Eric H., and Jill Rubalcaba. *The Ancient Egyptian World.* California ed. New York: Oxford University Press, 2005.

Gleason, Katherine. *Ancient Egyptian Culture.* New York: Newbridge Educational Pub., 2006.

Kramer, Ann. *Egyptian Myth: A Treasury of Legends, Art, and History.* Armonk, NY: Sharpe Focus, 2008.

Kudalis, Eric. *The Royal Mummies: Remains from Ancient Egypt.* Mankato, MN: Capstone High-Interest Books, 2003.

McCall, Henrietta. *Gods & Goddesses in the Daily Life of the Ancient Egyptians.* Columbus, OH: Peter Bedrick Books, 2002.

Mitchnik, Helen. *Egyptian and Sudanese Folk-Tales.* New York: Oxford University Press, 1978.

Schomp, Virginia. *The Ancient Egyptians.* New York: Marshall Cavendish Benchmark, 2008.

Wyly, Michael J. *Death and the Underworld.* San Diego, CA: Lucent Books, 2002.

Greek/Roman

Bingham, Jane. *Classical Myth: A Treasury of Greek and Roman Legends, Art, and History.* Armonk, NY: M. E. Sharpe, 2008.

Hepplewhite, Peter, and Mark Bergin. *The Adventures of Perseus.* Minneapolis, MN: Picture Window Books, 2005.

Lister, Robin, Alan Baker, and Homer. *The Odyssey.* Reformatted ed. Boston: Kingfisher, 2004.

McCarty, Nick, Victor G. Ambrus, and Homer. *The Iliad.* Reformatted ed. Boston: Kingfisher, 2004.

Mellor, Ronald, and Marni McGee. *The Ancient Roman World.* New York: Oxford University Press, 2005.

Roberts, Russell. *Athena.* Hockessin, DE: Mitchell Lane Publishers, 2008.

Roberts, Russell. *Dionysus.* Hockessin, DE: Mitchell Lane Publishers, 2008.

Roberts, Russell. *Zeus.* Hockessin, DE: Mitchell Lane Publishers, 2008.

Schomp, Virginia. *The Ancient Romans.* New York: Marshall Cavendish Benchmark, 2008.

Spires, Elizabeth, and Mordicai Gerstein. *I Am Arachne: Fifteen Greek and Roman Myths.* New York: Frances Foster Books, 2001.

Whiting, Jim. *The Life and Times of Hippocrates.* Hockessin, DE: Mitchell Lane Publishers, 2007.

Hindu

Choudhury, Bani Roy, and Valmiki. *The Story of Ramayan: The Epic Tale of India.* New Delhi: Hemkunt Press; Pomona, CA: Distributed in North America by Auromere, 1970.

Dalal-Clayton, Diksha, and Marilyn Heeger. *The Adventures of Young Krishna: The Blue God of India.* New York: Oxford University Press, 1992.

Ganeri, Anita. *The* Ramayana *and Hinduism*. Mankato, MN: Smart Apple Media, 2003.

Ganeri, Anita, and Carole Gray. *Hindu Stories*. Minneapolis: Picture Window Books, 2006.

Ganeri, Anita, and Tracy Fennell. *Buddhist Stories*. Minneapolis: Picture Window Books, 2006.

Husain, Shahrukh, and Bee Willey. *Indian Myths*. London: Evans, 2007.

Kipling, Rudyard. *The Jungle Book*. New York: Sterling Pub., 2008.

Parker, Vic, and Philip Ardagh. *Traditional Tales from India*. Thameside Press; North Mankato, MN: Distributed in the United States by Smart Apple Media, 2001.

Sharma, Bulbul. *The* Ramayana *for Children*. Penguin Global, 2004.

Staples, Suzanne Fisher. *Shiva's Fire*. 1st ed. New York: Farrar Straus Giroux, 2000.

Judeo-Christian

Geras, Adele. *My Grandmother's Stories: A Collection of Jewish Folk Tales*. New York: Alfred A. Knopf, 2003.

Kimmel, Eric A., and John Winch. *Brother Wolf, Sister Sparrow: Stories about Saints and Animals*. 1st ed. New York: Holiday House, 2003.

Schwartz, Howard, and Barbara Rush. *The Diamond Tree: Jewish Tales from Around the World*. 1st Harper Trophy ed. New York: HarperTrophy, 1998.

Schwartz, Howard, and Stephen Fieser. *Invisible Kingdoms: Jewish Tales of Angels, Spirits, and Demons*. 1st ed. New York: HarperCollins Publishers, 2002.

Self, David, and Nick Harris. *Stories from the Christian World*. Englewood Cliffs, NJ: Silver Burdett Press, 1988.

Senker, Cath. *Everyday Life in the Bible Lands*. North Mankato, MN: Smart Apple Media, 2006.

Taback, Simms. *Kibitzers and Fools: Tales My Zayda (Grandfather) Told Me*. New York: Puffin, 2008.

Native American

Ardagh, Philip, and Syrah Arnold. *South American Myths & Legends*. Chicago: World Book, 2002.

Berk, Ari, and Carolyn Dunn Anderson. *Coyote Speaks: Wonders of the Native American World*. New York: Abrams Books for Young Readers, 2008.

Brown, Virginia Pounds, Laurella Owens, and Nathan H. Glick. *Southern Indian Myths and Legends*. Birmingham, AL: Beechwood Books, 1985.

Curry, Jane Louise. *The Wonderful Sky Boat and Other Native American Tales from the Southeast.* New York: Margaret K. McElderry, 2001.

Monroe, Jean Guard, and Ray A. Williamson. *They Dance in the Sky: Native American Star Myths.* Award ed. Boston: Houghton Mifflin, 1993.

Parker, Victoria. *Traditional Tales from South America.* North Mankato, MN: Thameside Press. Distributed in the United States by Smart Apple Media, 2001.

Philip, Neil. *The Great Mystery: Myths of Native America.* New York: Clarion Books, 2001.

Pijoan, Teresa. *White Wolf Woman: Native American Transformation Myths.* 1st ed. Little Rock, AR: August House Publishers, 1992.

Ramen, Fred. *Native American Mythology.* 1st ed. New York: Rosen Central, 2008.

Schomp, Virginia. *The Native Americans.* New York: Marshall Cavendish Benchmark, 2008.

Vogel, Carole G. *Weather Legends: Native American Lore and the Science of Weather.* Brookfield, CT: Millbrook Press, 2001.

Near Eastern/Islamic

Ganeri, Anita. *Islamic Stories.* 1st American ed. Minneapolis, MN: Picture Window Books, 2006.

Grimal, Pierre. *Stories from Babylon and Persia.* Cleveland, OH: World Pub, 1964.

Ibrahim, Abdullahi A. *Enuma Elish.* Austin, TX: Steck-Vaughn Co., 1994.

Jabbari, Ahmad. *Amoo Norooz and Other Persian Folk Stories.* Costa Mesa, CA: Mazda Publishers, 2000.

León, Vicki. *Outrageous Women of Ancient Times.* New York: Wiley, 1998.

Marston, Elsa. *Figs and Fate: Stories about Growing Up in the Arab World Today.* 1st ed. New York: George Braziller, 2005.

Marston, Elsa. *Santa Claus in Baghdad and Other Stories about Teens in the Arab World.* Bloomington: Indiana University Press, 2008.

McCaughrean, Geraldine. *Gilgamesh the Hero.* Oxford: Oxford University Press, 2002.

Podany, Amanda H., and Marni McGee. *The Ancient Near Eastern World.* New York: Oxford University Press, 2005.

Schomp, Virginia. *The Ancient Mesopotamians.* New York: Marshall Cavendish Benchmark, 2008.

Walker, Barbara K. *Turkish Folk-Tales.* Oxford: Oxford University Press, 1993.

Norse/Northern European

Andersen, H. C., Diana Frank, Jeffrey Frank, Vilhelm Pedersen, and Lorenz Frolich. *The Stories of Hans Christian Andersen: A New Translation from the Danish.* Durham: Duke University Press, 2005.

Ardagh, Philip, and Stephen May. *Norse Myths & Legends.* Chicago: World Book, 2002.

Branford, Henrietta, and Dave Bowyer. *The Theft of Thor's Hammer.* Crystal Lake, IL: Rigby Interactive Library, 1996.

D'Aulaire, Ingri, and Edgar Parin. *D'Aulaires' Book of Norse Myths.* New York: New York Review of Books, 2005.

Evan, Cheryl, and Anne Millard. *Usborne Illustrated Guide to Norse Myths and Legends.* London: Usborne, 2003.

Jones, Gwyn, and Joan Kiddell-Monroe. *Scandinavian Legends and Folk-Tales.* New ed. Oxford: Oxford University Press, 1992.

Osborne, Mary Pope. *Favorite Norse Myths.* New York: Scholastic, 2001.

Porterfield, Jason. *Scandinavian Mythology.* New York: Rosen Central, 2008.

Web Sites

American Folklore. http://www.americanfolklore.net/ (accessed on June 11, 2008).

The British Museum: Mesopotamia. http://www.mesopotamia.co.uk/menu.html (accessed on June 11, 2008).

The Camelot Project at the University of Rochester. http://www.lib.rochester.edu/CAMELOT/cphome.stm (accessed on June 11, 2008).

Common Elements in Creation Myths. http://www.cs.williams.edu/~lindsey/myths (accessed on June 11, 2008).

Egyptian Museum Official Site. http://www.egyptianmuseum.gov.eg/ (accessed on June 11, 2008).

Internet History Sourcebooks Project. http://www.fordham.edu/halsall/ (accessed on June 11, 2008). Last updated on December 10, 2006.

Iron Age Celts. http://www.bbc.co.uk/wales/celts/ (accessed on June 11, 2008).

Kidipede: History for Kids. http://www.historyforkids.org/ (accessed on June 11, 2008).

Mythography. http://www.loggia.com/myth/myth.html (accessed on June 11, 2008). Last updated on April 17, 2008.

National Geographic. http://www.nationalgeographic.com/ (accessed on June 11, 2008).

NOVA Online: The Vikings. http://www.pbs.org/wgbh/nova/vikings/ (accessed on June 11, 2008).

Perseus Project. http://www.perseus.tufts.edu/ (accessed on June 11, 2008).

Sanskrit Documents. http://sanskritdocuments.org/ (accessed on June 11, 2008). Last updated on February 2, 2008.

United Nations Educational, Scientific and Cultural Organization. http://portal. unesco.org/ (accessed on June 11, 2008).

World Myths & Legends in Art. http://www.artsmia.org/world-myths/artbyculture/index.html (accessed on June 11, 2008).

Index

Italic type indicates volume number; **boldface** type indicates main entries and their page numbers; (ill.) indicates photos and illustrations.

A

Aborigines, *1:* 144–49
    assimilation, *2:* 317
    creation stories, *1:* 147; *2:* 315–17
    Dreamtime, *1:* 145–49; *2:* 320–22, 321 (ill.);
      5: 888
    floods, *2:* 390–91
    giants, *3:* 433–34
    serpents and snakes, *5:* 931
Abraham, *5:* 906
Achilles, *1:* **1–4**; *2:* 272; *3:* 530, 568–71
    Aeneas, provoked to join Trojan War, *1:* 12
    Agamemnon, feud with, *1:* 39–40;
      3: 489
    Amazon queen Penthesilea, killed by, *1:* 54
    Apollo, helped to kill, *1:* 92
    Balder, similar to, *1:* 166–67
    Chiron, teacher of, *2:* 221
    and Hector, *3:* 489–90
    Hephaestus, made armor for, *3:* 508
    Hera, protector of, *3:* 513
    Odysseus, encounters with, *4:* 774, 780
Achilles' heel, *1:* 1, 3
Acoetes, *2:* 311
Acrisius (King), *2:* 286, 287; *4:* 826, 829
Acropolis, *1:* 133–34
Actaeon, *1:* 111
The Acts of King Arthur and His Noble Knights
    (Steinbeck), *1:* 119
Adad, *5:* 923

Adam and Eve, *1:* **4–8,** 6 (ill.), 77; *2:* 260
    Cain and Abel, *1:* 5; *2:* 203
    cherubim, *2:* 230, 231
    fruit appearing in the myth of, *2:* 409, 410
    Garden of Eden, *2:* 331–33
    refusal of a jinn to bow down to, *3:* 425
    impact of sin on the rose, *2:* 396
    Lilith, first wife of Adam, *3:* 646–48, 647 (ill.)
    Satan, as tempter of, *5:* 910
Adam's rib, *1:* 5, 6–7
Adapa, *5:* 925
Adaro, *4:* 689
Adilgashii. See Skinwalkers
"Adonais" (Shelley), *1:* 11
Adonis, *1:* **8–11,** 10 (ill.), 86; *3:* 555
    association with the anemone flower, *2:* 393
    similar to Egyptian myth, *3:* 588
    similar to Semitic myth, *1:* 87; *2:* 296 (ill.),
      398; *5:* 924
The Adventures of Baron Munchausen (film), *1:* 88;
    3: 510
The Adventures of Robin Hood (film), *3:* 535;
    5: 893, 893 (ill.)
The Adventures of Sharkboy and Lavagirl in 3-D
    (film), *4:* 820
Aeëtes (King), *1:* 101
Aegeus, *4:* 682; *5:* 980, 981
Aegisthus, *1:* 38, 40–41; *2:* 208, 348
Aeneas, *1:* **11–16,** 15 (ill.), 135; *2:* 271 (ill.);
    5: 898–99
    Cerberus, *2:* 223

omphalos, *5:* 1073
Orpheus, *4:* 800
Theseus, *5:* 980
Demeter, *2:* **293–97,** 294 (ill.); *3:* 457
birth of, *2:* 265
Cybele, association with, *2:* 273
and the cycle of the seasons, *2:* 311, 412;
    4: 823–25
and Dionysus, *2:* 311
and Hecate, *3:* 487
and Persephone, *2:* 412; *3:* 461, 472–73, 487;
    4: 823–25; *5:* 1021
and Poseidon, *4:* 850
Roman counterpart, *5:* 896
Titans, *3:* 471
underworld, *5:* 1024
and Zeus, *2:* 311; *5:* 1074
The Demonata #1: Lord Loss (Shan), *2:* 306
Demophon, *2:* 293–94
Deucalion, *3:* 460; *4:* 810
Devaki, *3:* 622
Devi, *2:* **297–300,** 299 (ill.); *3:* 514, 537, 540;
    5: 944
The Devil. *See* Satan
"The Devil and Daniel Webster" (Benét), *5:* 911
Devils and demons, *2:* **301–6.** *See also* Evil; Satan
Ahriman, *1:* 42–45
female, *3:* 648
Lilith, *2:* 302; *3:* 646–48, 647 (ill.)
Persian mythology, *4:* 831–32
The Dharma Bums (Salinger), *1:* 201
Dhritarashtra, *4:* 659, 660
Diana. *See* Artemis
Diana (painting), *3:* 464
Dibbuk. *See* Dybbuks
Dictys, *2:* 287
Dido, *1:* 13–14, 16, 18, 20; *2:* **307–10,** 308 (ill.)
Dido, Queen of Carthage (Marlowe), *2:* 309
Dido and Aeneas (opera), *1:* 21; *2:* 309
Diomedes, *3:* 489
Dion, *2:* 285
Dione, *1:* 86, 87
Dionysius the Younger, *2:* 285
Dionysus, *1:* 81; *2:* **310–15,** 312 (ill.); *3:* 457,
    458; *5:* 896

Aphrodite, *1:* 86
Apollo, *2:* 314
Ariadne, *1:* 104, 105
Baucis and Philemon, *1:* 173
centaurs, *2:* 222
fruit, *2:* 410
Graces, *3:* 453
Hephaestus, *3:* 508
Hera, *3:* 513
Midas, *4:* 710
Orpheus, *4:* 800
Pan, *4:* 809
satyrs, *5:* 912
Semele, *3:* 513
The Dioscuri. *See* Castor and Pollux
Disabilities and physical deformities, *3:* 509–10
Disney movies
Aladdin, *1:* 50 (ill.), 51; *3:* 428, 535; *4:* 711
Aladdin and the King of Thieves, *4:* 711
Atlantis: The Lost Empire, *1:* 139
Chicken Little, *2:* 210
Darby O'Gill and the Little People, *1:* 168; *2:*
    219; *3:* 640
The Emperor's New Groove, *3:* 579
Fantasia, *3:* 510; *4:* 755
Fantasia 2000, *2:* 385, 392
Hercules, *1:* 4; *2:* 225, 361, 366; *3:* 474, 516,
    523, 526, 535; *4:* 725, 802, 817; *5:* 914,
    998
Jungle Book, *2:* 383
The Lion King, *5:* 972
The Little Mermaid, *4:* 699
Pirates of the Caribbean, *5:* 984, 1005
Sleeping Beauty, *1:* 144, 194
Snow White and the Seven Dwarfs, *2:* 326, 413
Song of the South, *1:* 29, 191
The Sword in the Stone, *1:* 119
Uncle Scrooge, *4:* 664
Disorder. *See also* Chaos
in Aztec mythology, *5:* 978
in creation myths, *2:* 355
and the Garden of Eden, *1:* 121
and Malsum, *3:* 442
symbols of, *3:* 643, 979
and Tezcatlipoca, *5:* 978, 979

F

Q

R

Ra, *5:* **873–75**, 966
    Amun, *1:* 57
    Aten, *1:* 127
    Bast, *1:* 170–71
    dragons, *2:* 318
    Egyptian mythology, *2:* 335, 336, 338, 339
    floods, *2:* 388–89
    Hathor, *3:* 477–78
    Isis, *3:* 585–87
    Nut, *4:* 764
    serpents and snakes, *5:* 930
    Set, *5:* 935
    Thoth, *5:* 989
    twins, *5:* 1013
Rabbit Hood (cartoon), *5:* 894
Racism
    African mythology and, *1:* 29
    Cain and Abel, *2:* 204
Radha, *3:* 623
Radish, *5:* 1024
Ragnarok, *5:* **875–79**, 877 (ill.)
    Fenrir, *2:* 367
    Freyr, *2:* 404
    Heimdall, *3:* 494
    Loki, *3:* 653
    Norse mythology, *4:* 756, 761
    Odin, *4:* 770
    Thor, *5:* 986
    Valhalla, *5:* 1035, 1037
    Valkyries, *5:* 1038
    Yggdrasill, *5:* 1067
The Raiders of the Lost Ark (film), *1:* 108
Rain
    Artemis, *1:* 113
    Baal, *1:* 157–61
    Indra, *3:* 579–80, 580 (ill.)
    Tlaloc, *1:* 151–52; *5:* 1000
Rainbow Mars (Niven), *5:* 1068
Raise High the Roofbeams, Carpenters (Salinger),
    1: 201
Rakshasas, *2:* 303; *5:* 880–81
Raktavira, *2:* 298

Rama, *3:* 540, 542; *5:* 879–83, 1046. *See also*
  Vishnu
Ramayan 3392 A.D. (comic book), *5:* 882
Ramayan (television series), *5:* 882
The Ramayana, *3:* 536; *5:* **879–83**
    heroes, *3:* 530–31
    Surya, *5:* 973
    Vishnu, *5:* 879–80, 1043, 1045
Ran (film), *3:* 638
Rangi and Papa, *2:* 256; *4:* 838, 839; *5:* **883–86**,
    884 (ill.)
Raphael, *1:* 70; *2:* 231 (ill.); *3:* 430, 453
Ravana, *2:* 303; *5:* 881, 1045
The Raven and the First Men (sculpture), *2:* 264
Ravi. *See* Surya
Re. *See* Ra
Reaper (television series), *5:* 912
Rebirth. *See* Death and rebirth
Regan, *3:* 637
Regulus. *See* Basilisk
Reign of Fire (film), *2:* 319
Reincarnation, *5:* **886–90**
    Buddhism, *1:* 196, 197, 200
    Dreamtime, *2:* 322
    Hinduism, *3:* 541–42
    Lethe, *3:* 641
Rembrandt, *2:* 288
The Remorse of Orestes (painting), *2:* 416
Remus. *See* Romulus and Remus
Reprobus. *See* Christopher, St.
Republic (Plato), *3:* 485, 641
Revelation, *1:* 69
Revenge
    Achilles, *1:* 3–4
    Artemis, *1:* 111
    Brunhilde, *1:* 193–94
    Electra, *2:* 348–49, 349 (ill.)
    Furies, *2:* 413–16
    Hera, *3:* 512–13
    Hunahpú and Xbalanqúe, *3:* 553–54
    Nala and Damayanti, *4:* 733
    Nibelungenlied, The, 4: 745–50
Rhea, *2:* 265, 266 (ill.), 273; *3:* 459, 512; *5:* 996
Rhea Silvia, *5:* 900
Das Rheingold (opera), *3:* 654

S

Sabrina, the Teenage Witch (television show), *5:* 1053

Sacrifice, *5:* **905–8**

Achilles, *1:* 4

Aeneas, *1:* 20

Agamemnon, *1:* 112; *2:* 348

Andromeda, *1:* 65–66

Ares, *1:* 97–98

Aztec mythology, *1:* 149, 152 (ill.), 153, 154–55; *2:* 248; *5:* 1000

in *Beowulf,* *1:* 180

Coatlicue, *2:* 248, 250

creation stories, *2:* 258

Daedalus, *2:* 279, 280

Delphi, *2:* 290

Devi, *2:* 298

Elijah, *2:* 351

Golden Fleece, *3:* 445–46

Hindu mythology, *3:* 538–39; *4:* 730; *5:* 905

Huitzilopochtli, *3:* 551

Hunahpú and Xbalanqúe, *3:* 553

Inca mythology, *3:* 575

Ishtar, *3:* 583

Judeo-Christian, *5:* 906

Juggernaut, *3:* 617

Laocoön, *3:* 632–33

Manu, *4:* 667

Mayan mythology, *4:* 675, 679; *5:* 906–7

Melanesian mythology, *4:* 690

Mesopotamian mythology, *5:* 926

Mexican mythology, *4:* 700

Mimir, *4:* 712

Minotaur, *4:* 716

in the myth of Sedna, *5:* 916

Noah, *4:* 754

Odin, *4:* 770, 771–72; *5:* 906

Odysseus, *4:* 781

Perseus, *4:* 827

Poseidon, *4:* 852

Proteus, *4:* 859–60

Quetzalcoatl, *5:* 871, 872

Shiva, *3:* 540–41

Tezcatlipoca, *5:* 977

Tyr, *5:* 1020

Xipe Totec, *5:* 1061

Ymir, *5:* 1070–72

Sadb, *4:* 789

Saint Seiya (cartoon), *3:* 561

Sakra. *See* Indra

Saktasura, *3:* 622

Sambhu, *2:* 298

The Sandman (comic book), *2:* 361, 416; *4:* 773

The Sandman Presents: Bast (comic book), *1:* 172

Sangreal. *See* Holy Grail

Sankara, *2:* 298

Santa Claus. *See* Nicholas, St.

Santa Claus is Comin' to Town (cartoon), *4:* 752

The Santa Clause (film), *2:* 326; *4:* 752

Satan, *2:* 303; *5:* **908–12**, 911 (ill.). *See also* Devils and demons; Evil

Adam and Eve, *1:* 6

Ahriman, *1:* 45

angels, *1:* 67, 69

Armageddon, *1:* 109–11

Beelzebub, *1:* 160

dragons, *2:* 318

dybbuks, *2:* 327

griffins, *3:* 465

hell, *3:* 504

Job, *3:* 614

serpents and snakes, *5:* 933

The Satanic Verses (Rushdie), *4:* 666

Saturn, *1:* 136; *2:* 266, 267. *See also* Cronus

Saturn Devouring One of His Children (painting), *2:* 267; *5:* 998

Satyavrata. *See* Manu

Satyrs, *1:* 76; *2:* 223, 287, 303; *5:* **912–15**, 913 (ill.)

Dionysus, *2:* 311

fruit, *2:* 410

Lares, *3:* 636

nymphs, *4:* 767

Pan, *4:* 807

Saul (King), *1:* 159, 160

Savita. *See* Surya

Savitri, or Love and Death (Arnold), *3:* 542

Savitri (opera), *3:* 542

REF 201.30 MYT VOL 4

UXL encyclopedia of world
mythology

		DATE DUE		